Controversy in the Classroom

In a conservative educational climate that is dominated by policies like No Child Left Behind, one of the most serious effects has been for educators to worry about the politics of what they are teaching and how they are teaching it. As a result, many dedicated teachers choose to avoid controversial issues altogether in preference for "safe" knowledge and "safe" teaching practices. Diana E. Hess interrupts this dangerous trend by providing readers with a spirited and detailed argument for why curricula and teaching based on controversial issues are truly crucial at this time.

Through rich empirical research from real classrooms throughout the nation, she demonstrates why schools have the potential to be particularly powerful sites for democratic education and why this form of education must include sustained attention to authentic and controversial political issues that animate political communities. The purposeful inclusion of controversial issues in the school curriculum, when done wisely and well, can communicate by example the essence of what makes communities democratic while simultaneously building the skills and dispositions that young people will need to live in and improve such communities.

Diana E. Hess is an Associate Professor of Curriculum and Instruction at the University of Wisconsin-Madison.

The Critical Social Thought Series
Edited by Michael W. Apple,
University of Wisconsin–Madison

Controversy in the Classroom
The Democratic Power of Discussion

Diana E. Hess

Routledge
Taylor & Francis Group

NEW YORK AND LONDON

First published 2009
by Routledge
711 Third Avenue, New York, NY 10017

Simultaneously published in the UK
by Routledge
2 Park Square, Milton Park, Abingdon, Oxon OX14 4RN

Routledge is an imprint of the Taylor & Francis Group, an informa business

© 2009 Taylor and Francis

Typeset in Minion by
Swales & Willis Ltd, Exeter, Devon

Library of Congress Cataloging in Publication Data
Hess, Diana E.
    Controversy in the classroom: the democratic power of discussion/
Diana E. Hess.
        p. cm. – (Critical social thought)
    Includes bibliographical references and index.
    1. Education – Curricula – Political aspects – United States.
    2. Democracy and education – United States.   3. Academic freedom –
United States.   I. Title.   II. Series.
    LC89.H43 2009
    379.1'55 – dc22   2008048438

ISBN 10: (hbk) 0–415–96228–5
ISBN 10: (pbk) 0–415–96229–3
ISBN 10: (ebk) 0–203–87888–4

ISBN 13: (hbk) 978–0–415–96228–5
ISBN 13: (pbk) 978–0–415–96229–2
ISBN 13: (ebk) 978–0–203–87888–0

I dedicate this book to the memory of my parents, Herbert and Charlotte, whose spirited discussions in the living room shaped my own interest in controversial political issues.

D. H.

Contents

Series Editor Introduction

Among the lessons educators and committed citizens have learned over the years is that very often the question of "What knowledge should we teach?" has been turned into the question of "Whose knowledge should we teach?" There are very complicated issues associated with these questions. But, one thing has become clear: the curriculum is part of what the great cultural critic Raymond Williams called "the selective tradition" (Williams, 1961). That is, from the vast universe of possible knowledge, only some knowledge and only some perspectives tend to get declared as official or legitimate. In the process, other knowledge is declared as popular, as not real, as not important (Apple, 2000).

Yet, given the changing nature of the world and of our understanding of it, it is now harder for an individual or a group to simply assert that they have a lock on the truth. Thus, the assumption that the knowledge that is and should be in schools will be unquestioned is an increasingly untenable one. There is nothing new about this, of course. The curriculum has always been subject to intense debate, as have the ways in which teachers organize and teach it (Kliebard, 2004). While such debates over what and whose knowledge should be represented in the school curriculum are not new, there has clearly been an increase in the intensity of these debates. From the math and reading "wars" to the role of schooling in preparing workers for our economy to the tensions over secularity and religion—all of these and more have created a situation where schools and teachers are sitting on a series of fault lines where the equivalent of educational earthquakes seem almost bound to happen. And as we have seen multiple times, they do with a good deal of frequency.

What are the kinds of things that are so powerfully in the public eye? Even a partial list of these issues shows the nature of controversies that surround us— the environment and global warming, economic inequalities, immigration, racism, religion, sexuality, war, terrorism and how it should be dealt with. The list could go on and on and could extend to education well beyond the borders of the United States. Given the salience of these issues and the need for all of us to think through them, this is both an exciting time and a difficult time to be an educator.

What is the role of schooling in dealing with these powerful concerns? With what kinds of issues should teachers and curricula engage? How should teachers and curricula respond? Should teachers be totally neutral or should they say what their own positions on these issues are?

There are strong ideological differences involved in the varying answers to these questions. As I noted, schools have become the center of political conflicts over what values a society should uphold. In *Educating the "Right" Way* (Apple,

2006), I devote a good deal of the book to analyzing the contending forces at work here and show how conservative groups have been more than a little successful in bringing their own values to the core of the debate over the content and processes of schooling. But it is not just conservatives who have weighed in on all of this. A considerable number of groups across the ideological spectrum have asked of schools and teachers that they provide students with ways of understanding the realities and dilemmas we face nationally and internationally.

There have been thoughtful surveys of things such as the political orientations of youth and of their religious values (see, e.g., Smith & Denton, 2005). While such research is very valuable, much of this kind of research is often left to the level of "what youth think." But a key issue is what youth *do* and the ways in which they make sense of *new* situations, new ideas, things that are perhaps out of their commonsense comfort zone. And for those of us involved in the public sphere, what do they do and think in the institutions that structure so much of their lives, such as schools?

I know of no other book that provides us with as cogent an analysis of what the questions I raised earlier mean and how we might answer them than in this book, Diana Hess's *Controversy in the Classroom.* Its arguments about why schools must face the controversies head on are powerful. Its descriptions of how it can be done and how it is being done are more than a little illuminating. In addition, its commitment to forms of democratic schooling that respond to the best in us comes through in compelling ways.

Hess brings together a range of political and educational reasons for engaging with controversy in authentic ways in schools. That alone makes the book worthwhile reading. But she goes much further. This is the first widespread picture of what happens in diverse classrooms when controversial issues actually arise and become a focus. The results are eye-opening and challenge many preconceptions that many of us may hold. We see close up what this looks like, how teachers teach, and how they organize that teaching.

But Hess doesn't focus only on teachers and curricula. She provides a detailed and insightful analysis, one based on rich sources of data, of what actually happens in classrooms, how students themselves respond, what their beliefs are, and how they seriously engage with issues that undoubtedly can and will affect their lives. A good deal of what she says is strikingly new. Students are much more open to discussions of controversial issues than one might expect. Even on topics where they seem quite conservative, discussions that are respectful of people's beliefs and yet open and serious can and do go on. The ideological diversity both within and among student groups is more than a little interesting. Indeed, I must admit that after reading what Hess has given us in this book, I can never go into a classroom that is dealing seriously with meaningful material without seeing it in a different and more complex manner than I did before.

What is Hess proposing? As she states, "Schools have not just the right, but also the obligation, to create an atmosphere of intellectual and political freedom that uses genuine public controversies to help students discuss and envision political possibilities." As this quote shows, Diana Hess is clearly committed to a responsive and responsible set of democratic beliefs. She rightly understands that democracy is not simply a set of slogans that politicians use to generate votes or a set of abstract principles that students are to learn for tests. Rather, democracy is a *way of life*. It is best learned in schools by actually engaging in and practicing it. In her words again:

> Democratic education is a form of civic education that purposely teaches young people how to *do* democracy. It stands at the crossroads of authenticity and transformation. In other words, democratic education both honestly addresses the political world outside of school and represents the political realm as dynamic, thereby emphasizing the ongoing transformation of society. In such an education, the democratic ideal is simply stated: people can build a better society.

Hess is deeply aware that there will be different positions on any serious controversy among teachers and students. But to her, this should be seen as a resource and a benefit. We should focus on the advantages of diversity of opinion and should have students engage with these differences in ways that demonstrate how respect for both difference and the nature of serious civic deliberation are to be lived out in this society.

> Building on the central claim that schools should activate students' awareness and appreciation of the inherent link between authentic controversy and democracy, I argue that the single most important policy aim we should work toward is transforming schools into communities that honor and put to good use the advantages of diversity—especially the ideological differences that are so necessary for high-quality deliberation.

There are well-known schools that exhibit some of these tendencies currently (see, e.g., Apple & Beane, 2007). But what Diana Hess has found is that throughout the nation there are a considerable number of teachers and classrooms where serious, critical, and respectful deliberations go on. This is an important finding, since it means that what she is proposing is not simply a Utopian vision. Indeed, we can move, and diverse classrooms are moving, toward this model *now*.

Politically, conceptually, empirically, and educationally, *Controversy in the Classroom* is a fine book. With its rich sources of data, detailed descriptions, nuanced arguments, and programmatic suggestions, the book gives us much to consider. Anyone who cares about how our youth are prepared to face an uncertain future with knowledge and courage should read it.

Michael W. Apple
John Bascom Professor of Curriculum and Instruction
and Educational Policy Studies
University of Wisconsin–Madison

References

Apple, M. (2000). *Official knowledge*, 2nd ed. New York: Routledge.

Apple, M. (2006). *Educating the "Right" way: Markets, standards, god, and inequality*, 2nd ed. New York: Routledge.

Apple, M., & Beane, J. (2007). *Democratic schools: lessons in powerful education.* New York: Heinemann.

Kleibard, H. (2004). *The struggle for the American curriculum, 1893–1958,* 3rd ed. New York: Falmer.

Smith, C., & Denton, M. (2005). *Soul searching: The religious and spiritual lives of American teenagers.* New York: Oxford University Press.

Williams, R. (1961). *The long revolution.* New York: Columbia University Press.

Acknowledgments

I want to thank Michael Apple, whose wise counsel and "you can do it" spirit enabled me to conceptualize and write this book, and to Catherine Bernard, the masterful editor at Routledge who provided such sage advice and crucial support. I am so appreciative of the invaluable feedback on the content of this book I received from Keith Barton, Connie North, Shannon Murto, Abigail Janowiec, Bennett Singer, John Smithson, Paula McAvoy, Jeremy Stoddard, Alan Lockwood, Taehan Kim, Lauren Gatti, Lee Arbetman, and Simone Schweber.

It would be impossible to list all the people who have influenced my ideas about democratic education, schools, teaching, and research, but I am especially grateful for what I have learned from Gloria Ladson-Billings, Beth Graue, Dawnene Hasset, James Gee, Betty Hayes, Anand Marri, Scott DeWitt, Louis Ganzler, Hilary Conklin, Kelly Elver, Kristen Buras, Shannon Murto, Eric Freedman, Wayne Au, Sohyun An, Alexander Miletta, Julie Posselt, Carole Hahn, Patricia Avery, Bruce Larson, John Zola, Lori Mables, Wendy Ewbank, Carolyn Pereira, Fred Newmann, Elizabeth Chorak, Sue Hess, Norma Wright, Laurel Singelton, Nisan Chavkin, Marshall Croddy, Judith Torney-Purta, Margaret Crocco, Linda Levstik, Todd Clark, Peter Levine, James Banks, Michael Knapp, Joe Kahne, and Joel Westheimer.

Forty teachers and 1,100 students participated in the three classroom studies that helped shape the contents of this book—because of confidentiality rules, they cannot be named, but I am enormously grateful to them for participating in the research. For funding the research, I am indebted to the Center for Information and Research in Civil Learning and Engagement, the Carnegie Corporation, The McCormick Foundation, the Graduate School at the University of Wisconsin-Madison, and the Spencer Foundation. Thanks also for the help I have received from Adam Gamoran and the staff at the Wisconsin Center for Education Research, where my ongoing study is housed.

A number of ideas in this book have been developed and helpfully challenged in teacher institutes, conference papers, and published manuscripts in the past several years. Without exception, every main idea developed in the book had a "try out" with the teachers who attended the Center for Education in Law and Democracy's annual conferences in Denver, Colorado. I am enormously grateful to them and to my good friend Barbara Miller, the primary organizer of the conference, for providing me with intellectual stimulation that was so helpfully grounded in the classroom. I am also thankful for the support and encouragement I have received from my siblings, Chris Hess and Sue Maurer, and from my good friend Ron Dawson. And most significantly, I want to thank Walter Parker—a great scholar and amazing teacher.

Diana Hess

Throughout this book I have included excerpts from articles, columns, and book chapters I have written or co-authored. Thank you to the publishers and the co-authors for giving me permission to include the excerpts from the following publications:

Hess, D. (2002). Discussing controversial public issues in secondary social studies classrooms: Learning from skilled teachers. *Theory and Research in Social Education, 30,* 10–41.

Hess, D. (2004). Is discussion worth the trouble? *Social Education, 68,* 151–155.

Hess, D. (2007). From *Banished to Brother Outsider, Miss Navajo to an Inconvenient Truth:* Documentary films as perspective-laden narratives. *Social Education, 71,* 194–199 [followed by my response to a letter to the editor].

Hess, D. (2008a). Democratic education to reduce the divide. *Social Education, 72,* 373–376.

Hess, D. (2008b). Teaching and learning about controversial issues in social studies. In L. Levstik, & C. Tyson (Eds.), *Handbook of research in social studies* (pp. 123–136). New Jersey: Erlbaum.

Hess, D. (2009). Creating comprehensive controversial issues policies to improve democratic education. In J. Youniss, & P. Levine (Eds.), *Engaging young people in civic life.* Nashville: Vanderbilt University Press.

Hess, D. (in press). Teaching student teachers to examine how their political views inform their teaching. In E. Heilman (Ed.), *Social studies and diversity teacher education: What we do and why we do it.* New York: Routledge.

Hess, D., & Avery, P. (2008).What young people learn from issues-based democratic education. In J. Arthur, I. Davies, & C. Hahn (Eds.), *International handbook on education for citizenship and democracy.* (pp. 506–519). London: SAGE.

Hess, D., & Murto, S. (in press). Teaching against the threats to democracy: Inclusive pedagogies in democratic education. In S. Mitakidou, E. Tressou, B.B. Swadener, & C.A. Grant, (Eds.), *Beyond pedagogies of exclusion in diverse childhood contexts: Transnational challenges.* New York/London: Palgrave/Macmillan.

Hess, D., & Posselt, J. (2002). How students experience and learn from the discussion of controversial public issues in secondary social studies. *Journal of Curriculum and Supervision, 17,* 283–314.

Hess, D., & Stoddard, J. (2007). 9/11 and terrorism: "The ultimate teachable moment" in textbooks and supplemental curricula. *Social Education, 71,* 231–236.

Hess, D., Stoddard, J., & Murto, S. (2008). Examining the treatment of 9/11 and terrorism in high school textbooks. In J. Bixby & J. Pace (Eds.), *Educating democratic citizens in troubled times: Qualitative studies of current efforts.* (pp. 192–225) Albany: SUNY Press.

Introduction

One warm day in the spring of 2006, I visited a U.S. History class at a public charter school in a large Midwestern city. I was to listen to students engage in a spirited and thoughtful discussion about whether abortion should be legal or illegal in the United States. The classroom was a packed and bustling place. Hundreds of books and newspapers spilled out from the room's many bookshelves and student essays hung on the walls. The rest of the wall space featured posters blaring inspirational sayings: Challenge Each Other Intellectually, Seek Wisdom, Be Organized, Live a Healthy Lifestyle, Speak Your Mind Even If Your Voice Shakes, and Those Who Will Not Read Have No Advantage Over Those Who Cannot Read.

The 19 students in the class were all juniors—half were African-American, the other half Latino—a composition that mirrored almost exactly the student population of the school. Almost all of the students were from poor families with only one parent or guardian at home. Many hoped to become the first in their families to graduate from high school. During my prior visits to the school to observe the history class and interview these students, I had been impressed by their thoughtfulness, their obvious pride in their school, their ability to talk about their learning, and most strikingly, the glowing language they used to describe their history teacher. Without exception, the students with whom I spoke raved about him. As one student explained it, he expected them to work hard: "When you go home you do a lot of reading. And on your homework, he expects your answers to be very detailed." Many students described him as the best teacher they had ever had and gave him credit for preparing them for college.

The teacher seemed worthy of this praise. Incredibly committed, and superbly educated, Mr. Dunn had taught for seven years. During that time he had worked diligently to improve his ability to teach students how to talk with one another about highly controversial political issues—issues like abortion, affirmative action, and the war in Iraq. He had focused specifically on developing students' abilities to discuss these issues without using vitriol, taking cheap shots, or making personal attacks. By succeeding, he was teaching his students how to be better at engaging in these discussions than many of the adults we see on television or hear on radio shows. The students were not engaging in the class discussions to win over or beat up on their peers. Instead, as one student told me: "Mr. Dunn really gives us a chance to say what we believe and he gives us space to voice our opinions. His classroom gives us space so our opinions aren't shut out. He gives us space where we can all work together and figure out a problem. His class is just very nice. I enjoy it. I enjoy it a lot."

The abortion discussion I observed was an introduction to a short unit on how sex and gender roles had changed during and after the 1960s in the United States. Mr. Dunn explained that the class would have an *initial* conversation about their current opinions on abortion, followed by a study of the legal history of abortion in the United States. He planned to have students revisit the same question again in another discussion at the end of the unit. Students would also be asked to write an editorial on whether or not they thought that *Roe v. Wade* should be overturned.

Written on the board was the question: "Can a woman legally terminate her pregnancy?" After reading the question, one student—a female—said that the word "terminate" was loaded, and suggested that it should be changed to "Should a woman be able to legally choose to end her pregnancy?" Mr. Dunn nodded and said, "We want to phrase the question so it is not biased," and he replaced the original question with her version. Then he explained the ground rules for the discussion:

> If you want to participate, get your name on the speakers' list—just get my attention and I'll write your name down. This way you can focus on listening instead of waving your hands around. And you have to restate what the person before you said to the person's satisfaction before you share your idea. Not to pay attention to what others say is just rude and it's not fair just to hear yourself speak—you need to listen too—that's part of the bargain. And don't just speak to me—speak to the whole class. I may talk too—but I'll put my name on the speakers' list.

Mr. Dunn then directed the students to take out their notebooks and write down their current thoughts on the question, explaining they would have 3–4 minutes for silent writing. After giving them a one-minute warning, he announced that he was looking for hands for the speakers' list. Many hands went up and he wrote them down in order.

The student who had objected to the original question on the board also began the discussion by sharing her position: "A woman should be able to do it, it is her choice, the government should not be able to interfere." Another female student restated what she heard, and agreed: "The woman should have her *own* choice," at which point a male student said (after repeating), "Well, I agree that the women should have choice, but if the husband or father wants to have custody of the child then he should be able to have a say too." Another male student said that abortion was OK if a woman's life was in danger, but if not, she should give the baby up for adoption.

What was clear at this point was that the students had different positions on the issue, which they wanted to get on the table. However, they were not supporting their positions in any detail. Given that this was a discussion being used to kick off the unit, one would not expect the students to be doing much more than sharing their views. They seemed interested in simply mapping the landscape of perspectives from which they were starting.

I was not surprised by the variety of views in the room. I knew from a survey I had conducted that the students held different opinions on a number of issues—including abortion. While the majority of students had marked that they thought abortion should be legal, there was a significant minority who thought otherwise—and from the onset of the discussion it was apparent that the students in the minority felt quite comfortable sharing their positions. Despite this diversity of opinions, I knew, too, that this class was unusually and strikingly homogenous. For example, in selecting which candidate they would have voted for in 2004 for president, all but one marked Kerry.

Just a few minutes into the discussion, the students began explaining their positions in a bit more detail, with the female student who spoke first now saying: "I get what you and Jose are saying, but the woman is the person who holds the baby for nine months. She is the one in pain. He's not the one with the morning sickness, back pains, body aching." Another student reasoned, "I saw an ultrasound, and that convinced me that the only time it should be legal is if the woman has health problems." After a brief back and forth about whether adoption was a good option (e.g., "a lot of kids are up for adoption— no one wants them"), the discussion moved to whether the decision to have sex should bring with it attendant responsibilities. One male student was clearly conflicted. He explained that while he agreed that it is wrong for "kids to be having kids," which seemed to suggest he favored legalized abortion, he also stated bluntly, "but they made their bed, [and] have to lie in it," which seemed to suggest that biological parents need to keep their children.

After an extended exchange on this point among several students, one said, "I want to comment on what Salia said. Why make the child suffer for your mistakes? The child has a right to grow up to be somebody—and if you have the baby, the child won't be dead and you won't go to hell for sinning." At this point Mr. Dunn inserted himself into the content of the discussion for the first time: "Notice that in these comments the focus is not on the woman's right to choose, but on what will happen to the child. This illustrates that we often collide with other people's rights. So pay attention to the different categories (of arguments) not because they are bad, but because you might be speaking across one another." He was urging the students to directly engage one another's arguments, especially when there was such a clear tension between competing ideas.

Earlier a female student had commented that the central point in the controversy about abortion is who gets to decide: "Is it us? Or is it the government—most of whom are men?" Then another female student took up the idea of deciding, but turned it in another direction: "If the question is who gets to decide, you need to remember that you made a decision a long time ago when you decided to have sexual intercourse with a man—you made your choice—now you must raise that child." Another female student also argued against legalized abortion—using autonomy as the lever: "If it's your body then you should not be doing what a guy said—in other words, women's liberation is telling the guy you don't want to have sex." Another female student challenged this, "We're programmed to have sex—everybody's going to do it— and I disagree with the argument that a woman has made her bed, now lie in it because men were in those beds too—and nobody should get to tell you what to do—that's really putting women down."

Mr. Dunn announced that the discussion was going to end because the period was almost over but paused to compliment the students for responding directly to one another's points and behaving in such a civil manner. He asked the students to jot down one issue raised during the discussion that they had never thought of before this class. After a minute of silent writing, the period ended and the students immediately launched into the discussion again as they exited the class. The conversation was boisterous and a bit louder than it was during class. Mr. Dunn turned to me, chuckled and said, "Well, so much for civil."

But what struck me was that the students were highly engaged, and while speaking with a bit more volume as they exited the class, they *were* still clearly civil to one another. Reflecting back on the discussion, I noted three-quarters of the students had participated verbally and all seemed to listen intently. I left the school impressed—this was by no means the most sophisticated or intellectually rigorous discussion I had viewed, but it was pretty good—especially for an initial discussion that was to be followed by an intense focus on the history of reproductive rights, and would then conclude with another discussion.

That the topic of the discussion was abortion rights also impressed me because I often hear from teachers that they steer away from those issues in particular, fearing that they are just too politically charged, could upset administrators and parents, or may be emotionally difficult for students in the class with personal experiences related to abortion. A teacher once told me she refused to deal with abortion in her classroom because of her own religious beliefs—"I just cannot bear to hear the other side on this issue." Given the saliency of issues related to abortion in the political world outside of school, it has always concerned me that so few teachers seem willing to engage their classes in discussions about abortion and that so few states include it in the documents that increasingly drive decisions about what will be taught. Regardless of whether one agrees or disagrees with the Supreme Court's decision in *Roe v. Wade*, it is clearly a landmark case that continues to generate immense controversy. That fact that only six of the 50 states that list Supreme Court cases in their social studies standards include *Roe v. Wade* is suggestive of the views of many adults in the United States: that abortion is a political issue that should *not* be discussed in school.[1]

Many school districts have been riled by controversies about whether to include abortion in the sex education curriculum (or whether to have a sex education curriculum at all), and some schools have banned the mere mention of the word "abortion" in classrooms. In many communities, too, there is scant support for engaging young people in serious discussions of policy and constitutional issues related to abortion, or a host of other controversial issues for that matter.

This book makes a case for why people who hold that belief are wrong. A more enlightened and democracy-sustaining approach is to teach all young people to engage in high-quality public talk about controversial political issues. I am not suggesting that all young people need to talk about controversial legal and political issues related to abortion in schools, but I do think they should be learning *how* to talk about controversial issues—regardless of what kind of school they are attending—private or public, secular or sectarian. Ideally, this learning would occur throughout the young person's schooling in multiple subject areas and in extra and co-curricular activities. I aim to show why schools have the potential to be particularly powerful sites for this form of democratic education and to show how some schools are already doing just that. My central claim is that the purposeful inclusion of controversial political issues in the school curriculum, done wisely and well, illustrates a core component of a functioning democratic community, while building the understandings, skills, and dispositions that young people need to live in and to improve such a community.

What Is a Controversial Political Issue?

At the outset, I want to clarify my definition of controversial political issues. They are authentic questions about the kinds of public policies that should be adopted to address public problems. When glancing at recent newspapers, for example, I notice a plethora of issues embedded in many of the stories. Should the USA send more troops to Iraq or withdraw? Should the federal government grant amnesty to people in the USA without legal documents? What should be done to lower the high school drop-out rates? Should my community build a new school? What should my state do to provide all of its citizens access to healthcare? What should the international community do to combat terrorism?

Although these issues involve different policy actors and stakeholders, they are all authentic and likely to generate multiple and competing answers. Consequently, they are *controversial* and important to include in the school curriculum. Notwithstanding the apparent simplicity and obviousness of my criteria, defining what constitutes a controversial political issue is itself controversial. I therefore examine this matter in some detail later in the book.

Why Include Controversial Issues in the School Curricula?

When schools fail to teach young people how to engage with controversial political issues, or worse, suppress, ignore, or deny the important role of controversial issues in the curriculum, they send a host of dangerous and wrongheaded messages. One is that the political realm is not really important, especially in comparison to other content on which schools traditionally have focused. Another is that such issues are "taboo" and therefore dangerous for young people to encounter. Yet another is that people in the United States and the larger world fundamentally agree on the nature of the public good and how it can be fostered.

Furthermore, a school that shuns political controversy is not taking advantage of some unique features that make schools an especially good site for learning how to talk about highly controversial issues. One of these features is the *opportunity* the curriculum can provide for the inclusion of such issues. Note, for example, that Mr. Dunn developed the controversy-rich gender unit as part of a required history course. A second feature is *teachers*, who have developed (or can develop) expertise in fostering deliberation and inquiry among students. Another is the greater degree of ideological diversity among students in schools than exists in most other venues inhabited by young people. Most schools contain gender, religious, ethnic, and some degree of racial diversity. Moreover, even classes that are homogeneous along a number of these dimensions likely encompass broader ideological diversity than students encounter in their own homes. The relative diversity of schools makes them particularly good places for controversial issue discussions. Students likely will be exposed to views different from their own and have to explain their own views during such discussions. This kind of "cross-cutting political talk" is markedly different from talk that occurs in an "echo chamber" of similar views.

As a case in point, a study that I am directing examines the degree and impact of ideological diversity present in high school social studies courses. Not surprisingly, we are finding that schools generally reflect the ideological diversity of the communities in which they exist. However, even in classes that appear to be extremely homogeneous, students consistently report that they are more likely to recognize and appreciate the ideological diversity in their midst if their teachers include discussions of controversial issues in the curriculum. Many students state that the range of opinions expressed in their classes is far wider than in their homes, partially because there are simply more participants, and therefore a greater diversity of viewpoints, in class discussions. But students also note that teachers make a difference, especially when they are skillful at surfacing the differences of opinion that exist within the group.

For these reasons, I argue that schools have not just the right, but also the obligation, to create an atmosphere of intellectual and political freedom that uses genuine public controversies to help students discuss and envision political possibilities. Addressing public controversies in schools not only is more educative than quashing or ignoring differences, but it also enhances the quality of decision-making by ensuring that multiple and competing views about controversial political issues are aired, fairly considered, and critically evaluated.

Book Roadmap

This book draws on my experiences over time as a teacher in a public high school, president of a local teachers' union, curriculum writer and professional development facilitator for secondary teachers while a staff member of a national democratic education organization, and professor and researcher at a public university.

While all of these experiences have shaped my understanding of the benefits and challenges of teaching young people how to engage in high-quality public talk about controversial political issues, much of the book focuses on what I learned from four studies about addressing controversy in middle and high schools in the United States that I conducted between 1998 and 2008. Three took place inside classrooms and sought to address three overarching questions: What do teachers who skillfully teach their students how to engage in issues discussions do? How do students experience and learn from these discussions? What impact does participation in discussions have on the civic and political engagement of young people? The fourth study focused on curriculum that dealt with 9/11 and its aftermath.

The book has three parts. In the first, "The Case for Controversial Political Issues," I answer the following questions: Why are democracy and discussion so often linked, both theoretically and practically? What rationales and empirical warrants support this form of teaching and learning? How prevalent are discussions on controversial issues in the classroom? What barriers obstruct the robust deliberations of issues? Then, I detail a framework for conceptualizing controversial political issues. I go to some length to illustrate the difference between a topic (Immigration, for example) and an issue (Should the United States increase the number of people who can legally enter?), as well as the difference between public issues that demand public decisions and impact many people (Should the United States reinstate the military draft?), and private issues that, while clearly linked to public decisions, are made by an individual (Should I join the military?). I also explore the different ways in which policy and constitutional issues are conceptually distinct, yet overlap.

Part II, "Inside Classrooms," begins with an analysis of what middle and high school teachers who skillfully teach their students how to engage in high-quality public talk about political issues actually do. Although the practices of the teachers vary tremendously, important similarities exist—it appears that skillful teaching in this realm is marked by a combination of the explicit instruction of discussion skills, adequate preparation so that students have enough infor-mation about which to talk, and the creation of a learning environment in which students want to participate.

Because of the importance of disparate opinions in high-quality political talk, I next turn to an analysis of ideological diversity in classrooms and how teachers in predominantly left-wing, right-wing, and mixed classes of students work to prevent "group think" or its evil twin, "classroom bedlam." These case studies investigate the role of ideological diversity among teachers and students as a "pillar" of effective democratic education. We know, for example, that race, gender, class, religion, and a host of other factors inform and influence what happens in schools and classrooms. I am broadening this concept by analyzing the extent to which ideological diversity within schools and classrooms matters.

Teachers who engage students in issues discussions need to make a number of decisions about what I label "controversial pedagogical issues," or the aspects of this kind of teaching that generate debate among their colleagues, parents, and the public. Among the general public (and certainly among many political pundits), a pervasive belief is that teachers indoctrinate students into a political paradigm or policy perspective when they share their views on hot issues with them. Thus, in a chapter co-authored with Paula McAvoy, I examine the question of whether teachers should disclose their own views to students or remain silent.

In the third part, "Controversy in the Curriculum," I complicate the task of defining the controversial political issues that I began in Part I by detailing a process I call "tipping." Tipping involves the movement of important questions alternately between open questions (for which there are multiple and competing answers) and closed questions (those that are taught with the aim of helping students develop a specific answer). The chapter on tipping introduces what I have come to believe is the key controversy attached to controversial political issues in the classroom: determining what should be considered an issue in the first place. Following that chapter, I examine the portrayal of the 9/11 attacks and their aftermath, as well as terrorism more generally, in curriculum developed by democratic education organizations, the U.S. government, and social studies textbook companies.

In a brief final chapter, I turn to what needs to be done to create climates in which more students are taught how to discuss highly controversial political issues. Specifically, I call for detracking courses because the trend toward separating students based on their perceived ability interferes with the goals of democratic education. I also support enhancing professional development opportunities for teachers to learn and/or improve their ability to infuse their courses with controversy. I end with a call to parents and the general public to demand that schools do more than simply reflect their own ideological positions on hot button political issues.

I
The Case for Controversial Political Issues

1

Why Democracy Demands Controversy

In the "Bong hits for Jesus" case (*Morse v. Frederick*, 2007), the United States Supreme Court wrestled with the question of whether its traditional, albeit muted, support for the free speech rights of students in public schools should be curtailed if the student "speech" could be interpreted as promoting the use of illegal drugs. The Court's split decision in the case illustrates different views about the purposes of public schools in a democratic society. Writing for the majority, Chief Justice Roberts said that when a school principal suspended a high school student for unfurling a banner proclaiming "Bong hits for Jesus," she was acting within the bounds of the Constitution because the speech could be interpreted as advocating illegal drug use. Justices Alito and Kennedy, while agreeing with Roberts, were careful to draw limits on a public school's ability to restrict the right of students to speak on public issues. Conversely, Justice Thomas wrote that the very idea of students possessing First Amendment speech rights in school was spurious: "In light of the history of American public education, it cannot seriously be suggested that the First Amendment 'freedom of speech' encompasses a student's right to speak in public schools. Early public schools gave total control to teachers, who expected obedience and respect from students" (Thomas, J., concurring, p. 10). Notably, even on a Supreme Court that is considered quite conservative, Justice Thomas was unable to garner any support for his position.

The *Morse v. Frederick* (2007) case is important because even though the majority opinion did place some limitations on students' free speech rights in public schools that the Court had not articulated previously, both conservative and liberal justices, with the exception of Justice Thomas, went to great pains to stipulate that students *should and do* have a constitutionally enshrined right to speak about important political issues while in public schools. Liberals and conservatives alike lauded extending some free speech rights to young people in schools—at least theoretically. They asserted the importance of maintaining schools' traditional role of educating citizens for political participation *and* exposing young people to multiple and competing views about controversial issues. For example, in his dissent, Justice Stevens encouraged schools to engage students in discussions about contemporary drug policy, likening current drug laws to prohibition, which was a hot controversy during the time he attended secondary school. He explicitly argued that silence about controversial issues, both in schools and in society, makes it more likely that bad policies will prevail. Specifically, he argued:

> Even in high school, a rule that permits only one point of view to be expressed is less likely to produce correct answers than the open discussion of countervailing views. *Whitney*, 274 U.S., at 377 (Brandeis, J., concurring); *Abrams*, 250 U.S., at 630 (Holmes, J., dissenting); *Tinker*, 393 U.S., at 512. In the national debate about a serious issue, it is the expression of the minority's viewpoint that most demands the protection of the First Amendment. Whatever the better policy may be, a full and frank discussion of the costs and benefits of the attempt to prohibit the use of marijuana is far wiser than suppression of speech because it is unpopular (Stevens, J., dissenting, p. 16).

I disagree with the Court's decision in the *Morse v. Frederick* (2007) case because it sends a message to the lower courts that students' speech rights can be whittled away. However, I strongly support some of the justices' position that speech, schooling, and democracy are inextricably linked. Unlike those justices, Thomas ignored the reality that public schools *are* the government. Although suppressing student speech may be acceptable in a totalitarian state, it surely has no place in a democratic nation. Nevertheless, merely refusing to suppress student speech in schools does not promote the development of democrats (note the small "d") either. As noted in the introduction, a more enlightened policy would teach all young people to engage in high-quality public talk about controversial political issues.

There are four main points I make in this chapter. First, there is an intrinsic and crucial connection between the discussion of controversial political issues, especially among people with disparate views, and the health of a democracy. This is so because participating in political discussion can have two powerful effects: it makes people more politically tolerant and it causes them to learn more about important issues. Second, there is mounting evidence that relatively few people in the United States currently engage in such political talk and the trend is clearly moving in a non-deliberative direction. Fewer people now are likely to engage in political talk with people who do not share their views than in the past. The political consequences of this trend are harmful for individuals and for society at large. Third, one especially powerful way to work on lassoing this trend is to use the schools as sites for transformation by teaching young people how to engage in such discussions. This is clearly an ambitious goal— and we know from a myriad of past efforts that using the schools as a lever to change society does not always work. Schools, after all, are a reflection of society, so their transformational potential has both theoretical and practical limits. Fourth, notwithstanding the promise of schools as powerful sites for this form of democratic education, there are many, many barriers that stand in the way of mining the deliberative potential of schools. However, there is evidence that many teachers are teaching their students to engage in high-quality discussion of controversial political issues—that they have found ways to hurdle the barriers—which benefits their students and, I will argue, has the potential to benefit the rest of us as well.

Before turning to my first point—which is that discussion and democracy go hand in hand—it is important to define what I mean by two central concepts used throughout the book: discussion and democratic education.

What Is Discussion?

There are numerous approaches for how to include controversial political issues in the classroom, such as simulations, role-plays, and writing assignments. Although this book will detail a number of ways in which teachers combine these activities with discussions, its primary focus is on teaching young people how to engage effectively in high-quality *discussions* of controversial political and constitutional issues. For that reason, it is important to define discussion, which is a contested concept both on the theoretical front and in practice. Within the context of democratic education, educators commonly focus on the importance of controversial issue discussions: public discussions that in their process include, nurture, and honor diverse views, and in their content, focus on authentic political issues. Authentic political issues do not constitute the sole discussion subjects that democratic educators support (Parker, 2006), but they have a stronger presence in the theory, studies, and reports of researchers in this area than other kinds of discussions, such as text-based seminar discussions; however, as we shall see in Chapter 4, there are teachers who use seminar discussions for the purposes typically associated with classroom talk about issues.

Consider the following definitions advanced by scholars with expertise in classroom discussion: (1) "the free exchange of information among three or more participants (which could include the teacher)" (Christoph & Nystrand, 2001, p. 250); (2) "an alternatively serious and playful effort by a group of two or more to share views and engage in mutual and reciprocal critique" (Brookfield & Preskill, 1999, p. 6); (3) "a particular form of group interaction where members join together in addressing a question of common concern, exchanging and examining different views to form their answer, enhancing their knowledge or understanding, their appreciation or judgment, their decision, resolution or action over the matter at issue" (Dillon, 1994, p. 8); (4) "a kind of shared inquiry the desired outcomes of which rely on the expression and consideration of diverse views" (Parker, 2003, p. 129); (5) "[public] talk about something upon which the group seeks to improve its knowledge, understanding and/or judgment and it will be of an appropriate form" (Bridges, 1979, p. 27).

Notice the differences among these definitions. The first is minimalist—requiring only a small number of participants and the simple exchange of ideas. The next describes the ethos of discussion ("alternatively serious and playful") and its content ("sharing views and critique"), but not the goal. The third identifies a precondition for discussion (there must be a question of common concern), the content (exchanging and examining views), and the purpose of the discussion (to form an answer, or to build knowledge, understanding, appreciation, or judgment). The fourth definition focuses on the process of discussion—inquiry-based on the exploration of multiple perspectives. The final definition combines purpose and form, but also specifies that the forum must be public—a particularly important point for classroom discussion.

Notwithstanding the differences among these definitions of discussion, there are common features that help distinguish discussion from other forms of classroom talk, among which are lecture and recitation. First, discussion is dialogue between or among people. It involves, at a minimum, the exchange of information about a topic (e.g., a controversy, a problem, an event, a person, etc.). Second, discussion is a particular approach to constructing knowledge that is predicated on the belief that the most powerful ideas can be produced when people are expressing their ideas on a topic and listening to others express theirs. Moreover, the multiple definitions quoted above illustrate an area of consensus regarding discussion: it takes many forms and is used for many purposes. This is especially the case when discussion is employed as a form of democratic education—a type of education framed by multiple, and seemingly contradictory, goals. Among the dilemmas faced by democratic educators are their desires to simultaneously forge community and nurture controversy, to develop in their students commitments to particular values while respecting their rights to hold ideas that are not shared, and to encourage the expression of political "voice" without coercively demanding participation.

Differentiating Democratic Education from Civic Education

good

Throughout the book, I use the term "democratic education" instead of civic education. I do so deliberately because the label "civic education" suggests "fitting in" to society as it currently operates, whereas my deliberate use of "democratic" highlights the dynamic and contested dimensions inherent in a democracy. I saw this distinction most clearly while spending time in schools in two nations that were—in my view—far from democratic: the USSR in the 1980s and Cuba just before the dawning of the new century. Both nations had robust and startlingly effective civic education in their schools. Students learned a lot about the history of their nations, their own roles and responsibilities in daily life, and why their system of governance was vastly superior to others in the world at the time, especially that of the United States. I frequently heard young people talk about why their nation was the "best in the world."

Doing a good job teaching civic education seemed to be pretty uncomplicated in these two nations. Fights about how history should be represented in the official government textbooks did not consume the time and energy of administrators, teachers, students, and community members. The principals also did not have to respond to parents who were angry about a guest speaker spouting controversial views with which they disagreed, as guest speakers who did not support the state's version of events typically were not invited into classrooms. Nor did teachers have to carve out instructional time to introduce multiple perspectives on controversial public issues. Only one "official" perspective was included in the curriculum. Thus issues were not issues, *per se*; they were answers.

The supposed consensus on these official curricula was a ruse. Indeed, it masked deep tensions and divisions in both of those societies. Yet, my experiences in the USSR and Cuba also poignantly exposed the difference between civic and democratic education. In a nutshell, democratic education is a form of civic education that purposely teaches young people how to *do* democracy. It stands at the crossroads of authenticity and transformation. In other words, democratic education both honestly addresses the political world outside of school and represents that political realm as dynamic, thereby emphasizing the ongoing transformation of society. In such an education, the democratic ideal is simply stated: people can build a better society. This ideal, with its Enlightenment roots, certainly is not unique to the United States, which is the first thing we need to make sure young people understand. It is also not without controversy, for multiple and competing conceptions of what constitutes a better society abound. Consequently, different conceptions of what citizens in a democracy should do to work toward that end also abound. With these definitions of discussion and democratic education in mind, I will widen the analytic lens to consider how democracy and discussion go hand in hand.

Why Democracy Demands Discussion

To many democratic theorists and practitioners, discussion is a proxy for democracy itself. Discussions in democratic societies, especially if characterized by inclusion and widespread participation, are markers of what Robert Dahl (1998) calls "intrinsic equality"—the fundamental assumption that the good of every human being is intrinsically equal to that of any other (p. 65). The ideal of discussion supports the validity of intrinsic equality by implying, at least symbolically, that all members of a community are political equals and are therefore equally qualified to participate in discussion and decision making. The listening *and* talking that constitute discussion physically represent a core goal of democracy: self-governance among equals (Gastile & Levine, 2005). Thus, one rationale for discussion in democracy is that you cannot *have* democracy without discussion. As Mansbridge (1991) posits, "Democracy involves public discussion of common problems, not just silent counting of individual hands" (p. 122). In short, to be *against* discussion is akin to opposing democracy.

But there are other reasons bolstering the need for the discussion of public problems in a democracy, and some are much more tightly focused and pragmatic. Engaging in discussion of public problems—as long as there are people in the group with views different from your own—builds political tolerance, teaches people, and may result in better policy decisions. Recall Justice Stevens' point in his dissent in the "Bong hits for Jesus" case. He argued that "a rule that permits only one point of view to be expressed is less likely to produce correct answers than the open discussion of countervailing views."

Building Tolerance Through Cross-cutting Political Talk

The causative relationship that exists between discussion and tolerance has long been one of the most powerful rationales used by those who advocate the need for discussion-rich environments in a democracy. By tolerance, I am not referring to a society in which it is legally and morally permissible for people to do whatever they want, but instead I refer to *political* tolerance, which is the willingness to extend important and significant rights (such as free speech) to people who are different from oneself. While all democracies, it can be argued, have a need to foster political tolerance, this is an especially important set of beliefs for highly diverse democracies, such as the United States, to cultivate. For without it, putting into practice the democratic ideal of intrinsic equality would be virtually impossible.

We know from research that engaging in discussion with people whose opinions are different from your own builds political tolerance—even if the discussion was not with a person from a different group. In a powerful series of studies assessing the impact that "cross-cutting political talk" has on attitudes and actions, Diana Mutz (2006) set out to examine political talk as it "naturally occurs" as part of routine social life in the United States. She was most interested in what happened when people were exposed to political perspectives different from their own. She called this kind of exposure "cross-cutting" in order to distinguish it from talking with people who share one's political views—a form of interaction which is much more common in the United States.

While Mutz was well aware of a plethora of research that indicated powerful effects that accrued from highly structured deliberative experiments (such as Fishkin's deliberative polling which we will turn to in a moment), her concern was whether or not some of the most powerful theoretical supports for political talk pan out in the practice of the kind of talk that people are more likely to engage in via their social networks. In particular, she wanted to know the answer to a fundamental question: What are the benefits of hearing the other side? She found that people who engage in this kind of political talk (and their numbers are low, approximately 23% of the adult U.S. population) do become more politically tolerant. This is so for two reasons: cross-cutting political talk familiarizes them with legitimate rationales for opposing views and normalizes and legitimizes a political conflict.

For example, imagine that I engage in a conversation with one of my work colleagues about whether or not our state should increase funding for stem cell research. I think they should, but my colleague disagrees, arguing that other needs are more pressing. Through our "cross-cutting" exchange we explain why we believe the way we do. Neither one of us changes our mind on the issue, but we come to better understand the reasons a person might have for an opposing position while simultaneously framing the issue itself as legitimate. This combination, according to Mutz, translates into a greater willingness to extend civil liberties even to those groups whose political views one dislikes a great deal (2006, p. 85). More specifically, she claims:

> Ultimately, political tolerance is about formalized ways in which people agree to disagree. It is primarily about restraint and not doing, rather than political action. Thus carrying on conversations across lines of political difference, conversations in which one must agree to disagree at a micro-level, may teach important lessons about the necessity of political tolerance. After all, political tolerance is just the macrolevel, public policy rendition of agreeing to disagree. (p. 86)

The rationale for discussion in democracy as a way to build political tolerance only has power, of course, if there is a reason why extending important rights to people who significantly differ from oneself (either on the micro or macro level) enhances the health, stability, or sustainability of democracy. While there is a plethora of reasons why political tolerance and democracy go hand in hand, the most obvious is that a society without political tolerance is likely to enact policies that deprive some people of their right to influence the political agenda and to have an influence on what is decided. That is, there will be no political equality. And absent political equality, there really is not a democracy.

Talking with people who disagree with one's political views can build political tolerance. So too can it produce learning—especially if the nature of the talk is structured to make it more likely that people will share, hear, and interrogate a variety of different interpretations about such important questions as what caused a problem and what the relative strengths and challenges associated with alternative solutions are.

Learning From and Through Deliberation

By producing learning, I mean that individuals will become better informed— quite simply, they will *know and understand* more. People who are lucky enough to have had experience with high-quality political talk often recognize that they are learning—both from what they hear and what they say. When a person says, "I never thought of it that way," she is really saying, I have learned a different way of conceptualizing something than I had prior to the discussion. Or when someone says, "I never really understood what I meant until I had to put it into words," he is explaining how you can talk yourself to understanding—literally. I know I am much better able to understand my own views and those of others as a consequence of discussion and I have often heard others say the same thing. The idea that discussion produces learning appeals to our common sense and is often rooted in personal experience.

There is also powerful empirical evidence that certain forms of political talk—most notably, the deliberation of political issues among a diverse public—can produce learning. Political scientist James Fishkin was one of several people who undertook a series of studies on a form of political talk he developed called a "deliberative poll." These studies examined a number of fundamental questions about what is produced by political talk, including the key question of whether talk is simply a way to demonstrate verbally what one knows, or is actually a process that builds knowledge (Fishkin & Farrar, 2005).

A deliberative poll is a process by which a random sample of adults in a community is brought together to deliberate about an authentic political issue (such as whether property taxes should be shared across town boundaries, or what to do about prison overcrowding) in a highly structured format. As such, they cannot occur spontaneously, because as Fishkin and Farrar (2005) note: "Discussions that arise spontaneously tend to bring together people who already know one another and share an interest or a concern" (p. 72).

Deliberative polls have occurred in numerous communities in the United States and a number of other nations. A few years ago I spent some time in Northern Ireland working with teachers and professors on how to produce high-quality issues discussions in classrooms and heard about how deliberative polling was being used there to bring Catholics and Protestants together to talk about important political issues. The conveners realized that a cessation of violence, while a stunning accomplishment, was only one step in what would be a long process to build a healthy democracy.

While there are surely differences in how deliberative polls are put into practice, the basic components are designed to meet two criteria: political equality (the consideration of everyone's preferences) and deliberation (weighing competing arguments based on their merits). Balanced background materials are prepared, moderators are well trained, and experts are available for plenary sessions to respond to participants' questions. Most of the deliberation occurs in small groups, and participants are formally surveyed about their views before and after the deliberation polling process.

Research on the effect of deliberative polls compares people who participated in a poll on a particular issue with those who did not. Quite consistently, the results support the theoretical claim that deliberation can produce learning, and moreover, that learning can influence opinion. Specifically, people usually come away from the deliberative poll much better informed. Also, people may change their views on the issue (pre-post) and when that occurs, it is because they have learned. That is, it is those people who show an increase in knowledge about the issue who change their views. Moreover, in some important follow-up studies, deliberative polls have been shown to spark further learning about the issue for many months, and often cause people to engage in political action about the issue (Fishkin & Farrar, 2005, pp. 68–79).

How Much Political Talk Actually Occurs in the United States?

Given the positive effects gained from engaging in talk, it is not surprising that many deliberative democracy theorists are quite concerned about evidence showing that in some democratic nations, few people actually engage in much political discussion of this kind. In a study of adults in six communities in Britain and the United States, Conover, Searing, and Crewe (2002) found that 30% of the sample in the United States and 50% in Britain are "silent citizens." That is, a large percentage of each nation's respondents discuss issues in private only. Virtually no one discussed in public only, and a mere 18% of U.S. citizens and 9% of British citizens reported speaking in both contexts. Further, Conover et al. (2002) suggested that these discussions are often marred by inequality and a lack of analysis and critique.

It is important to recall that Mutz found that only 23% of adults in the United States engaged in "cross-cutting" political talk, and notwithstanding the power of deliberative polls, these types of conversations are certainly not commonplace—very few people in the United States have participated in one, or other forms of public discussion for that matter. In the 2007 America's Civic Health Index research, researchers asked people if they had "been involved in a meeting—either face-to-face or online—to determine ideas and solutions for problems" *and* whether people who held views different from their own had participated. People who said yes to both were termed "deliberators" and 18% fit into this category (National Conference on Citizenship, 2007).

However, there is evidence to suggest that the vast majority of people in the United States support the *idea* of engaging in discussions of political issues. In the Civic Health Index of 2008, the researchers added a question to assess how much support there is among people in the United States for deliberation and found that 80% favored a proposal developed by AmericaSpeaks to "involve more than one million Americans in a national discussion of an important public issue and requiring Congress to respond to what citizens say" (National Conference on Citizenship, 2008, p. 12).

Researchers who have explored why there is so much rhetorical support for engaging in political discussions with people with different views, but so little of it in reality, have provided a variety of explanations. Two seem particularly compelling: the creation of ideologically homogenous environments and the aversion to political conflict.

With respect to the first, there is powerful evidence to suggest that fewer adults engage in cross-cutting political talk now than in the past because they have chosen to live in ideologically homogeneous communities. In *The Big Sort*, Bill Bishop demonstrates that "as Americans have moved over the past three decades, they have clustered in communities of sameness, among people with similar ways of life, beliefs, and in the end, politics" (2008, p. 5). Consequently, legislative districts are being ideologically gerrymandered to an extent that was unheard of in the past. For example, in 2004 more than 50% of people in the United States lived in a county where one of the presidential candidates won by a landslide—compared with only 26% in 1976 (Bishop, 2008). In these communities, people are more likely to talk with others who share their views, access media that reinforces and makes more extreme what they already believe, and then generally marinate what they hear in an echo chamber of like-mindedness about the most important issues facing the society.

In one particularly fascinating study, researchers convened adults in two Colorado communities that were notable for a lack of diversity—Boulder and Colorado Springs—to create an experiment they called "Deliberation Day" (Schkade, Sunstein, & Hastie, 2006). On deliberation day, they brought together citizens from liberal Boulder and conservative Colorado Springs. They asked each person to record their views on the issues that would be deliberated anonymously. Working in small groups with others from their *own* cities, they then deliberated three especially hot issues: global warming, affirmative action, and civil unions for same-sex couples.

Unlike the deliberative polling process previously explained, there was no moderator, they did not have background papers that explained alternative views, and there were no "experts" to question. There were simply small groups of people—five in each group—talking about the issues with the goal of reaching a group decision, if possible. After the deliberations they recorded their views once again, individually and anonymously. What happened on Deliberation Day? The researchers reported the following: First, the groups from Boulder became even more liberal on all their issues; the groups from Colorado Springs became even more conservative. Deliberation thus increased extremism. Second, while each group showed substantial heterogeneity before they started to deliberate, after a brief period of discussion group members showed much more agreement, even in anonymous expressions of their private views. Thus, deliberation increased consensus and decreased diversity. Third, deliberation sharply increased the differences between the views of the largely liberal citizens of Boulder and the largely conservative citizens of Colorado Springs. Before deliberations began, there was considerable overlap between many individuals in the two different cities. After deliberation, the overlap was much smaller.

In short, this study provided a particularly powerful example of how talking with people who agree with you can cause what the researchers termed ideological amplification—a process by which your pre-existing ideological tendencies become more pronounced and more extreme (Schkade, Sunstein, & Hastie, 2006, p. 2).

At the same time people are moving to ideologically homogenous communities, they are also increasingly becoming adverse to normal and legitimate political conflict. Hibbing and Theiss-Morse (2002) have identified the aversion that many adults in the United States have toward political conflict and the relationship that exists between that aversion and unwillingness to participate in the political realm. Certainly, Hibbing and Theiss-Morse are not the only scholars documenting the low level of political engagement among citizens of the United States. Their study (Hibbing & Theiss-Morse, 2002) is particularly compelling, however, because it pinpoints the fact that people in the United States generally *like* conflict and controversy (witness the addiction to viewing competitive sports), but dislike conflict and controversy when it is related to politics, policy issues, and governance. Consequently, the aversion to conflict and controversy causes low levels of political engagement. Moreover, it dampens the appetite for a wide range of political views, which may account for why visitors to the United States from other democracies so frequently comment on the relatively narrow range of political views available in newspapers and television news compared to what they are used to. People in the United States do not demand wide diversity in their political news climate—and, not surprisingly, they do not receive it.

The effects of these trends are undeniably dangerous for a democracy. When people live in Balkanized communities, they are likely to become increasingly hardened in their opinions, less able to view people with disparate views as even comprehensible, and more likely to become intolerant. Although this extremism might be combated by the exposure to differing views through national media like television and the internet, the tendency towards "shouting heads" on television, and the self-selection aspect of the internet, prevent these media from serving as a balancing force to the increasing extremism that can result from communities of sameness.

This produces a politics that is so polarized that cases of developing acceptable solutions to significant problems may increasingly become something only read about in history books. It is hard to imagine forging the kinds of legislative achievements—such as Social Security, the Civil Rights Act of 1964, or the Americans with Disabilities Act—in a climate where so many people are so sure that their opinions are not just right, but the only *legitimate* way to think.

For the purposes of this book, the recommendations that many of the researchers whose work I have summarized in this chapter make for how to improve the quantity and quality cross-cutting political talk are perhaps more salient than the findings. Researchers who report low levels of political talk and its effects are clearly worried, and most typically one solution they propose is to promote political discussions *within* schools as a way to improve the political world *outside* of school. Through the creation of more high-quality, cross-cutting, and public political discussion, schools thus become the lever by which society can be changed rather than merely reproduced—a recommendation that I believe deserves support.

Why Schools Are Good Sites for Political Talk

Schools of various types (public, private, urban, rural, secular, sectarian) are especially appropriate and powerful places to give young people the very opportunity that we know many adults do not have—to engage in "cross-cutting" political talk. More importantly, schools are places in which young people can be taught *how to* engage in such talk wisely and well. Thus, the most significant reason I am putting forward to encourage this particular kind of democratic education is that while it is *inauthentic* to the world outside of school, it is *authentic* to what a healthy democracy demands. More significantly, they are probably the best sites we currently have if our interest is using schools as a lever to improve the quality of U.S. democracy.

Schools are prime sites for this type of education for three reasons. One, they have curricular opportunities for issues discussions. Two, they have teachers who are or could become skillful at teaching students how to participate, and three, in schools, there is a degree of ideological diversity that can be turned into a deliberative asset.

As an illustration, consider the assets available to Mr. Dunn and his students. First, there were opportunities for students to discuss issues because they were taking a course in which issues easily fit. Recall, Mr. Dunn infused historical and contemporary issues in a *required* course on 20th century U.S. history. There were also curricular opportunities in the form of free high-quality resources that Mr. Dunn regularly used to help his students prepare for discussions, and he even involved his students in a multi-school deliberation program.

Even though there is good reason to be concerned about the narrowing of the curriculum that is caused by high stakes standardized tests, it is still the case that in many schools there are required and elective courses that students take that either are or could be appropriate venues for controversial political issues discussions. The forums for discussion created by courses with this type of content, curricular materials, and opportunities for multi-school engagement are simply not present in many other venues inhabited by young people. This is why it is quite common for students in classes where they are being taught how to participate in controversial issues discussions to remark that they are rarely provided these opportunities in other venues—not at home, on the soccer field, while playing video games, or in church.

A second deliberative asset was Mr. Dunn, who knew quite a bit about how to teach his students to engage one another in a civil manner, and possessed the kind of rich and deep content knowledge that enabled him to create powerful curricular units and courses. And as we shall see in Chapter 4, teacher skill matters to the success of issues discussions in schools. I am not suggesting that the mere presence of a teacher in the classroom is all that is needed, but many teachers do have considerable skills they can put to the task of teaching their students how to discuss political issues, and most who do not, can learn.

Finally, it is obvious that even in a class with an unusually high degree of political agreement, there were still enough ideological differences among the students to create an environment in which they were going to hear opinions that differed from their own. Some of my own work examines the degree and impact of ideological diversity present in high school social studies courses (Hess & Ganzler, 2007).[1] Not surprisingly, we are finding that schools generally reflect the ideological diversity of the communities in which they exist. However, even in classes that appear to be extremely homogeneous, students consistently report that they are more likely to recognize and appreciate the ideological diversity in their midst if their teachers include discussions of controversial issues in the curriculum. Many students state that the range of opinions expressed in their classes is far wider than in their homes, partially because there are simply more participants, and therefore a greater diversity of viewpoints, in class discussions. But students also note that teachers make a difference, especially when they are skillful at surfacing differences of opinion that exist within the group.

Barriers to Teaching about Controversial Political Issues

The idea that schools in democratic nations should foster the maintenance of democracy and, ideally, its positive transformation, is not new or novel. Nevertheless, several studies suggest that many parents do not really want schools to take on this task, especially when they consider other roles of schooling, such as credentialing for further education and workplace preparation. Our market economy promotes such emphasis on the latter roles. As Peter Levine (2005), the executive director of the preeminent civic learning and engagement research center in the United States, argues, markets "pose special problems for *civic* education. The civic development of young people will be undervalued in any market system, unless we take deliberate and rather forceful efforts to change that pattern." A recent study supports his claim (Campaign for the Civic Mission of Schools & Alliance for Representative Democracy, 2004); when asked to rate whether preparing young people for democratic participation was a very important goal of schooling, just over 50% of adults in the United States agreed, while other goals, such as workplace preparation (which 64% rated as very important) and basic academic knowledge in reading, math, and science (80% agreed) garnered much more support. Thus, one of the barriers to any form of democratic education—including issues teaching—is that much of the support for it is rhetorical rather than substantive.

Even when people authentically support democratic education, they disagree about the *kind* of participation schools should foster (Westheimer & Kahne, 2004). This disagreement stems from larger questions about what "good" citizens in a democracy are supposed to do. Is it more important for the populace to monitor and critique political leaders or to volunteer to help community members in need? Is it more important to vote in every election or to use the marketplace to voice political views via buying and boycotting? Is it more important to deliberate political issues with people whose political views are different from your own or to join with like-minded people to advocate a partisan position on a political issue? While these activities are not mutually exclusive, research shows that very few people regularly engage in *all* of these forms of political involvement.

Given this disagreement about what constitutes effective democratic participation, it is not surprising that people also disagree about what kind of democratic education young people should experience. While some conceptions of what "good" citizens should do line up well with teaching issues in schools, others do not. For example, many service-learning programs that focus on individual volunteerism lack any meaningful discussion of controversial political issues. Even some political advocacy programs rely on the assumption that students *agree* about the best position on controversial issues. Otherwise, they would not have a position in common for which to advocate.

Ironically, the very reason that Hibbing and Theiss-Morse (2002) give for low levels of political engagement (i.e., aversion to political conflict) explains why the solution they propose is so difficult to implement. That is, the controversies emanating from democratic education programs that address contentious political issues may be just the kinds of political controversies that people want to avoid. Many adults either want schools to mirror their ideas or fear that adding controversy to the curriculum *creates* controversy, as opposed to simply teaching young people how to deal more effectively with the kinds of political controversies that exist outside of school. As one of Jonathan Zimmerman's (2002) students remarked, "You'll never see a parents' group called 'Americans in Favor of Debating the Other Side' in our schools" (p. 197).

Besides the general aversion to controversy in the United States, other barriers to enacting issue-rich democratic education programs persist, too. These include differing views about the purposes of democratic education; fears that teachers, other students, or instruments of the "official curriculum" (such as textbooks and films) will indoctrinate students into particular positions on issues; and sharp conflicts about what should rightly be considered an issue in the first place. The rancorous divisions permeating the current political climate, coupled with the aftermath of September 11, 2001, make the terrain of controversial issues teaching especially treacherous in this historical moment. For example, the Civic Mission of the Schools report (Carnegie Corporation of New York & CIRCLE, 2003) that I referenced earlier notes, "[T]eachers need support in broaching controversial issues in classrooms since they may risk criticism or sanctions if they do so" (p. 6). In the most dramatic instances, teachers were disciplined and even fired for addressing 9/11 as a controversial issue. More commonly, teachers were instructed to eliminate or curtail plans to teach about such issues. In New York, for example, a principal ordered a teacher to spend no more than two 50-minute class periods teaching about 9/11-related controversies (such as whether the United States should bomb Afghanistan). The special challenges presented by September 11th do not expose new barriers to addressing contemporary political issues in schools—this approach to democratic education is always challenging. However, those challenges are even more difficult to address effectively in the current climate.

Rising to the Challenge

In a time when threats to democracy are numerous and powerful, the very possibility that schooling can play any kind of meaningful role in the creation, maintenance, or transformation of democracy may seem both idealistic and hopelessly naïve. Yet, many teachers continue to talk with passion and fervor about themselves as democracy workers. In my research in middle and high school social studies classes, I regularly encounter teachers who say they hope their practice can not only shape how young people view democracy, but also help them develop the ability and desire to engage politically and civically, thereby improving the overall health of democracy in the United States. These teachers see contemporary threats to democracy as barriers, to be sure. But they also see them as indicators of why schools must take up democratic education and act as a catalyst for action (Hess, 2002; Hess & Posselt, 2002; Hess & Ganzler, 2007).

2
Rationales for Controversial Issues Discussions in Schools

Teaching young people how to talk about highly controversial political issues in schools is not a new concept. For almost a century, many advocates of democratic education, especially within the social studies, have called for the infusion of such issues into the curriculum. In the early 20th century, for example, a number of scholars creating the new field of social studies encouraged teachers to focus on the "problems of democracy" through the analysis of authentic political issues. Subsequently, in a 1948 issue of *Social Education*, Richard E. Gross promoted this kind of teaching with the pithily titled article, "Teaching Controversial Issues Can Be Fun" (Gross, 1948). By the 1960s, a "jurisprudential" approach to analyzing historic and contemporary policy issues was introduced into the curriculum as part of the Harvard Social Studies Project, which itself was embedded within the "new social studies" (Oliver & Shaver, 1974).

More recently, the teaching of controversial political issues has come to describe a lesson, unit, course, or curriculum that engages students in learning about such issues, analyzing them, deliberating alternative solutions, and, frequently, taking and supporting a position on which solutions may be based. Often educators and scholars advocate this type of teaching and learning in secondary-level social studies courses, but, increasingly, those in the field of science (Zeidler, Sadler, Simmons, & Howes, 2005) and mathematics (Gutstein, 2003, 2006) are infusing political issues into courses so as to make the curriculum more authentic to the discipline, the world outside of school, and democratic goals. For example, the Northwest Association for Biomedical Research in Seattle, Washington, has developed a program to encourage science teachers to include highly controversial political issues in their courses. One set of materials focuses on the science and ethics of stem cell research. After learning about the science involved in stem cell research, students become familiar with the history of federal policy and the regulation of this kind of research, and then they participate in an elaborated decision-making process to develop a position on what policies about this highly controversial topic should be adopted by the government (Northwest Association for Biomedical Research, 2008).

Moreover, in English, literature, and language arts classes, students report regularly encountering political issues (Conover & Searing, 2000). Although evidence shows that controversial issues are more likely to be included in secondary schools than in elementary schools, it is not unheard of for elementary school teachers to engage their students in deliberations of controversial issues (Bolgatz, 2005; Paley, 1992; Parker, 2009).

Infusing controversial political issues into the curriculum now remains within mainstream conceptions of democratic education. For example, the broadly disseminated Civic Mission of the Schools Report makes only six research-based recommendations for improving civic education in the United States (Carnegie Corporation of New York & CIRCLE, 2003). One of these is to "incorporate discussion of current local, national, and international issues and events into the classroom, particularly those that young people view as important to their lives" (pp. 26–27). This recommendation is based on accumulated evidence from research dating back to the 1970s, which indicates that teaching young people about controversial issues in a supportive classroom environment that encourages the analysis and critique of multiple and competing viewpoints is positively correlated with important civic outcomes (p. 41). The Civic Mission of the Schools report summarizes the civic power of controversial issues discussions in a bold and straightforward manner:

> Studies that ask young people whether they had opportunities to discuss current issues in a classroom setting have consistently found that those who did participate in such discussions have a greater interest in politics, improved critical thinking and communications skills, more civic knowledge, and more interest in discussing public affairs out of school. Compared to other students, they also are more likely to say that they will vote and volunteer as adults (p. 8).

Rationales for Controversial Issues Discussion

Discussion as a Key Aspect of Democratic Education

Support for engaging young people in classroom discussions as part of democratic education comes from various quarters. Teachers and students from many democratic nations report their affinity for discussion (Avery, Simmons, & Freeman, 2007; Hahn, 1998; Yamashita, 2006). Political theorists also advocate discussion as a vital component of democratic living (Fishkin, 1991; Gutmann, 1999). Additionally, democratic education researchers laud classroom discussion—especially of the authentic political issues that animate political communities—as a key component of the pathway toward greater political knowledge and participation (McDevitt & Kiousis, 2006; Torney-Purta, Lehmann, Oswald, & Schultz, 2001). Issues discussion is thus advanced as both a pedagogical form and as a critical part of democratic education

(Parker & Hess, 2001). Advocates of classroom discussion view it as a particularly powerful instrument for developing critical thinking skills, teaching content, and increasing tolerance. But many also advance discussion in classrooms because they hope it will help young people learn how to be more effective discussants, thereby fostering their participation in discussions in other public venues. In short, discussion is not only a *way* to learn, but is also a skill to be learned. It cultivates skills and habits and a deeper understanding of public issues. Given these goals, it is not surprising that discussion has tremendous cachet in the field of democratic education.

Discussion as Authentic

As suggested above, much advocacy for discussion in democratic education emerges from the belief that a healthy democracy requires necessary and ongoing political discussion among citizens. That is, there is no end-point to discussion. But not just any talk will do. To cultivate democracy, students need to learn how to engage in high-quality public talk. Thus, advocates for the inclusion of controversial issues in the school curriculum aspire to prepare young people to participate fully and competently in a form of political engagement that is authentic to "the world outside of school" (Newmann & Wehlage, 1995).

Although this idea has been widely accepted and seems reasonable, the authenticity rationale has one stunning flaw. As we learned from Chapter 1, evidence shows few people actually engage in much political discussion—and when they do, it is likely to be with people who have the same views. There is no reason to believe that teachers are unaware of this reality. In fact, I consistently hear teachers advocate for issues discussions because they are concerned about what is happening in the "world outside of school." As Joe, a teacher whose practice we will learn about in Chapter 4, told me:

> I want my students to become part of the great conversations that take place in our society, and are taking place increasingly poorly. One of the things that drives me crazy is what goes for political conversations in our society, on TV especially, and in talk radio. They are shouting matches that have absolutely nothing to do with thoughtful dialogue and the complexities of issues. And that, I think is anti-democratic. (Hess, 1998, p. 75)

I frequently notice that when teachers talk about reasons for teaching their students how to discuss highly controversial political issues, they cite high-quality political discussion as a goal they hope society will achieve at some point, as opposed to a contemporary reality. Like Joe, they are not satisfied with the nature of the "great conversations" that occur now. They hope that teaching students how to participate in these types of discussions will make it more likely that they develop into adults who are *better* at creating a deliberative democracy than the generations that came before them have been.

Discussion as a Means to an End

Some scholars argue that discussions serve as *vehicles* for a host of outcomes, some of which are explicitly connected to democratic education. For example, discussions of political issues facilitate students' understanding of and commitment to democratic values, such as tolerance, equality, and diversity (Lockwood & Harris, 1985; Oliver & Shaver, 1974); increase their comfort with the nature and ubiquity of conflict existing in the world outside of school (Hibbing & Theiss-Morse, 2002); enhance their sense of political efficacy (Gimpel, Lay, & Schuknecht, 2003); advance their interest in engaging in public life (Zukin, Keeter, Andolina, Jenkins, & Delli Carpini, 2006); and teach them how to break down historic divides and, in turn, forge bonds between social groups in a community or nation where people are markedly different from one another (McCully, 2006). Advocates also associate issue discussions with schooling outcomes writ large, such as learning important content (Harris, 1996), improving critical thinking (Oliver & Shaver, 1974), and building more sophisticated interpersonal skills (D. W. Johnson & R. Johnson, 1995). In sum, an ambitious set of aims accompanies the use of discussion in democratic education.

Just as scholars have a plethora of reasons for supporting and advocating issues discussions in schools, teachers who create courses that emphasize such discussions often have multiple aims. In a study I conducted, one high school government teacher gave the following answer when asked about her rationales: "My number one goal is that my students will vote. If they do nothing else, they walk out of my class understanding why it is important to vote. The second goal, an overarching one, is for them to have opinions on issues and be able to state them, defend them, and know how to do it." Clearly, both of these goals are as noble to strive toward as they are challenging to realize, but this teacher also hoped that issues discussions would make it more likely that students would be able to critically evaluate how government works, how it affects them, *and* to learn important content. She recounted how she explained this to her students:

> I was telling a class that when Jay Leno stops you on the street (it is called Jay Walking), and puts a microphone in your face and asks you, "What is a Supreme Court?" you should be able to tell him. You should never be on the Jay Leno show because if you are on, you are the person that was not able to answer the question.

The Effects of Controversial Issues Discussions

With these rationales for controversial issues discussion in mind, I will now examine empirical evidence about how discussions affect students with respect to three dimensions: democratic values, content knowledge, and political and civic engagement.

On Democratic Values

Research on the development of democratic values provides strong support for the inclusion of controversial issues in democratic education. The strongest line of research in this area involves the relationship between issues discussions (and other forms of conflictual pedagogy) and the development of tolerance, as examined in a study of 338 middle and high school students (Avery, Bird, Johnstone, Sullivan, & Thalhammer, 1992; Bickmore, 1993). Defining tolerance as "the willingness to extend civil liberties to groups with whom one disagrees," researchers worked with a group of teachers to develop a four-week unit that involved a variety of active learning strategies, many focusing on controversial issues related to freedom of expression. Using a quasi-experimental design with control and experimental classes, the researchers found that the curriculum caused most students to move from mild intolerance to mild tolerance, regardless of their previous achievement levels in schools, gender, or SES. Moreover, in a follow-up study four weeks later, these gains did not dissipate. However, for a small number of students who demonstrated low levels of self-esteem and high levels of authoritarianism, the curriculum actually caused them to become less tolerant. While this backlash effect is troubling, it is significant that the effect of the curriculum for most students is increased tolerance.

On Content Understanding

Given the increased emphasis on testing in many nations, some teachers report that it is hard for them to justify spending time on issues discussions unless they can show a link to enhanced content knowledge. However, much of what students learn from issues discussions typically does not appear on the most commonly used measure of content knowledge: standardized tests. Yet, as David Harris (1996) compellingly asserts, "The effort to produce coherent language in response to a question of public policy puts knowledge in a meaningful context, making it more likely to be understood and remembered" (p. 289). Because this situated knowledge varies with each issue, standardized assessments cannot effectively measure what students have learned from an issue-based discussion.

Despite this obstacle, some researchers have developed generalized content-related outcomes. For example, to test the effects of issue-based discussions on student learning, researchers compared high school students who studied an issue and then discussed it in classrooms (with teachers who were trained in the public issues approach) against high school students who were exposed to the same background information but did not discuss the issue (J. Johnston, Anderman, Milne, Klenck, & Harris, 1994). Information about the issue was delivered to all students via a Channel One news program. The students in the experimental group (who watched the program and *discussed* it) scored higher on the current events test and also showed more improvement in their ability to analyze public issues discussions: they had gained knowledge.

There is also evidence that students in government classes that address local issues learn more about how social change occurs. Kahne, Chi, & Middaugh (2006) used a quasi-experimental design to assess the effects of a curriculum that focused on learning about problems in the community that the students found personally relevant, and how local government addresses those problems. Personal relevance was the strongest predictor of the civic outcomes they measured, which included various civic norms, knowledge of social networks, and trust. With respect to social networks, students who were in classes that included a focus on discussions of personally relevant issues were much more likely to report knowledge of whom to contact with concerns about their community, the resources available to help them with a community project, and how to work effectively with organizations in their community (Kahne et al., 2006, p. 14).

On Political and Civic Engagement

The most compelling empirical evidence that issues-based classroom discussions advance democratic outcomes comes from a quasi-experimental longitudinal study of the Kids Voting USA program (McDevitt & Kiousis, 2006). Students who participated in this interactive curriculum, which included classroom discussions of controversial issues, were much more likely to engage in acts associated with deliberative democracy than students without such exposure. Although the curriculum has a number of components, three were found to have the most dramatic influence on the long-term civic development of young people: frequent classroom discussions of election issues, teacher encouragement for expressing opinions, and student participation in get-out-the-vote drives (McDevitt & Kiousis, 2006, p. 3).

To summarize, there is evidence that participating in controversial issues discussions can build pro-democratic values (such as tolerance), enhance content understanding, and cause students to engage more in the political world. However, much more research is needed to understand the causal pathways between issues discussions and these outcomes.

How Students Experience Controversial Issues Discussions

Although theoretical and practical claims about what young people *could* or *should* learn from controversial issues discussions abound, to date we do not have a clear understanding of what students *do* learn and why. As discussed in the preceding section on the effects of controversial issues discussions, empirical evidence bolsters some claims about the beneficial outcomes of using discussion in classrooms, but generalizing these results is more problematic than one might expect. As Hahn (1996) pointed out in her review of research on issues-centered education, educators use many approaches to discussion, and virtually all of them are embedded in a course of study that includes a number of other components as well. Thus, measuring the influence that discussion of controversial issues has on particular outcomes is difficult.

Classrooms are complicated social spaces experienced differentially by different students. Thus, although the majority of students may find conversations about controversial issues engaging and relevant, others may view them as dull or, worse, as instigators of unequal power relations amongst students (Hess & Posselt, 2002; Rossi, 1995). Related to the latter point, Annette Hemmings's (2000) study of discussions in two high school classes illustrated how sociocultural divisions within each class influenced how and why students participated. She found that student displays of tolerance actually masked deep class and race-based divisions.

Hemmings's (2000) research raises a troubling challenge for teachers who want to include controversial issues discussions in their courses. Much of the theory supporting issues discussions rests on the assumption that diversity is a deliberative strength (Gutmann, 1999; Parker, 2003). According to this logic, discussions of controversial issues in classrooms with students who are similarly situated would yield less powerful results than a classroom with students from different socioeconomic and sociocultural backgrounds because there would not be enough difference of opinion to produce a meaningful consideration of competing perspectives. Simply put, students are not likely to develop respect for the opinions of others as a consequence of discussions if they are not given the opportunity to deliberate in a heterogeneous group. Given the multicultural nature of U.S. society, this argument goes, the classroom must represent that diversity rather than reify divisions based on race, class, religion, etc. However, just as diversity can be a deliberative strength, it can also re-inscribe social divisions if students feel they are being silenced or simply do not want to voice opinions that differ from the majority. In fact, David Campbell's (2005) analysis of the International Association for the Evaluation of Educational Achievement (IEA) data from the United States suggests an inverse relationship between exposure to controversial issues and racial diversity in a class. Specifically, he finds that African-American and White students are more likely to report issue discussions in their classrooms as the proportion of students who share their racial identity increases. He calls this phenomenon the "racial solidarity effect" (p. 16).

Although most of the research about how issues discussions work is based in classrooms and involves face-to-face discussion, a number of researchers are investigating how students experience online discussions. One study (Larson, 2003) compared students' experiences in both formats—face-to-face and online—and found that the online format sparked the participation of some students who often were silent in classroom discussions. However, the online discussion had drawbacks, too. In particular, the online discussions took longer for students because they had to read the postings. More significantly, Larson noted that many students simply responded to the teacher's prompts instead of to their classmates' comments—creating an online environment akin to the oft-used pedagogy of IRE in which the teacher initiates a question, elicits a response from a student, and then offers an evaluation of the student's response. Just as IRE is a form of classroom talk that is typically not considered discussion, Larson found that the online exchanges included few of the hallmarks of effective issues discussions.

It should not be a surprise that students experience controversial issues discussions in different ways, as that is the case for virtually all pedagogical practices. However, the public nature of students' participation in controversial issues discussions necessitates the creation of a classroom environment that students interpret as welcoming. Otherwise, these discussions may reify some of the inequalities that exist in the deliberative world outside of school. Although Campbell's research (2005) suggests that teachers may be more likely to engage students in issues discussions in racially homogeneous classrooms, students need to learn how to discuss issues in heterogeneous groups because differences of opinion that typically result from heterogeneous groupings can produce meaningful consideration of competing perspectives.

Accordingly, Parker (2003) argues that tracking practices in schools are harmful to issue-based deliberations. Moreover, evidence shows that in class-rooms where teachers activate students' ideological differences through contro-versial issues discussions, students begin to see political conflict as a normal and necessary part of democracy (Hess & Ganzler, 2007). This normalization of conflict is linked to enhanced political engagement (Hibbing & Theiss-Morse, 2002). Researchers routinely report that discussions in which students air and examine strong and genuine differences of opinion in a civil climate are also highly engaging to students (Hess & Ganzler, 2007; Hess & Posselt, 2002; McDevitt & Kiousis, 2006; Rossi, 1995), which may account for the correlation between participation in issues discussions and increased political engagement.

Further complicating researchers' attempts to understand how students experience and learn from controversial issues discussions is the fact that few schools or school districts in any nation have infused controversial issue discussions in the curricula in systematic, developmentally-sequenced ways. Not surprisingly then, researchers who study the effects of a single course that includes some attention to controversial issues discussions find that even exceptionally well-taught courses do not result in significant gains on specified outcomes (Avery et al., 2007; Hahn & Tocci, 1990; Hess & Posselt, 2002). A final and perhaps more serious obstruction to a well-warranted understanding of the relationship between stated goals for discussion and their realization in practice is the contradiction between what teachers and students say about the prevalence of issue discussions in schools and what researchers who do large-scale field studies observe.

The Prevalence of Controversial Issues Discussions

Given the frequency of arguments for including controversial issues discussions in democratic education, we could logically conclude that they are a fairly standard component of school-based democratic education. In the 1999 IEA Civic Education Study of students in 28 nations, items such as "teachers encourage us to discuss political or social issues about which people have different opinions" and "students feel free to disagree openly with their teachers about political and social issues during class" were included on a survey measuring open classroom climate. This survey construct measured the "extent to which students experience their classrooms as places to investigate issues and explore their opinions and those of their peers" (Torney-Purta et al., 2001, p. 138). The researchers of this study reported that an open classroom climate for discussion is an especially significant predictor of civic knowledge and political engagement, as measured by whether young people say they will vote when they are legally able (2001, p. 155).

Although there was variance within and across nations with respect to the number of students who assessed their classrooms as open, well over half of the students reported that their classrooms were "sometimes" or "often" open. More specifically, when asked whether students "feel free to disagree openly with their teachers about issues," 67% said that was "sometimes" or "often" the case (Torney-Purta et al., 2001, p. 207). The teacher reports from several nations, when compared with past teacher assessments, showed an increase in rich controversial issues discussion taking place in democratic education programs. In Britain, 58% of teachers reported that "exploring, discussing and debating issues" occurred often in their classes. Just two years earlier, only 47% indicated that was the case (Kerr, Lopes, Nelson, White, Cleaver, & Benton, 2007, p. 59).

In contrast to these promising student and teacher self-reports, large-scale observational studies described virtually no classroom discussion of any sort. For example, when Martin Nystrand, Wu, Gamoran, Zeiser, and Long (2003) analyzed discourse in 106 middle and high school social studies classes in the United States for a year-long study, they found that "despite considerable lip service among teachers to 'discussion'," little discussion occurred in any classes (p. 178). Joseph Kahne, Rodriquez, Smith, and Thiede (2000) described similar findings in their secondary analysis of observers' reports of 135 middle and high school social studies classes in the Chicago Public Schools. In over 80% of the classes, social problems were not mentioned. Even when teachers brought up problems, discussion of possible solutions, connections to contemporary life, or action rarely followed suit.

Given that many studies of issues-based curricula rely on student self-reports, these conflicting findings merit consideration. One explanation for these disparate conclusions is that students and teachers alike tend to conflate classroom talk with discussion (Hess & Ganzler, 2007; Larson, 1997; Nystrand et al., 2003). Wendy Richardson's (2006) study about how U.S. high school students interpret the IEA Civic Education survey questions offers evidence to support this theory. She found that the majority of students do not make a distinction between a controversial issue and a current event, and that their conception of discussion includes any talk with a teacher, even if it occurs outside of class (p. 171).

In a study of my own, which involves 1,100 high school students and 35 teachers in 21 high schools, we are finding that some students label their classroom climate as open although they do not engage in the robust discussion of issues (Hess & Ganzler, 2007). For example, in one classroom the teacher lectured on many days and did not facilitate any full-fledged issue discussions. Nevertheless, the students reported an open classroom climate on the items that were also used on the IEA Civic Education survey. We are also finding, however, that students are less likely to report an open classroom climate in classes with virtually no student talk. The latter conclusion raises the possibility that these survey items are not a proxy for issues discussions *per se*. Instead, students may be communicating that they are in classrooms with at least some modicum of a democratic ethos, student talk, and acknowledgment of controversial issues. Although discussion experts do not equate classroom talk with discussion (Nystrand et al., 2003; Parker, 2003), it appears that students do.

In sum, although the occurrence of controversial issue discussions influences democratic outcomes, students' sense of being in a classroom where they can speak and their opinions are respected also matters. Thus researchers may need to pay greater attention to how student perceptions of an open classroom climate affect the realization of democratic education goals like increased tolerance, political knowledge, and political interest.

The research drawn upon in this chapter clearly demonstrates the rationales for the inclusion of controversial issues discussions and the empirical evidence that both supports and clouds these rationales. Throughout, I have purposely avoided answering the seemingly obvious question of how to define what constitutes a controversial political issue. In the next chapter, I turn to the perhaps more difficult task of forming a concept of controversial political issues, as distinguished from other potential curricular components of democratic education.

3
Defining Controversial Political Issues

Given the long history of advocacy for issues-centered approaches to teaching discussed in the beginning of Chapter 2, it should not be surprising that a host of frameworks have been proposed as conceptual tools for thinking about how to define issues. For example, in an approach advanced in the early 1950s, Hunt and Metcalf (1955) advocated the inclusion of issues related to "taboo" topics (such as sexuality and racism) in the curriculum, while Oliver and Shaver's (1966) approach focused on policy issues that included the weighing and balancing of competing "democratic" values (such as liberty and equality). Some issues are defined as inherently public, while others, such as the moral dilemmas in Kohlberg's (1981) approach, are personal decisions for an individual to make in a morally complex situation. In addition, other dimensions of how issues are conceptualized and defined include time (an issue of the past, the present, or possibly the future), place (local, state, national, global), and scope (ranging from broad perennial issues to more narrowly focused "case" issues).

In this chapter, I explain what I mean by controversial political issues. My definition is by no means original. It is derived from how teachers and students define issues in their teaching and learning, coupled with ideas and frameworks developed in the past whose quality have passed the test of time (most notably, the work of Dewey, 1927; Kohlberg & Mayer, 1972; Hunt & Metcalf, 1955; Oliver & Shaver, 1966; Oliver & Newmann, 1967; Engle & Ochoa, 1988; Parker, 2003; Fineman, 2008).[1]

Defining the Term

I define *controversial political issues* as questions of public policy that spark significant disagreement. These are authentic questions about the kinds of public policies that should be adopted to address public problems—they are not hypothetical. Such issues require deliberation among a "we" to determine which policy is the best response to a particular problem. These are the public's problems, and as such, they both deserve and require the public's input in some cases (such as what policy a school board or other legislature should adopt) and the public's actual decision in others (often voiced through a ballot initiative or other "direct democracy" process).[2] Moreover, it is important to remember that the people crafting and adopting public policies *are* members of the public—school board members, state legislators, and the like. Thus, when such people engage in policy deliberations they are public actors. Controversial political issues are open questions, meaning there are multiple and often strikingly different answers that are legitimate—even though people frequently have strongly held and well-reasoned opinions about which answer they prefer.

The concept label *controversial political issue* is not without problems—notably the redundancy of the words controversial and issue. However, some issues *are* more controversial than others because they generate more disagreement, and I use both words in the label to signal my view that issues that generate more controversy often deserve and need public—and hence, students'—attention. In the past, I used the word "public" instead of political in the label, but I have come to believe that in an era when many people view political as pejorative, it is time to reclaim the word as the heart of democratic decision-making. That is, I am using political in the classic sense—the making of governmental policy, which in a democracy depends on the public, or should do so, if it is functioning well.

This definition of controversial political issues, it should be noted, is much narrower than the broader conceptions of controversial issues or academic controversies often used in a variety of school subjects. For example, it purposely does not include historical issues, such as what caused a particular event in history, which are frequently quite controversial and clearly appropriate for the curriculum. By excluding those issues from my definition I am not suggesting they should be excluded from the curriculum. In fact, I think there are a variety of types of issues that students should be asked to grapple with in schools—historical issues, moral issues, scientific issues, constitutional issues, and the list goes on.

It is also important to note from the outset that there are often significant disagreements about whether a particular controversial political issue is actually an issue or, conversely, whether it is a question for which there is one clear answer. In this chapter, I explain the critical attributes of the concept of controversial political issues. In Chapter 7, I complicate that very definition by describing a phenomenon I call "tipping," which illustrates that whether a question is a matter of legitimate controversy or one for which there is a right answer often shifts over time and varies by context.

Forming the Concept

When teaching the definition of controversial political issues to teachers and those preparing to be teachers, I often use a tool of concept formation that I learned from Walter Parker (and that he learned from Hilda Taba).[3] This pedagogical strategy begins with an analysis of examples of the concept (in our

Table 3.1 Concept Formation

Read through the questions below and then complete the exercise that follows:

---

1. Should public money be used for school tuition vouchers for students who attend private schools?
2. Should our democracy have the power to prohibit unauthorized public demonstrations?
3. Should the U.S. immediately initiate a withdrawal of armed forces from Iraq?
4. Should the states and the federal government pass legislation banning the death penalty?
5. Should our city have a curfew for youth?
6. What should the international community do to combat terrorism?
7. Should our state pass a law legalizing marriage between members of the same sex?
8. Should the U.S. drop its economic sanctions against Cuba?
9. Should the United Nations pass a resolution banning the cloning of human beings?
10. The new challenges of American immigration: What should we do?

EXERCISE: Working with a partner, please discuss the following:

---

1. What are the differences among these questions (see 1–10 listed above)?
2. What are the similarities among these questions?
3. Identify the similarities that seem most significant to you and craft a sentence with this stem: These are all questions that (or in which) . . .
4. Develop a label for these types of questions.

---

case, controversial political issue) being formed. Students read the following questions (Table 3.1) and then work through the exercise that follows.

When I developed this list of questions, I sought to include examples that clearly represented what I saw as the most essential "critical attributes" of the concept of controversial political issues: such issues are authentic, contemporary, and open. You will notice that these are all questions of public policy at the local, state, national, and international level. While the majority of the issues focus on a specific policy proposal beginning with the word "should," there are a few that are worded much more broadly. I did this purposely to represent the different approaches that curriculum developers and teachers use when framing issues for students.[4] Moreover, although it is possible that some of these issues are not considered legitimate matters of controversy, my experience has been that most of them are—although it is important to note that I have only used this lesson with teachers (pre and practicing) in the United States. It is likely that some of these topics would not be seen as issues in other nations. It is also possible that in the future some of these will no longer be considered legitimate matters of controversy in the United States. The goal of this lesson is not to debate whether or not an issue is controversial; rather, it is to help students identify the ways in which these issues are similar: they are authentic, are contemporary, and are really issues—that is, open questions.

This lesson lays the groundwork for the development of five key ideas about the differences between controversial political issues and other topics and issues—many of which are routinely conflated—which is problematic for a number of reasons that I detail. For each of the five ideas listed below, I explain the distinction embedded in the statement (for example, the difference between a topic and an issue), provide some examples, and then explain why the distinction is important in the curriculum. The five ideas are:

1. There is a difference between topics, problems, and issues.
2. There is a difference between current events and issues.
3. There is a difference between specific case issues and larger perennial issues.
4. There is a difference between public and private issues.
5. There is a difference between controversial political issues and constitutional issues.

Number One: Distinguishing Topics, Problems, and Issues

Topics, problems, and issues are three concepts commonly, although mistakenly, used in conversation to mean the same thing. This conflation is problematic because it can dampen the controversy unique to *issues*, which is what makes them such good topics for discussion. A topic can be an event (such as the Iraq War), a place (the Middle East), or an act or a process (such as immigration or nuclear disarmament). In the context of controversial issues teaching, topics are often used to articulate the primary content focus of a lesson, unit, or even a course.

For example, healthcare is a topic—not an issue *per se*. However, there are numerous controversial political issues related to healthcare, such as whether or not the United States should adopt a national healthcare system or whether or not businesses should be required to provide healthcare to their employees.

As another example, consider my experience in the spring of 2006, when I spoke at a conference for teachers from Northern Ireland and the Republic of Ireland that focused on the inclusion of controversial issues in the curriculum. I began my talk by asking the teachers to list issues that were important to them and/or their students. The teachers had no problem listing *topics*, all of which they saw as presenting *problems* the society needed to address. Religious strife, immigration, discrimination, racism, and healthcare were many of the *topics* listed by the teachers. I tried to probe their understanding of these topics and what typically followed was a fairly detailed explanation of the *problems* associated with each of the topics. For example, teachers described the problems that revolved around the topic of immigration, such as whether or not immigrants were being taken advantage of by employers, whether or not they were getting the access they needed to vital social services, and whether or not their children were being treated with kindness and respect in the schools. They also explained that some people believed the large number of recent immigrants was preventing people who already resided in these nations from finding work. It is notable and laudable in my view that many of these problems emanated from the teachers' human rights orientation about the need to ensure that all people within their borders were treated with dignity and respect. It wasn't until I asked additional questions that the teachers were able to identify policy proposals—the actual *issues*—that were being considered, or which they thought should be considered, to address some of the problems.

What was interesting to me about the trajectory of this discussion is how it mirrored the way in which many teachers and their students move from topics to problems to issues when determining what question will be the focus of classroom deliberation. In Chapter 4, I illustrate how this works in some classes, but suffice it to say for now, it is not unusual for a class to identify topics they are interested in (e.g., the Iraq War, access to higher education, student rights in the school) and then define problems related to those topics before focusing on an issue or issues for deliberation. This winnowing process often provides essential background and context, so it clearly has pedagogical value. It provides an understanding of the broader context in which an issue is embedded, and also helpfully focuses students' attention on deliberating about whether a proposed policy will have the desired effect. That is, will it solve the problem(s) without creating even larger problems?

That being said, deliberations that focus on controversial political issues, as opposed to topics or problems, tend to be much more effective because it is exceptionally difficult to create a high-quality discussion if the focus is too broad. It tends to lead to meandering, lots of talking past one another, and little depth. For example, having a discussion on the topic of healthcare would be quite challenging—it is simply too big and there are too many things that could be discussed. A discussion on the problem of lack of *access* to high-quality healthcare is more manageable because it is more focused. One can imagine a good discussion about who lacks access to healthcare and why; however, if the discussion ends there, the opportunity to consider what should be done to enhance access to high-quality healthcare—the important policy issue—would be lost. Thus, the reason I make a distinction among topics, problems, and issues is not to suggest that topics or problems lack importance, but to help clarify the central attributes of controversial political issues: they focus on policy questions that are authentic and contemporary.

Number Two: Distinguishing Current Events from Issues

Just as topic, problem, and issue are often conflated, there is evidence to suggest that the oft-used phrase "current events" is routinely used as a synonym for controversial political issues and vice versa (Richardson, 2006). There are instances when this is accurate—that is, many current events are issues, and many issues are current events. For example, many of the issues listed earlier in this chapter are currently on the public agenda and arise in the context of a current event. And often, public debate about an issue is itself a current debate (imagine, for example, a school board's public deliberations about whether or not to ask the public to approve a tax increase). As a result, to urge that distinctions be made between current events and issues may seem inaccurate at worst and nitpicking at best. Still, I think there is a very powerful reason to make this distinction, which is that the way in which current events are often included in the classroom can work to depress controversy and focus students' attention on topics that may be interesting but are not as important as controversial political issues. In other words, the opportunity cost for conflating current events and issues is high. This is so because many events that are currently in the news are not very important and not at all controversial. Drawing the distinction clarifies the difference between staying informed about popular news and becoming aware of the issues that face society.

Of course, there are some current events that are worth class time—and we should be concerned that so many teachers believe they can no longer take the time to help students understand contemporary events because of the pressures of standardized curriculum and high-stakes tests. As a case in point, in the fall of 2001, I was struck by the number of teachers who told me that they did not spend much (and in some cases, any) time helping students understand the attacks of 9/11 because they feared it would detract from the time needed to "cover" the curriculum. In one case a teacher said that she only had two class periods to "do" the War of 1812 and so she simply could not spare the time to focus on 9/11. I remember thinking at the time that it was downright bizarre that we had so reified what is considered core knowledge that teachers felt like they could not spare the time to teach about what was clearly one of the most significant events of our time. Thus, I think it is certainly helpful when students learn about current events that are important. In fact, this is often a powerful precursor to focusing students' attention on controversial political issues. Moreover, it is likely beneficial for teachers to engage students in activities that are designed to teach them the skills and habits needed to pay attention to what is in the news. But my concern is that too many teachers stop at the level of awareness of current events, and thus students are deprived of learning how to deliberate issues. Thus, it is critically important to make clear distinctions between what is an event and what is an issue, and not to think that the question of *what is* happening is the same as the question of what we should do about it.

Number Three: Distinguishing Specific Case Issues from Perennial Issues

One distinguishing and extremely useful feature of the Harvard Public Issues Project (Oliver & Shaver, 1966) was the inclusion of perennial issues and subsequent specific topical issues that were presented as "cases of" the larger, more transcendent issue. Often, these perennial issues are said to cross time and place. It is not difficult to find historical examples of issues that have transcended time, and there are also contemporary issues likely to arise in the future that will remain relevant long after they are first generated. For example, in a set of curriculum materials emanating from a project that was developed by Donald Oliver and Fred Newmann called the Public Issues Series, there is a distinction made between general topics (e.g., The New Deal, Revolution, Organized Labor), perennial issues (e.g., Under what circumstances should the government intervene in the economy?), and case issues (e.g., Was the New Deal justified?). Notice that the case issue is not perennial because it emanates from a specific controversy in a particular time and place. But the question about when government intervention is justified is perennial—there were certainly many examples of it before and after the New Deal, and it is fairly easy to predict that this question will continue to arise in the future. It is frequently the case that teachers select controversial political issues because they are "cases" of perennial issues they deem important for their students to experience deliberating. The teachers know that the perennial issues will arise frequently in their students' futures and want to give them very concrete experiences wrestling with the value tensions that so often undergird and are embedded in perennial issues—tensions between liberty and security for example, or between autonomy and equality. Doing so in the context of a specific issue is helpful because the discussion is more focused. For example, a discussion about when a nation is justified in going to war tends to fall flat unless there is a specific case of the question to deliberate. But it is enormously helpful for teachers to select controversial political issues that are clearly examples of the perennial issues that they want to engage their students in deliberating. Moreover, especially powerful learning can occur when teachers are able to help students move inductively and deductively between cases and the perennial issue they exemplify.

Number Four: Distinguishing Public from Private Issues

Many of the most interesting discussions in classrooms focus not on public issues but on private ones—questions about what individuals should do in morally complex situations. For example, in a curriculum developed by Lockwood and Harris (1985), students are asked to discuss what an individual will do when faced with an especially challenging question. For example, the question of whether or not a person should join the military in the United States is a private decision. Contrast that with the question of whether the United States should reinstitute the military draft—this is a controversial political issue. It is important to distinguish private issues from public issues, in that the type of controversial political issues discussion I advocate requires deliberation among a group of people to determine which policy is the best response to a particular problem facing the group. Instead of focusing on individual choices, this type of discussion focuses on the public's problems, problems that deserve and require the public's input and/or the public's actual decision.

Again, I am not suggesting that drawing students' attentions to the complexity of individual decisions is out of bounds in schools—we know much of good literature teaching focuses on just these types of questions. However, they are quite different from controversial political issues. There is a critical distinction that needs to be made between what an individual might do in a situation and what the society writ large should be allowed or forbidden from doing. Focusing only on personal or private issues masks that difference and could lead students to believe that whatever they decide to do is what everybody should do.

Number Five: Distinguishing Constitutional and Public Policy Issues

The distinction between constitutional issues and controversial political issues regarding public policy is especially important because it illustrates a critical difference between the kind of work that is done in legislatures compared to courts. Moreover, the kind of thinking and the sources on which the thinking is often based are different when people engage in discussions of constitutional issues compared with policy issues. We should want people to understand both types of issues; but equally as important is ensuring that the distinction between them is clear, even though, as we shall see, there is considerable overlap in practice and in pedagogy.

Constitutional issues are questions about the meaning of the Constitution that spark significant disagreement. Such issues require us to consider whether or not an existing government policy or action is constitutional. That is, *can* the government exercise power in a particular way without violating the Constitution? Or, in some cases, *must* the government act in a certain way because of the Constitution? For example, the question of whether or not the United States Constitution should be interpreted to prohibit the execution of juveniles who commit capital crimes prior to turning 18 years of age is a constitutional issue, as is the question of whether or not laws banning same-sex sodomy violated the 14th Amendment. In both of these cases, the United States Supreme Court has recently ruled that the government action (executing juveniles and criminalizing sodomy) did violate the Constitution; therefore, it is no longer constitutionally permissible for such policies to exist, and the option is off the policy-making table absent a subsequent decision that opens it up again (to amend the Constitution, for example, or a reversal of precedent by the Court). But had the Court gone the other way and said these actions did not violate the Constitution, then the policy question—should "we" do these things—would be on the public's platter. It is also important to recognize that just because a government action or policy is constitutional (that is, allowed), it does not necessarily follow that it is a good idea or has to be done. For example, it is constitutional for a school district to drug test some students, but it is not required by the Constitution, and there is real dispute about whether or not it is a good idea. Constitutional issues discussions are primarily designed to help students develop deep knowledge about the Constitution—what it means and how it influences what the government can and cannot do. Such knowledge is critical in a law-based society. The Constitution, after all, is the "highest law" in the land. Consequently, I am a strong supporter of engaging students in discussions of constitutional issues, which is frequently done through an analysis of specific cases that have come before a court (often an appellate court).

However, it would be misleading to suggest that courts never consider whether or not a policy is a good idea or whether or not alternative policies might be better suited to the problem at hand. In some cases, the courts will evaluate the importance of a goal and whether or not there is a way of achieving a goal that is less intrusive on individual rights in order to determine if a particular policy is constitutional. For example, if an individual right is considered "fundamental" (such as the right to travel and the right to marry), then the courts will apply what is known as "strict scrutiny" when judging whether or not a government policy violates the Constitution. Strict scrutiny asks whether the goal of the government is a "compelling one" (i.e., really important) and whether there is a close relationship between the goal and the policy. These questions, by definition, are policy-focused.

Even when a case does not involve a fundamental individual right, the courts often let policy analysis seep into their decision-making about constitutionality. As an example, in the most recent school voucher case, some Supreme Court justices explicitly focused on the question of whether public or parochial schools provided students with a better education. During oral arguments, one justice even went so far as to state that "there are extensive studies that show that parochial schools do a better job" (*Zelman v. Simmons-Harris*, 2002, official arguments transcript, p. 64). Arguably, this claim was both factually erroneous and irrelevant to the constitutional question at hand, which was whether or not a particular school voucher program violated the establishment clause. This example illustrates that courts do not employ a bright line separation between the questions of whether or not a policy is constitutional or wise. Consequently, it is challenging for teachers to determine how much of a distinction they should help their students draw between constitutional and policy issues, which in my experience can often lead to a conflation of the two with problematic results. To explain this, let's examine the difference between what students could learn in a constitutional versus policy discussion.

WHAT STUDENTS LEARN FROM CONSTITUTIONAL AND PUBLIC
POLICY ISSUES DISCUSSIONS

Because of the core difference between constitutional and public policy issues, the types of arguments and the evidence used to discuss each should differ. A constitutional issue discussion should focus on the actual text of the Constitution and should explore competing interpretations of what a particular part of the Constitution means (or should mean) relative to a particular government policy and significant case precedents. If a discussion of a constitutional issue is effective, students should achieve a variety of important educational goals, including building a deeper and broader understanding of the meaning of the particular part of the Constitution that the issue is about, recognizing that meaning is socially constructed and changes over time (i.e., "a living Constitution"), understanding the important precedents for the issue and various interpretations of how they apply to the issue at hand, knowing the facts of a case (or cases) about the constitutional issue, and understanding the process used by courts (and other branches of government) to make decisions about the issue.

To engage in public policy discussions effectively, students need the faculty to weigh different types of arguments and evidence. Consequently, the content knowledge they build should *include* but also *extend beyond* constitutional understanding. A public policy issue discussion stems from core questions, such as, "is this policy fair?" and "will it work?" In such a discussion, one would expect to hear many different types of arguments (and evidence) used: ethical, economic, historical, personal experience, sociological, etc. The discourse should focus also on the history and nature of the particular problem the policy is designed to address, as well as the goal the policy will work toward. The discussion will center on what the desired end of an issue should be and whether or not a particular policy will accomplish it. If a discussion of a controversial public policy issue is effective, students should build a deeper and broader understanding of the following things: the causes and nature of the particular problem(s) that the policy issue is about; the origin(s) and history of the public policy; what makes the public policy controversial, including who supports it and who does not; and arguments in favor of and against the public policy that are based on a variety of different types of evidence and analyses (e.g., economic, historical, etc.). Many teachers hope that as a consequence of controversial issues discussions, students will become more motivated to act politically.

SIMILARITIES BETWEEN CONSTITUTIONAL AND POLICY DISCUSSIONS

It is especially easy to see the overlap between these two types of issues by examining what resources a teacher might draw on to help students prepare for discussion. In preparing for a constitutional discussion, background knowledge of various public policies is helpful because it can provide context in which to consider the constitutional question. Similarly, a public policy discussion can benefit from knowledge of the Constitution—it is, after all, supposed to be the guiding framework for the entire system.

First, if a class is exploring a constitutional issue, then the resources a teacher provides students to prepare for the discussion should focus *mostly* on the text of the Constitution, not resources debating whether or not the policy is a good idea. After all, "bad" policies can be constitutional, just as "good" ones can violate the Constitution (for example, some citizens might argue that Washington, DC's recently stricken-down handgun ban was a good policy). Teachers, then, should consider carefully if some evidence about whether or not a policy is a good idea belongs in the preparation materials for a constitutional issue discussion. There are cases (such as those involving fundamental rights) when it certainly is necessary. But because it is often difficult to focus students' attention on constitutional issues in the face of questions about whether or not a policy is a good idea, it may be wise to err on the side of preparation materials that focus intensely and explicitly on the constitutional arguments during constitutional issue discussion.

Conversely, resources that will adequately prepare students to participate in public policy issues discussions need to cover a broader range because there are so many types of arguments (and forms of evidence) that should be employed when making policy decisions. For example, making a decision about whether or not to initiate a school voucher program should involve weighing educational claims (e.g., "What do we know about what students learn in different types of schools?"), economic arguments (e.g., "What effect will a voucher program have on the funds available for public schools?"), and so forth.

In some cases, information about whether or not a policy is constitutional is an important part of the preparation for a public policy discussion. This is the case when there is a genuine question about whether or not a proposed policy will pass constitutional muster or when a legislature is deliberately trying to provoke a change in constitutional interpretation. For example, after the Supreme Court ruled that drug testing student-athletes did not violate the Constitution, some school districts passed policies extending the testing to students in other forms of extracurricular activities. It would be important to understand how the Court viewed the constitutional question involved with drug testing student-athletes when participating in a policy discussion about whether or not to extend the reach of a testing program.

This distinction between what is being decided with controversial political issues compared to constitutional issues is a crucial one that if misunderstood, can lead to both bad pedagogy and bad governance. For example, I frequently encounter teachers who use constitutional cases as the only preparation for engaging students in policy decisions, which is exceedingly problematic because, as noted above, effective policy discussions should draw on a much broader range of sources. Moreover, it makes it exceedingly difficult for students to understand that just because something *can* be done it *should* be done.

As an alternative, I strongly encourage teachers to include both types of issues in their classes—and to link them when possible while still maintaining critical distinctions. For example, I recently examined a high school teacher's unit on "Contemporary Trends and Issues of Race in the United States" and had a conversation with him about how the unit worked in practice. One part of the unit focused on affirmative action. The students engaged in a moot court of an affirmative action case that the Supreme Court recently decided in which they ruled that some forms of affirmative action in university admissions are constitutionally permissible. The moot court required them to examine and evaluate the multiple and competing perspectives on whether affirmative action should be constitutional. In other words, it was through the moot court that the teacher engaged students in the topic as a constitutional issue—and during this part of the unit the students focused primarily on the 14th Amendment and key precedents. But it also showcased for the students the ways in which courts rely on policy, as in sources to make decisions, because in this case there were a plethora of amicus briefs that relied primarily on policy analysis—and some of these clearly had influence on some of the justices' thinking about the issue.

After the moot court, students broadened their inquiry to prepare for a controversial political issue discussion on whether affirmative action policies should be enacted. They examined a much wider range of sources and moved dramatically beyond the constitutional question. The teacher reported to me that while there was often overlap between how the students felt about the constitutional and policy issues that was not always the case. Some students believed that affirmative action should be constitutional, but was not a good idea as a matter of policy. Others believed that while it was a good policy, it should not be considered constitutional. The unit impressed me because while it seemed to focus on the critical distinctions between constitutional and policy issues, which prevented their conflation, it still showed the ways in which they overlap. This seemed much more sophisticated than an approach I frequently encounter that uses a constitutional case as the only source to set up a policy discussion or writing activity.

Conclusion

In developing a definition of controversial political issues that is useful to both educators and students alike, I have sought not only to explain what is meant by "controversial political issues" – questions of public policy that spark significant disagreement among a group of people – but also to show how these issues differ from topics, problems, current events, and other issues that have an important, but different, role to play in the classroom (i.e., constitutional issues). At the same time, as illustrated in the case of constitutional issues, there is often some overlap between controversial political issues and other types of issues. Moreover, it is clearly the case that students can benefit from engaging in discussion of a range of different types of issues. So I do not mean to suggest that controversial political issues are the only types worth curricular attention.

The definitions and distinctions I have explained in this chapter only go so far, however. They beg the important questions of what issues should be in the curriculum to begin with, and what happens when there is disagreement about whether a question that is clearly a controversial political issue to some people is considered a question for which there is a right answer to others. In short, there are significant controversies about what should be considered rightfully and legitimately controversial—which is the topic I shall return to in Chapters 7 and 8.

II
Inside Classrooms

4
Skillful Teaching of Controversial Issues Discussions

While there are many factors influencing whether or not students learn how to discuss highly controversial issues effectively in classrooms, the single most important factor is the quality of a teacher's practice. Consequently, this chapter presents three examples of teachers effectively engaging students in controversial issues discussions, and for contrast, one example of a controversial issues discussion that falls completely flat. I will start with that one.

This discussion took place in a classroom of high school seniors. The day *after* a school referendum had failed, the teacher came in and tried to spark a discussion about why it had failed and what the consequences would be for students and teachers.

Unfortunately, many of the students knew nothing about the referendum, which caused them to remain silent. A handful of students participated—and they actually did have interesting things to say—but the majority sat quietly. During the discussion, some said they did not vote because they just did not know enough to make a decision, and clearly they did not know enough to participate in the discussion either.

Moreover, even though the teacher asked the students to identify and critically evaluate reasons in support of and against the referendum as a way to understand why it did not pass, it became very clear very quickly that he really did not want the students to thoughtfully consider multiple perspectives. When a student gave a reason against the referendum, he quickly refuted either the factual claim on which it was based or added a counterpoint argument. However, when students articulated and positively evaluated reasons in favor of its passage, he would nod in agreement, often elaborate on the points, and in one instance, banged on the table and said, "that's right—please say that again so everyone gets it."

When he was interviewed after class, it became evident that the teacher was unaware of how few students had participated. Because he and a small number of students had kept the discussion going for most of a class period, he believed it had been a success, although he did say that he may have gone a bit overboard in his critique of students who had articulated the position that did not comport with his own, an issue we will return to in Chapter 6.

[handwritten margin note, left: MISTAKE]

[handwritten margin note, right: TEACHER, NO!]

There were a number of problems with this discussion. First, waiting until after the election was a mistake because the students could have benefited from an opportunity to learn about this important issue before the day of the vote, especially given that a number of them were old enough to participate in the election. Second, the students were not prepared to participate, as evidenced by the fact that many did not have even a rudimentary understanding of what a referendum was, what this one called for, and what arguments had been marshaled in support or opposition to its passage. This clearly accounts for why so many remained silent. Third, the teacher did not engage students in a rigorous analysis of the competing points of view that *were* voiced by the students who did talk because he could not control his own bias. All of these problems were in the teacher's power to correct—which illustrates why I believe that the quality of a teacher's practice is the key ingredient to the creation of high-quality issues discussions.

I do not mean to suggest that teachers who are skillful at teaching their students to participate effectively in issues discussions have to be what Levy (1998, p. 3) calls, "classroom wizards," those individual teachers who "overcome apparently insurmountable odds to succeed where others have failed." Unfortunately, the portrayals of strong teachers that are so often shown in the media reinforce this conception of effective teachers (Barton & Burroughs, in press). Instead, I have learned that what marks these teachers as skillful is their ability to put into practice well thought-out and thorough lesson plans about controversial issues that are informed by a sophisticated understanding of the purpose of discussion and its link to democracy writ large. Moreover, they are able to "carry off" their theoretical ideas and goals—that is, they have sound ideas about what they are trying to teach as well as the skill to translate these ideas to practice.

In the case studies below, all three teachers believed in education as a tool to help students better understand and participate in democracy, and one critical part of their practice that aligned with this theory was the use of controversial issues discussions. As we shall see, the teachers also agreed with deliberative theorists who argue for an intrinsic connection between the health of a democracy and high-quality political talk among citizens. But there were different elements of what specific attributes of high-quality political talk the teachers thought should receive the most attention in issues discussions. You will notice that the teachers showcased here are aligning their teaching practice—what they and their students actually do in the classroom—with their specific interpretations of which elements of deliberative democracy are most important for their students to learn.

The case studies below also tell the stories of three teachers who have developed strategies for managing the complexities of this kind of teaching. Some of these strategies are not unique to issues discussion teaching. Developing sound lesson plans and having high expectations for students, for example, are strategies evident in virtually all instantiations of skillful teaching. Other strategies and elements of their practice, however, clearly resulted from decisions the teachers had made about core methods questions that arise more frequently with issues discussion teaching than they would in many other pedagogical approaches: Should students be required to participate verbally in class discussions, or simply be encouraged to do so? Should students be grouped with peers with similar discussion skills, or be grouped with students who have a variety of skills? Should students have an influence on selecting the issues to be included in the curriculum?

These core questions are themselves controversial issues. Specifically, they are *pedagogical issues* that are especially important for teachers to address. Many of these issues are controversial for teachers, students, and their parents. For example, the question of whether or not it is acceptable to require students to speak during discussion often provokes intense debate, as does teacher disclosure (discussed at length in Chapter 6). Notably, there are real differences among the teachers about what is the best answer to these questions—as one would expect given that they are controversial. Thus, woven throughout this chapter are illustrations of both the similarities and differences in pedagogical approach by teachers who are particularly skillful teaching their students to discuss controversial political issues.

Even though the practice of the three teachers differs in important ways, they share a rich and expansive conception of discussion, which shows up in one key similarity in their practice: they teach intentionally *for* and *with* discussion. Put another way, discussion is both a desired outcome and a method of teaching students critical thinking skills, important content, and interpersonal skills. According to Parker (2006) those two instantiations of teaching with and for discussion (seminar and deliberation) are important because "The two kinds of discourse are complementary in school practice, and neither is sufficient alone. They express the two goals of liberal education, both at risk today: enriching the mind and cultivating a democratic political community" (p. 12). Through discussion, students can learn deep content *and* important discussion skills.

To elaborate, teaching *for* discussion means that these teachers strive to teach students how to participate effectively in discussions in school and in other public situations. The teachers emphasize the importance of scaffolding discussion instruction so that students can participate in the "great conversations" of democratic society. Teaching *for* discussion cannot be achieved through the use of other instructional strategies. Put differently, students cannot learn to participate more effectively in discussions by writing papers. As another teacher from the first study exclaimed, "There has to be some sort of environment where kids practice [discussing]. They practice baseball batting, for God's sake, why can't they practice talking?"

Teaching *with* discussion, by contrast, represents a panoply of other reasons the teachers have for foregrounding issues discussions in their curriculum, such as learning important social studies content and developing the belief that many perspectives are necessary to fully understand the nuances and complexities of controversial political issues. By teaching *for* and *with* discussion, the teachers direct the full resources of their pedagogical content knowledge to the lesson planning process, and they devote a generous amount of classroom time to teaching students how to prepare for discussions, how to participate in them, and how to debrief them.

Background

The following three case studies are drawn from research I have done since 1997 (Hess, 2002; Hess & Posselt, 2002; Hess & Ganzler, 2007). In my work, I sought to follow Shulman's (1983) recommendation to study "good cases" because they allow us to learn from the possible, not only the probable. These "models of wisdom" studies are advocated when there is a sense that some commonalities may exist in practice and that if those were induced, made transparent, and thoroughly explicated, others could gain an understanding of what "good looks like." Although controversial issues discussions in Ann, Joe and Bob's classrooms are all unique, in each it is evident that, among many things, they are all thinking carefully about their pedagogy and aligning theory to practice, and this practice includes teaching *for* and *with* discussion. In each case, I begin by explaining the teacher's understanding of the purpose for using controversial issues discussion, followed by an in-depth look at how this theory plays out effectively in the classroom.

A Town Meeting in Ann Twain's[1] Class

Ann's Purpose

For Ann, central to effective participation in democracy is the understanding that multiple perspectives exist for every issue, and students (citizens) must be able to engage in discussion about these varying points of view. Therefore, the purpose of the controversial issues discussion in her classroom is to help students understand multiple perspectives and communicate effectively with people who have opinions contrary to their own.

Ann's Class

In 1998, at the time when I was observing in her classroom, Ann Twain had been teaching social studies at a magnet middle school in a suburb outside a large city in the Pacific Northwest for five years. Ann had created a mixed seventh and eighth grade social studies class that combined U.S. history, civics, and world geography, laced with an extensive service learning program and whole-class discussions of controversial issues in a format she labeled Town Meetings.

During the 1997–1998 school year, Ann Twain's students participated in eight Town Meetings on issues ranging from whether or not it was right to drop the atomic bombs to gun control. One criterion Ann used to select discussion topics was whether or not an issue was currently a matter of public deliberation. In the spring of 1998, an initiative banning local and state government affirmative action programs based on race and gender was being planned for the fall election ballot. Ann decided that this initiative would be an especially good topic for a Town Meeting in part because "discussing ballot initiatives gets kids talking to their parents about the importance of being informed on an issue that you're going to vote on." As an aside, Ann's hope that her inclusion of ballot issues would have "trickle-up" effect on the political engagement of her students' parents is not without warrant. One of the findings from the Kids Voting research is that students in discussion-rich classes that include the deliberation of public issues and the importance of voting do, in fact, enhance the political engagement of their parents (McDevitt & Kiousis, 2006).

The Town Meeting Model

As a first-year teacher, Ann had developed the Town Meeting discussion model, which she defines as "a public forum where participants air their views on an important controversial issue as a way to either affect public policy, or educate others, or persuade others to come around to their point of view." The primary reason she used Town Meetings was her belief that it helped her students better understand multiple perspectives on an issue.

The Town Meeting model was a large group discussion in which each participant assumed the role of a person with a particular perspective. Ann and her students crafted the roles to cover a broad spectrum. Ann encouraged students to pick roles that represented positions other than the ones they currently held. Additionally, Ann made sure there was a relatively equal distribution of roles for each of the various points of view on the issue.

Before the first Town Meeting in the fall, Ann taught the model to her students by explaining its assessment rubric and showing them a videotape of an especially good Town Meeting from the previous year. Ann occasionally stopped the videotape and pointed out students' contributions that met exemplary standards of the rubric. Thus, students first learned the model by viewing a positive example. Ann followed up with a negative example, showing a videotape of adults participating in an ineffective policy discussion. She had her students identify what the adults were doing wrong, such as monopolizing, not using evidence to support their opinions, and talking over one another.

Preparing for the Town Meeting

One week before the Town Meeting, Ann's students received a packet of background material on the affirmative action initiative. After one class period of didactic instruction on the issue, Ann and her students created the roles, which included the Governor of the state, a university admissions officer, a newspaper reporter, a white business owner, a minority student, and representatives of education and advocacy organizations. After selecting roles, students were given specialized reading packets that focused on the particular positions of their roles and a sheet that required them to state the position and identify pro and con arguments. For the next three class days, the students worked individually and in pairs reading the articles and preparing for their roles by watching videos, hearing speakers, searching the World Wide Web for information, and calling advocacy organizations.

The Town Meeting

As Ann's 29 seventh and eighth grade students entered the classroom, they immediately noticed that the furniture had been reconfigured for the Town Meeting. The tables were arranged in a large circle, and Ann had placed paper tents listing the various roles (intentionally mixing pro and con positions as she did so) on the tables. The students came into class and took their places.

Because Ann assessed each student's participation in the Town Meeting, she began the class period by reminding students of the categories on the assessment rubric: knowledge of subject matter, portrayal of role, and effectiveness as a participant. Ann briefly explained traits in each category while holding up the tally sheet.

The Town Meeting officially began with each student stating his or her role and its corresponding positions. Ann did this as a verbal warm-up and to remind students of the many roles. Next, Ann told the students to "stand behind that character; give him the benefit of your voice," and she stated the purpose of the Town Meeting. She said, "We're here to get the facts on how you feel about the initiative." She then asked, "What does the initiative say?" Several students quickly responded, explaining its major points.

For the next 90 minutes, all but two of the 29 students participated orally in the discussion about the affirmative action initiative. This was an unusually long Town Meeting; typically they last 50 minutes. Throughout the Town Meeting, students raised their hands and Ann called on them, going back and forth between roles that supported and opposed the initiative.

Because the initiative addressed affirmative action based on both race and gender, the discussion alternated between the two. For example, in the beginning of the discussion a student said, "The initiative says you can't discriminate [by preferring racial minorities and women]," and another student responded,

"But sometimes people are naturally racist, so affirmative action is really just trying to even out [the playing field]." A student immediately shifted the focus to gender when she said, "To add to that, 95% of management jobs in this state and in the nation are taken by men."

This shifting between race and gender continued throughout the Town Meeting, although several students contributed statements that contextualized the initiative within broader tensions, such as equality v. merit, and equality v. safety. One lengthy interchange about firefighters exposed the latter tension. A student remarked, "I don't think we should risk people's lives. Fire departments are forced to hire women because of affirmative action, and they can't do the job." Another student agreed and added, "Many women couldn't pass the physical tests that men had to pass to become firefighters, so they changed the tests. Again, that is risking people's lives." A few statements later, another student challenged this view, shifting attention to merit by telling a long story about how women are discriminated against in the local fire department even when they score the highest on the tests. Another student agreed, saying, "They [the fire department] should hire the person who is the most qualified."

The students' conflicting opinions on the affirmative action initiative paralleled those in the larger public debate. Some students thought there was still a lot of discrimination against racial minorities and women, while others disagreed. A student raised this issue by quoting from a study he had read: "A wom[a]n or minority has only a 2% chance of being hired by a company that is run by white men." Another student immediately challenged that statistic and asked for its source. The first student pointed to an article he had on his desk. Another student used stipulating language when he said, "Well, if what he said is true [the 2% statistic], that's why we need to keep affirmative action." Several students elaborated on this point, which finally caused one boy to ask, "Why do people discriminate when we're all one race – the human race?" This rhetorical question momentarily silenced the entire class.

Ann was incredibly busy throughout the discussion. She called on students who had their hands raised, assessed by marking on the tally sheet, and, on occasion, redirected the content of the discussion by asking clarifying questions and raising new issues. When there were factual disputes that needed to be clarified, Ann often inserted very short questions, such as "Are quotas legal?" and "Is the playing field level?" At other times, she helped students who were having difficulty by re-phrasing their questions or comments.

Ann also signaled the end of the discussion. The Town Hall meeting described above ended with Ann directing students to turn to their neighbors and say anything about the initiative that they had not had time to contribute during the discussion, which they did.

The Town Meetings in Ann's class often occurred on Fridays, so debriefing waited until the following Monday. Ann reported that two things typically occur after Town Meetings. First, the students talk about what went well and what did not. Second, Ann gives students her assessment of the Town Meeting, focusing on the traits listed in the rubric. Students also have their role sheets returned with comments from her, find out how she assessed their participation in the Town Meeting, and sometimes get individual feedback.

Considerations Unique to Ann's Case

There are elements of Ann's practice that in my experience clearly distinguish her from teachers who are less successful at teaching their students to engage in controversial issues discussions—notably the clear alignment between Ann's purpose for the discussion (understanding multiple perspectives) and the discussion itself. Instructionally, Ann did many things that intentionally met this purpose, such as choosing the Town Hall format that is founded on the sharing of various opinions, assigning roles that included many perspectives, and even seating students so that these perspectives were intermingled. In addition, Ann's intense focus on helping students form a conception of what good discussion looked like in practice, the preparation the students engaged in prior to the Town Meetings, and the ways in which she gave students some power as a way to emphasize that it was their forum—their voices— that mattered made this an effective discussion. Finally, unlike many novice discussion teachers, Ann was able to hold herself verbally in restraint—she facilitated, but did not dominate. Consequently, her students responded to one another, which is rare in many classrooms.

The next case study is set in a high school with students who are five years older than Ann's, and is another example of a course with a highly scaffolded and intense focus on issues discussions. However, this teacher, Joe, focuses on constitutional issues, rather than on policy issues as Ann did, by engaging his students in seminar discussions about important United States Supreme Court cases.

A Seminar on a Supreme Court Case in Joe Park's Class

Joe's Purpose

Although he has many reasons for including discussion in his courses, Joe is most interested in developing critical thinking. Specifically, he wants his students not only to critically analyze the Constitution, but also to understand that embedded in any Supreme Court ruling is controversy concerning *interpretation* of the Constitution. According to Joe, to participate effectively in democracy, students (citizens) must understand the Constitution *and* be able to think, and so the purpose of constitutional issues discussions in his classroom is twofold: first, to learn about the Constitution and second, to promote critical thinking.

Joe's Class

Joe Park has taught middle and high school social studies for 22 years, the last five at a "break the mold" high school in a university community. Because his school does not require teachers to follow a specific curriculum, Joe is able to create courses that closely mirror his conceptions of the social studies knowledge and skills most important for students to develop. He taught *Important Supreme Court Decisions* for nine weeks in the fall and winter of 1997; this unit served as the basis for my learning about how Joe teaches issues discussions.

Joe's course focused on historically significant issues related to freedom of speech and press. He designed the course around Supreme Court cases because "you would be hard pressed to find a more authentic text than a Supreme Court decision." Although all nine cases the students read were about the First Amendment's speech and press clauses, Joe also hoped his students would gain an understanding of content that extends beyond the amendment. On the first day of class, he said to his students: "I want to grow old in a society that has many people understanding the way the Constitution and the Supreme Court works."

The 24 ninth through twelfth grade students enrolled in the course met three times per week, for a weekly total of four hours. Most weeks, the students read one First Amendment Supreme Court case, prepared to participate in a discussion on the case by completing an assignment called a "ticket," worked in small groups to review the facts of the case, participated in a seminar, and wrote and issues-analysis paper.

The Seminar Model

The seminar model of discussion that Joe used was pervasive throughout New Horizons High School. Joe learned the model from the school's principal, who participated in the seminars as a model participant and, on occasion, as a facilitator. The model, labeled simply "seminar" at the school, is a text-based, large group discussion designed to help participants develop a deeper under-standing of the issues, ideas, and values in the text (Gray, 1989). Joe favors the model because of its potential to enhance critical thinking and the generation of new ideas.

Preparing for the Seminar

This day's seminar focused on the Supreme Court's decision in *New York Times Co. v. United States*, the famous "Pentagon Papers" case decided in 1971. Examining the tension between freedom of the press and national security, Joe's students read the 50 pages of the case and completed a 'ticket' assignment, a data retrieval chart that identified the basic arguments made by each of the justices in the nine separate opinions issued. Joe's ticket assignments required students to read and interact with the text; the seminar discussions were designed to help them understand it. The day before the seminar, the students worked in small groups to review the basic facts of the case as well as the movement of the case to the United States Supreme Court.

As the students entered the classroom on seminar day, Joe checked whether or not their "tickets" were completed. Graded as a "pass" if completed and a "fail" if not, the tickets determined who could participate in the discussion. Students who failed were assigned an observer role and had to sit outside the circle and take notes on participation patterns. These notes would later be shared with the group during the debriefing of the seminar. Requiring completed "tickets" is one way that Joe navigates the difficulties involved with talking across difference. He said:

> The only thing that we know we have in common in a seminar is the text that we share. We've been raised differently. We have studied different materials in this class. We may have had U.S. History classes, but others have not had U.S. History classes. All sorts of things. But what we do know is that we all have the text in common. A good discussion, a good seminar, begins from the premise that we are talking about a shared text.

As the two-hour class period began, Joe, 19 students, and the school principal were seated in the seminar circle. The one student who did not complete the ticket was creating a list of participants, preparing to check off each time they talked. Before the seminar began, Joe reminded the students to "do the work of the seminar," by which Joe meant adhering to the guidelines created by the students at the beginning of the course, which were currently posted on butcher paper on the wall. Some of the guidelines included: "listen, respond to ideas out there, make the agenda yours, and refer to the text."

The Seminar

Joe began the discussion with a focus question: "What was the most compelling argument in the case?" Joe had developed this focus question using specific criteria: it could not be answered without using the text; it was open-ended in that there was no right or wrong answer; and it was a question about which he, as the seminar facilitator, had some genuine curiosity.

A student immediately responded by changing the question. "Well, I can tell you the least compelling argument." The student then pointed the class to a part of Chief Justice Burger's dissenting opinion that laments the short amount of time the Court had to spend on the case, and he said, "He is just whining here." Later, I asked Joe why he didn't direct the student to stick with the question that was asked. Joe responded, "That's a no-brainer. Just because I asked a question, doesn't mean that I asked the right question . . . Just because I was fishing for trout doesn't mean I'm going to ignore the bass that bites." Moreover, Joe believed the student's response accomplished the primary purpose of his focus question, which was to open a door to the text in a way that would focus students on the reasoning of the justices.

None of the other students commented on Burger's reasoning; after a short pause, several chimed in to say that Justices Douglas and Black had particularly compelling arguments. Joe asked the students to find where the Douglas opinion began, and they turned to a specific page in the text. Joe immediately probed with a question to one of the students who liked the reasoning of Justice Douglas: "Betty, what was your sense of what Douglas was arguing?" She responded by paraphrasing, and Joe followed up by labeling Douglas' reasoning: "So he was a First Amendment absolutist?" Students agreed, and Joe followed up again: "Talk to us more about Douglas' arguments." This type of interchange continued for several minutes: students referring to the text, locating specific points, and talking about the basic tenets of the two First Amendment absolutists. During the opening several minutes of this seminar, Joe asked quite a few questions, continually reminding students to find the specific part of the text about which they were talking.

During the seminar, it became apparent that most of the students supported the opinions of the court majority, which held that publishing the Pentagon Papers was protected by the First Amendment. One student, however, dissented. Joe then said to the class, "There's our lone conservative, this time. We actually don't have to support Logan, but let's . . . pretend to do so for a minute. Okay? Let's try to construct and give credence to the argument of the government in this case." For several minutes, the seminar continued with students identifying and explaining parts of the dissenting opinions. Joe explained to me why he refocused the seminar on the dissenting arguments:

> I think a real important critical thinking skill is the ability to take a different position and to argue it with credence and credibility. I think it's an incredible skill for citizens, enlightened citizens in a democracy, because it's rare that issues are completely black and white. It's important to give minority voices a really serious airing in a classroom. Because then people will give their true opinion. I think it's also real important to have kids take on different viewpoints as a way of better understanding their own viewpoints . . . Doing the work of seminars is trying on ideas.

The fact that the Pentagon Papers were stolen government documents became the focus of conversation toward the end of the seminar. Joe asked the students, "So, what should the *New York Times* have done when Daniel Ellsberg came to them with boxes of stolen government documents? If Logan steals a TV and gives it to me, and I know that he stole the TV, have I done something wrong?" Several students exclaimed, "Yes." Joe asked, "Is that the same thing as what the *New York Times* did with the documents?" A student replied, "They didn't know." Another countered, "Oh yes, they knew." A third said, "But they thought the public had a right to know." Joe then took them back to the text: "Doesn't one of the justices say something to the effect that there is this right to know right now and the *New York Times* feels a responsibility to provide that information? Who said that?" After a few seconds of looking, someone shouted, "Page 749," and Joe read an excerpt from that page. Joe then prompted, "You guys, most of you believe that what the Supreme Court did was right in this case." Several students concurred, and Joe continued, "Did the *Times* do the right thing?" One student agreed, and another added, "It's like this pull—they were publishing stolen documents, which was basically not the right thing to do, but yet it was important to let the public know what the government was doing. I have a question. Did anything happen to the *New York Times* as a result of this?" Joe answered, "The *New York Times* was fine, Daniel Ellsberg was tried for taking the Pentagon Papers—do you want to know now or later what happened to Daniel Ellsberg?" One student said, "Not right now, Joe." Another jokingly added, "We have a right to know." This excerpt illustrates a move Joe frequently made to spark discussion of larger moral questions—in this instance, 'Is it ever right to steal?'

While students were not required to participate orally in the seminar discussions, they were required to share their critique of the discussion during a debriefing period held immediately after each seminar. This particular seminar was the final one in the nine-week class. In a celebratory manner, Joe began the debriefing session with the statement, "Give yourselves a round of applause, you guys got this thing." Following enthusiastic applause, one student exclaimed, "I was terrified when I first saw it." Joe responded, "I would like to know what your sense of this seminar was as it compared to others and on its own merits." A student volunteered:

> I'll start . . . I just thought this was a really comfortable seminar, not a lot of people talked, but those people who did really know what their ideas were about the case, and that helped me, a person who didn't understand it a whole lot, to get a better sense of it all. I enjoyed the relaxed energy of it because it made it a lot more easy to get into.

Although many students agreed the seminar had a relaxed pace, views about the text differed. Some students liked the text, but a few others said it was confusing or worse. One student plainly stated, "This text sucks." Another student critiqued her own participation in the seminar:

> I finally completed my goal, which was to not talk during the seminar. I kept wanting to talk because I think this case was very confusing, but the seminar cleared it up. I thought it was pretty good, but it is kind of weird trying not to talk. I think I listen more when I am talking because I listen in order to respond.

Compared with Ann, Joe took a more active role in the discussion. In this hour-long discussion, we counted 150 different contributions: 104 (or 70%) made by seminar participants and 46 (or 30%) by Joe. Of the 19 students in the seminar circle, 13 verbally participated. Twenty of the 104 statements, however, were from the principal (21%). In comparing this seminar to the eight others in the course, I found that the overall participation rates remained fairly constant. Joe talked quite a bit, although most of his participation was in the form of questions to students.

Considerations Unique to Joe's Case

Like Ann, Joe also successfully aligned his theories about the purpose of discussion to his practice. His choice of a seminar format that revolves around a close-reading of a common text, which is a Supreme Court ruling, is an obvious result of his intended dual purpose for the discussion: understanding the Constitution and developing critical thinking skills.

It is also worth comparing the seminar discussion in Joe's class to the Town Meeting in Ann's because it illustrates the differences between the content of constitutional and policy issues discussions. Joe is mainly interested in helping his students talk about differing interpretations of what the First Amendment means—in the context of a particular factual situation. Ann, on the other hand, is focusing her students on a policy question—one that is authentically in the public sphere in their state. Note that both teachers assume that there is an *open* question that is worth discussing. In Joe's class, the question is whether or not the Supreme Court made the correct decision in the Pentagon Papers case, while in Ann's the question is whether or not the state should have a policy that allows or forbids affirmative action. Both are "cases" of a larger and more perennial issue.

In the next case study we will see how teachers draw on constitutional content to prepare students for policy discussions.

Public Issues Discussions in Bob Martin's[2] Class

Bob's Purpose

While Ann's purpose was to help students engage and understand multiple perspectives, and Joe's was to think critically and better understand the Constitution, Bob's was to improve students' abilities to effectively discuss controversial issues. According to Bob, democracy is rooted firmly in free speech and participatory citizenship; therefore, engaging students' minds through discussions of controversial policy issues enables them to practice a fundamental aspect of that citizenship. Ultimately, he claims, citizens need to deliberate with one another to form opinions on issues that are then communicated to political leaders in our democratic republic. From Bob's philosophy of democracy comes his attempt to create a democratic classroom in which the free marketplace of ideas reigns within a climate of mutual respect.

Bob's Class

Bob Martin taught social studies for 33 years, and he was in his final year of teaching at Midland High School in the Midwestern city of Franklin (population approximately 200,000) when I observed his class.

Bob designed his school's initial Discussion of Public Issues (DPI) course in 1972 with a since-retired colleague and university professor/researcher with expertise in democratic education. The DPI course is a required, non-tracked class that is focused explicitly on improving students' abilities to discuss controversial policy issues.

The specific discussion presented here was on the topic, which Bob selected, of physician-assisted suicide because it focused on a clear moral issue that he felt students could understand and because there was such powerful reasoning supporting different positions on the issue. Moreover, at the time of my observation, this issue was being deliberated in the state legislature, which accounts for why the teachers framed the question as a matter that jurisdictionally would most likely be acted on within the state. Specifically, the students deliberated the following question: Should the state legislature legalize physician-assisted suicide? It is important to point out that three years prior to this time the United States Supreme Court had ruled in a pair of cases that there was no constitutional right to physician-assisted suicide, and it was clear that Congress was unlikely to give citizens that option through national legislation. Thus, framing the question in the way that most closely aligned with how and where it was deliberated in the world outside of school reflected Bob's desire to deal with topics that are not hypothetical, but are actual contemporary policy debates.

It is also important to note that few students initially saw this issue as relevant to their own lives. It most likely would not have been an issue the students themselves would have selected to deliberate had they been given the choice. Yet, when we asked the students to rate which issues were their most and least "favorites" at the end of the course, 31% ranked this issue as their second *most* favorite, while 21% said it was their second *least* favorite. As an aside, this disparity among how students resonated to issues was also the case with the free speech and juvenile crime topics. While many teachers think it is important for students to select which issues they will deliberate, this data indicates that it is unlikely that students will agree on which issues are important to them. Moreover, we learned from the interviews that many students changed their minds about whether or not they were interested in the issue as a consequence of the discussion. That is, they did not know if they were interested in an issue until they actually knew something about the issue.

The Public Issues Discussion Model

Just as Ann used Town Meetings and Joe seminars, Bob used a specific form of classroom discussion—the Public Issues model, developed in the 1960s (Oliver & Shaver, 1966). The model uses three specific types of questions (factual, definitional, and value-oriented) to guide the discussion of larger public policy issues, defined in the DPI course syllabus as "significant, contemporary, and unresolved political, social, and moral issues in our society."

Preparing for the Discussion

During the semester I observed the course, students spent two weeks learning the discussion model and then studied five major public issues, which had been pre-selected by Bob (Table 4.1).

Students studied a general issue (e.g., gambling) and then considered dimensions of and possible resolutions to a more specific case (e.g., Should the state legislature allow the operation of privately owned casinos?) in a scored discussion.

The unit in which the physician-assisted suicide discussion occurred was relatively early in the semester. Previously the students had learned about the discussion model, worked on developing a number of specific speaking,

Table 4.1 Course Schedule and Topics of Scored Discussion in Bob Martin's Class

Week	Topic
Week 1	Taking a Stand
Week 2	
Week 3	*Gambling:* Should the state legislature legalize privately owned casinos?
Week 4	*Physician-assisted Suicide:* Should the state legislature legalize physician-assisted suicide?
Week 5	
Week 6	
Week 7	*Juvenile Crime:* Should the U.S. Congress pass stricter gun control laws to reduce school violence?
Week 8	
Week 9	Public Service Announcement activity
Week 10	
Week 11	*Title IX:* Should Congress repeal the sports equity provision of Title IX of the Education Amendments Act of 1972?
Week 12	
Week 13	Advocacy speech research
Week 14	Spring break
Week 15	*Free Speech:* Should the U.S. Congress prohibit internet sites from publishing materials that threaten public safety?
Week 16	
Week 17	Mary Beth Tinker visit
Week 18	
Week 19	Advocacy speech presentations
Week 20	Review and final exams

listening, and analysis skills, and participated in one full-fledged scored issues discussion on the topic of gambling. Consequently, coming into this unit the students were beginning to understand the characteristics of effective participation in issues discussions, but most of them were still quite novice in their participation. Some students had never been required to participate in class discussions before, and they were not used to voicing their views, using various kinds of evidence to warrant their claims, or having to respond to questions from other students. For virtually all students this was their first experience in a class where participation in discussion "counted," and Bob went to great lengths to explain the rationale for placing so much emphasis on discussion. Before the discussion, Bob taught each of the elements of the discussion scoring checklist so that students understood what it meant to engage in the forms of discourse it valued. He also placed the students in heterogeneous groups based on verbal prowess and comfort level in discussion so they would feel comfortable participating.

The Public Issues Discussion on Physician-assisted Suicide

We watched six different groups discuss the physician-assisted suicide issue. Most of the discussions were 30–40 minutes long. While some students came into the discussion with a clear position on the policy issue, many were undecided, which, in my experience, tends to be a deliberative asset. These students were less interested in supporting their position, and more interested in understanding multiple positions. They tended to ask more questions and verbally balance conflicting ideas for the group. It was not uncommon to hear such a student say, "well, on the one hand, people should have a right to make this decision, but terminally ill people are already very vulnerable, and they may be pressured by others to do something they don't really want to do." There was a lot of talk about the potential for this kind of abuse, about creating a culture in which elderly and ill people are expected to end their lives. Religion came up frequently as well. One student said that physician-assisted suicide was a violation of God's will, but then immediately countered her own statement by saying, "but he [God] gave us free will, and the current policy that makes physician-assisted suicide illegal actually takes away our free will." There was a lot of emphasis on reasoning and evidence—it was clear that simply saying, "because I think so" was not considered adequate in the discussion. But students did not have to take a public position, which was a good thing because it was clear that many were wrestling with the moral ambiguities and challenges inherent in this issue and were not ready to form an opinion.

Similar to Ann's facilitation style, Bob did not say much, but when he did it was typically to push students' analysis, point out contradictions in their reasoning, or encourage them to deal more seriously or in a more detailed way with another students' comments. It was common for Bob to insert four or five such comments or questions during each scored discussion, but because he was sitting outside the students' circle, they did not look to him for help, nor did they seem to resent it when he did participate. He was clearly an occasional "coach" as opposed to a traffic cop, full participant in the discussion, or agenda setter. After each discussion he would give the students a short verbal assessment of how they did as a group, and then each student would receive a score for her his or her own participation. In addition, the group would receive a score for the overall quality of the discussion.

Considerations Unique to Bob's Case

Bob's choice of discussion format, intensive focus on preparation, explicit instruction of discussion techniques, and clear explanation of guidelines and requirements show that his instruction is aligned to his purpose.

I was particularly intrigued by the grouping practice that Bob used because it so directly challenged my previous beliefs about the strengths of heterogeneous grouping practices in classrooms and raised, in practice, perplexing contradictions. Before the first scored discussion, Bob divided his students into three groups based on verbal prowess and comfort level in discussions. There were three groups of 9–10 students. Each group had its own discussion in a circle, which Bob facilitated (very lightly) from the side and also scored, while the other students worked on other assignments for the course.

In each of the classes there was one group comprised of students who were quiet in class, another group with students who did participate, but without a lot of confidence or frequency, and a third group with students who were quite vocal. These decisions were made after the first two-week unit in which students participated in a number of whole class and small group activities. The groups were not permanent, and some students were moved to different groups as the semester progressed. Cooperative learning research suggests that this kind of grouping might simply reify differences among the students, but for the most part that is not what we saw happening during the discussions. The quiet students talked—they could not *all* stay quiet after all—and the particularly vocal students had to learn to yield the floor. However, when we interviewed students about which group they were in, how it functioned, and what they thought of the other groups, we were struck by how the students in the most vocal groups had been reinforced in their feelings of superiority. Conversely, many of the students in the other two groups indicated that they thought they had talked more and learned how to be better participants because they did not have to compete against verbally aggressive students.

At the time I remember thinking that because the grouping practices were working for the students who often are shut out of class discussions by their peers and/or allowed to remain silent by their teachers, it made sense. But after spending two more years observing discussions in classrooms, I am more conflicted because I have watched a number of other teachers create hetero-geneous groups in which students were not dominating—in large part because they saw domination as an indication that students simply had not developed the skills to participate wisely and well. Consequently, these teachers worked hard to teach such students that they had to tone it down and learn to listen more carefully. Instead of simply giving the floor to students who talked continually (which is what many students reported to us was the norm in many other classes), the teachers utilized a variety of strategies—both formal and informal—to reign-in over-talkers.

Another issue unique to Bob's case is that at least once during a semester, parents or other adults who were connected to the students in some way were invited to come to evening political issues discussions about the same topics the students were studying in class. During the semester we studied the classes, the parent discussion was about physician-assisted suicide. They were given the same background materials about the issue that the students had used in class and then participated in discussions facilitated by the teachers. Students participated in the discussions, too, although often not in the same group as the parents/adults they had invited. The discussions were quite lively, and I heard many of the adults make comments to the effect that they wished they had experienced such a course when they were in school.

What was particularly interesting was how much more personal the discussion among the parents was compared with the students' discussions. Many of the parents were in the "sandwich" period of their lives—simul-taneously caring for children and for their parents or other elderly relatives. Many had watched their relatives struggle through long and painful illnesses and had wrestled with end-of-life medical care decisions. They were quite divided about the policy issue, and some even challenged its fundamental assumptions. One parent, a medical doctor, advocated legalizing physician-assisted suicide because, as he recounted, so many of his patients wanted a peaceful ending to their lives. At which point, another parent shot back, "why should doctors have this much power—why should people need *your* involvement to make such a crucial and personal decision." Many told personal stories, which were used to support differing positions on the issue or to explain why it was so difficult to make a decision about the issue. One parent sighed, "I am glad I am not a legislator," while another said, "but I wish we all could vote on this policy." Compared with the students' scored discussions in class in which they had used a lot of "factual" evidence to evaluate the strengths and weaknesses of policy options, the parents used more personal narrative to fuel the discussion. Both have an important place in policy discussions, of course, which probably accounted for why the discussions involving the students and the adults were so rich.

Clearly, many aspects of this program would not work in all schools or for all parents. The program presumes that parents do not work at night (which is certainly not the case for many), and it is predicated on parents having a comfort level with school, and with talking in public with strangers—attributes many people simply do not have. As a result, this program might be criticized as reeking of privilege. However, in this program I think there is a nugget that is worth exploring, which is generating cross-generational issues discussions in order to further expand the diversity of perspectives and to provide an opportunity for different political generations to hear one another's views. An added benefit, I think, might be to generate support among adults in the community for the inclusion of controversial issues in the schools by involving them in the process.

Learning from Teachers' Practice

From the similarities and differences among these teachers' controversial issues discussions conceptions and practices, it is possible to draw some conclusions about what skillful discussion teaching entails.

Teachers Understand that Preparation is Paramount

Successful controversial issues discussions are intricately planned and everyone involved is expected to prepare. These discussions are not *ad hoc*, nor are they scheduled at the last moment. I have often had teachers ask, "How much difference do you think that makes in whether an issues discussion will be successful?" What has become clear to me from studying classroom discussion is that the difference is significant. Students and teachers who prepare well for issues discussions tend to have greater success. This does not mean that spur of the moment discussions are doomed to failure. In my own teaching and observations of other teachers, I can think of a few such discussions of issues that worked well. But, as a general rule, it is unwise to expect that students without exceptionally well-developed discussion skills (and there are few of those students) can create a good discussion without preparation. In Ann's class, students studied background material on the issue, created roles, and studied both effective and ineffective discussion. In Joe's class, students created guidelines for discussion, read material before the discussion, and prepared a "ticket" that allowed them to enter the discussion. In Bob's class, students studied the discussion model extensively, and learned about both the specific case they would discuss as well as general issues surrounding this case.

Each of the teachers in the case study gave their students a significant amount of time and materials to prepare for the discussion, which led to effective discussion. As the story at the beginning of this chapter illustrates, when students do not come to the discussion prepared, it falls flat.

Teachers Make Thoughtful Decisions about Assessment

Literature on classroom assessment suggests that the most valuable assessments of students' learning are classroom-based (as opposed to district or state level-based) and tightly aligned to curriculum and instruction (Miller & Singleton, 1997; Stiggins, 1997). Additionally, assessment experts (Martin-Kniep, 1998; Newmann & Wehlage, 1995) recommend that teachers assess students' progress toward goals that are valued in the world beyond school, which is one aspect of authentic assessment. Educators who specialize in the assessment of issues discussions (Miller & Singleton, 1997; Harris, 1996) recommend formal assessment of students' participation in discussion as a way to communicate to students that discussion is valued and to provide students with the specific feedback they need to improve their discussion skills. While both Ann and Bob formally evaluated their students' participation in some discussions, Joe did not, and throughout my work with many teachers who use discussion, it is clear that even the most highly effective discussion teachers approach assessment differently.

For example, Ann used codified rubrics to assess her students' preparation for and participation in issues discussions. She also counted how her students prepared for and performed in discussion as a formal part of their grades. Holding students accountable for their preparation and performance in issues discussions and rewarding oral participation reflects Ann's concern about aligning assessment procedures to what is valued in her classroom.

Similarly, in Bob's class, discussion skills, especially taking a position and defending it with evidence, were central both to the scored discussions and to his goals for the course (see Table 4.2 for the scoring checklist Bob used to evaluate students' participation in the scored discussions).

Assessment in Bob's class took a variety of forms. Students completed an elaborate worksheet to prepare for each discussion and took a traditional written test at the end of each unit. The discussion and worksheet received approximately equal weight (23 and 27 points, respectively), and the written tests were worth 50 points each. Near the end of the semester-long course, students individually prepared "advocacy speeches" on other controversial public issues, orally defending a position before the class. Despite students' perceptions that their oral participation in scored discussions factored heavily into their final grade, it amounted to only about 10%; the advocacy speech and written tests made up the bulk of their grade.

Conversely, while Joe does informally assess his students' participation, he is adamantly opposed to the grading of seminar participation because he believes that "paying kids to talk" is inauthentic. That is, it does not represent the way public discourse operates in the world outside of school. Moreover, Joe believes that grading oral participation would be at odds with the creation of effective seminars, in which participants should talk because they have something to say, not because they are being rewarded by an authority figure.

Table 4.2 Bob Martin's Scoring Checklist for Scored Discussions

Positive	Negative
1. Making a relevant comment (+1)	1. Making an irrelevant comment (−1)
2. Using a probing question to elicit more information or to get someone involved in the discussion (+1)	2. Not paying attention (−1)
	3. Interrupting another discussant to prevent him from participating (−2)
3. Using evidence to support a statement (+1)	4. Lack of or inappropriate use of evidence when making a factual statement (−2)
4. Challenging the relevancy of a person's comment or use of evidence (+2)	
5. Using evidence from personally gathered sources to support a statement (+2)	5. Monopolizing/dominating a discussion to prevent other from participating (−3)
6. Summarizing the discussion (+2)	6. Making a personal attack (−4)
7. Recognizing a contradiction in someone's opinion (+2)	
8. Making a stipulation (+2)	
9. Making a concession (+2)	
10. Making a clear transition to a relevant issue (+3)	
11. Identifying and explaining a value conflict (+3)	
12. Stating and explaining an appropriate analogy (+3)	

Additional Notes
Individually, students may not receive more than 18 points per discussion.
An additional 1–5 points are added to each individual's score on the basis of the overall discussion's quality, for a maximum of 23 points.
A maximum of 3 points may be earned on #1 (positive) and a maximum of 8 points may be earned between #3 and #5 (positive).

Joe distinguishes between informally and formally assessing the quality of students' participation in seminar discussions. While Joe does provide each student with oral and written feedback on their seminar discussion skills, he does not factor their participation in seminars into their course grades because he believes the authenticity of the seminar would be harmed if students were graded on their verbal participation. The unique concept of seminars as discussions aimed to collaboratively create meaning makes the grading of individual verbal participation problematic for Joe:

> Seminars are about public performance [and]. . . about collaborative work. Seminars are about coming together in a public space to interact with people who are and are not like you, and that is freighted with different things, not less important, but different things than individual writing assignments are [which Joe does grade]. . . If I want us to make meaning together, I want only the contribution of authentic ingredients.

Another reason for Joe's refusal to grade seminars is his belief that students participate in seminars in various ways. He believes it would be impossible to create an assessment rubric for participation that would honor all those forms of participation.

Thus, comparing and contrasting the assessment practices of the three teachers makes apparent a tension between accountability and authenticity. Ann has chosen to privilege accountability because she believes that if she values discussion, assessing it in a fairly formal way with a rubric reinforces the message of its importance. Additionally, formal assessment gives her the opportunity to provide specific feedback to students about what they do well and what they still need to improve. Requiring and formally assessing participation are important for communicating the message that democratic discourse is a critical outcome of her curriculum. Bob shared this view.

Joe, on the other hand, has chosen to privilege authenticity. Because he believes that "paying kids to talk" will compromise the genuineness of students' contributions, he allows some students to remain silent. While students in Ann and Bob's classes can also make that choice, there is a cost involved. No such cost exists for students in Joe's class.

While Joe conceptualizes the way in which he is teaching and providing feedback to students as authentic, it does not match with another commonly held view that assessments that are authentic to the world beyond schools need to identify clear standards for what constitutes quality work. Common standards only work if there is agreement about what good performance looks and sounds like. It may be that discussions, especially those that occur in a large group, work best if participants are behaving in different ways. Authentic examples of issues discussions that occur in the world beyond school do not demand that all participate in the same manner or with the same frequency. Think of a particularly good discussion among community members about how to solve a public problem. We would expect that some people would talk more and some less. We would expect that some people would use analogies to explore the problem, while others would use statistical evidence. We would expect that some people would ask many questions, while others would use examples from their personal history to explore the problem or suggest solutions. In short, we would expect difference. Yet, discussion rubrics that are specific enough to be helpful to students often do not allow for these types of difference. They explicitly identify common ways that people should behave in a discussion.

Embedded in decisions about assessment is the choice of whether or not to require students to participate in discussion. Even with careful preparation, some students and parents get concerned about requiring students to participate in discussion. In Bob's class, for example, a majority of students in the beginning of the course believed they had a responsibility to contribute to class discussions occasionally, that verbal participation was an essential skill, and that students should be taught how to participate effectively in discussions. However, they were divided over whether or not participation in class discussion was a matter of personal choice and whether or not it was fair for a teacher to base part of their grade on the quality of their participation. As one student told us, "free speech should mean that we have the freedom *not* to speak."

To teachers like Ann and Bob, however, allowing students to opt out of discussion was off the table because it was an important academic and democratic skill. Bob reported that, in the past, parents had requested waivers from his course because "my child is the quiet type who does not talk in class." These waivers were not granted because Bob and the school administrators believed that learning how to talk about controversial political issues was important for *all* students.

Scoring discussions reinforced that point and clearly had an impact on student participation. For example, 74% of the students in the study at Bob's school indicated that a teacher's basing part of their grade on participation in discussions would cause them to speak more.

Teachers Make the Discussion the Students' Forum

First, having a students' forum means that students share some power with the teacher when key decisions about controversial issues discussions are made. For example, all three teachers involved their students in creating the guidelines that would be followed throughout the discussions. These guidelines were made public and referenced periodically as a way to hold students accountable for following them and to remind the students that the guidelines represent the group's will. For example, Ann's students helped set roles for the discussion and Joe's students helped set guidelines for the discussion.

In addition, the teachers' roles as facilitators of the discussions clearly demonstrate how the teachers work to enhance the likelihood that students will view the discussions as their own forum. Even though the teachers' facilitation styles differed, their common emphasis was on encouraging students to speak to one another directly. Furthermore, while students are encouraged to hold and state opinions on issues, the teachers' opinions are not explicitly stated. In all of the effective discussions I have witnessed, never did I hear a student ask the teacher his or her opinion on the issue, nor did I hear the teacher volunteer a position. This suggests that the teachers viewed these discussions not as a soapbox for themselves, but as a forum for their students. This is challenging because many teachers really like to talk, and their apprenticeship of observation has most likely taught them that teacher talk is what teaching is all about.

All three of the case studies also illustrate that students do not have to pick the topic in order to take ownership in the discussion. When the students have time to adequately prepare for a discussion, and when their voices are heard during the discussion, they can fully engage in discussions about a variety of topics.

Conclusion

I began this chapter with the position that the key ingredient for high-quality discussions of controversial issues in classrooms is the quality of teacher practice. As I have shown, there is no one right way to teach young people how to participate skillfully in such discussions. But there are some similarities that cross the practice of teachers who are having success with a form of teaching that is undeniably challenging. Aligning theory and practice, teaching *for* and *with* discussion, and thinking carefully about preparation, assessment, and student ownership all contribute to effective controversial issues discussions.

5

Diversity in Our Midst

Ideological Diversity in Classrooms and Its Impact on Controversial Issues Discussion

I would not say that I completely changed my opinions, but I have at least understood what the other side is and can be like, okay, that makes sense to me. And there are other times, too, when I still think that what I believe is right. The teacher had taught me that you cannot just have an opinion on something without looking at every side of it. Just because you believe in something one way does not mean you should not look at the other side and try and understand it and get a better understanding of the issue as a whole. (High School Senior in a Social Issues Class)

I think the closet conservatives do not feel comfortable. I think they are just not as knowledgeable as us [referring to the left-leaning members of the debate team in the class], so they feel like, 'if I say something, the *bulls* are going to attack me with their information,' which is probably true. But our views on issues are more informed—and more likely to be correct than theirs. (High School Senior in an International Relations Class)

Both of these students are in classes that include a robust and sustained focus on controversial political issues discussions, yet the first student is learning that it is important to listen to and consider disparate views, while the second seems to believe that some students, specifically he and his friends, have the *right* views and are justified in verbally attacking those with whom they disagree. What accounts for this difference? And what difference does it make? This chapter focuses on ideological diversity in high school classes. Its major purpose is to explore empirically and practically what is typically talked about theoretically— the influence that ideological diversity within a class has on how young people experience and learn from the discussion of controversial political issues.

As a backdrop, it is important to recognize that the heart of the deliberative enterprise is the foundational belief that multiple perspectives are an asset—not a hindrance—to democratic thinking, participation, and governance. After all, if people agreed on what should be done about important problems, what would be the purpose of deliberation? In such a circumstance, it would be logical to move forward with putting into place the solution that enjoyed such widespread support. But we know that many of the public's problems do, in fact, involve controversy because there are fundamental disagreements about which problems deserve attention in the first place, what has caused the problem, how much of a problem it really is, for whom it is a problem, what the strengths and weaknesses of proposed solutions are . . . and the list goes on. In short, while there are some things that vast majorities of people agree on in communities, it is also the case that there are many disagreements—as one would expect in democratic nations. In fact, the extent to which there are multiple and competing perspectives voiced about what "we" the people should do to address a problem facing the community is not a flaw of democracy, but a marker of how democratic a community is in practice.

Consequently, it is not surprising that many democratic educators share a basic belief that when you bring together a group of young people in a classroom, disagreements will happen, and those disagreements are something to be cultivated, not suppressed. It is not just educators who hold this view. It has been officially supported by those who spend little time in classrooms but are called upon to think about the relationship between diversity and learning, such as the United States Supreme Court.

As a case in point, *Grutter v. Bollinger* (2003) revolved around the question of whether the 14th Amendment's equal protection clause, which in almost all cases makes government decisions based on a person's race *verboten*, could be trumped by the *compelling interest* the state had in ensuring that students were exposed to differences as a part of their education (in this case, through affirmative action at the University of Michigan Law School). By a slim majority, the Court answered in the affirmative. Diversity, as the majority construed it, was not about redressing historic wrongs against people who had historically been discriminated against. The Court did not buy the claim that affirmative action in this case was a necessary form of redress, but instead asserted that it was an educational asset because students learn more when they are exposed to views that differ from their own. The Court's decision in the case is important because it represents—officially—the commonsense notion that if you are going to talk about hard problems, it is better to have more opinions represented at the table. This not only helps to ensure that the discussion's result does not just represent narrow interests, but also that people do not feel that their views were kept from consideration as a matter of course.

In the course of real democratic practice, however, we know that few people actually engage in political discussions in ideologically diverse settings. Recall, in Chapter 1, we learned that only 23% of adults in the United States engage in "cross-cutting" political talk (Mutz, 2006). It is much more typical for people to discuss political issues with likeminded others, especially given the migration to ideologically homogenous communities that Bishop (2008) has documented in his research. The effects of such discussions do not expand people's thinking, enable them to consider thoughtfully views that differ from their own, or build tolerance for people who do not agree with them. Instead, as the Colorado experiment discussed in Chapter 1 indicated, the views of people who talk with likeminded others are *ideologically amplified.* They become more extreme.

It is interesting to note that scholars report their findings about the impact of discussion with likeminded others with something akin to dread—it is clear that their belief in the deliberative ideal will not go down without a fight. Diana Mutz (2006) and Hibbing and Theiss-Morse (2002) have both called for schools to act as an intervention by giving young people concrete experiences with "cross-cutting" political talk and by teaching young people that conflict is natural, not something to be shunned. As we learned in Chapter 4, it is clearly possible to create a classroom environment in which students do hear multiple and competing perspectives on important political issues. But there is also evidence to suggest that the ideological views of young people in schools may well reflect their communities (which as Bishop reminds us, are becoming increasingly less diverse) and that racial segregation in schools may lead to few experiences with issues discussions. As mentioned in Chapter 2, David Campbell's (2005) analysis of IEA data from the United States makes the connection between racial diversity and decreased exposure to ideological diversity, showing an inverse relationship in schools between the diversity in a classroom and the amount of discussion students report about issues.

Studying Ideological Diversity in High School Classes

The study reported in this chapter and in Chapter 6 (Hess, McAvoy, Smithson, & Hwang, 2008) investigated what happened in high school classes that focus on controversial issues (compared with those that do not). The study is ongoing and will eventually analyze whether there is a pathway that exists between issues discussions in high school classes and future political participation, and if so, its elements.[1]

This is a mixed method study, which means that we used surveys that we analyzed quantitatively, and classroom observations and interviews with students and their teachers that we analyzed qualitatively. We collected data over a four-year period, beginning in the spring semester of 2005 and continuing through the spring semester of 2008. The study included over 1,100 students and their teachers in 35 classes in 21 high schools in three states in the Midwest (Illinois, Indiana, and Wisconsin), most in classes with at least some attention to controversial issues discussions, and some matched to classes in the same school where the teacher reported little or no inclusion of issues discussions. (See Appendix A for a more detailed description of the study's sample and methodology.)

After examining the research by Fishkin & Farrar (2005), Mutz (2006), Hibbing and Theiss-Morse (2002), and Campbell (2005), we knew going into the study that the ideological make-up of the students and teachers in the classes was potentially important. As a result, we were interested in exploring the following questions about the role of ideological diversity within classrooms:

1. How ideologically diverse are students, classes, and their teachers? And to what extent do students and teachers have "coherent" political views—that is, do they consistently lean to a particular position on the ideological spectrum or is there a lot of intra-person variation?
2. To what extent do students recognize the diversity in their classrooms? Do they accurately describe its nature and range? What causes them to access this accurately or not?
3. What influence does the ideological diversity within a classroom have on how students experience and learn from issues discussions?

While attending the classes we studied, students completed questionnaires about their views on political issues, what they thought constituted effective civic and political engagement, their knowledge of how politics and government work, and what they thought about key issues related to this form of teaching—such as whether their teacher did and/or should disclose his/her own views on the issues during discussion (this particular aspect of the survey is the focus of Chapter 6).

To explain what we have learned about ideological diversity in high school classes, the rest of this chapter is divided into two sections. The first explains our most important findings, notably that there is much more ideological diversity in classes than one would expect—even in unusually homogeneous communities—and for the most part students want to hear views that differ from their own. When they do hear disparate views, it has some positive effects, such as promoting open mindedness and the willingness to engage in political discussions outside of the classroom. In the second section are three short case studies—one of the most conservative classes in our study, another of the most liberal, and another of the most ideologically diverse. All our three teachers are interested in exposing their students to different points of view, but face different challenges when trying to do so. I then explain what the teachers in each class do pedagogically to maximize students' awareness of the ideological diversity in their midst.

Nature and Range of Ideological Diversity

To address our questions about ideology, we included items on the student and teacher surveys about important political issues, such as taxation, civil unions for gay people, and the death penalty. We also asked for whom they would have voted for in the 2004 presidential election had they been legally eligible. The teacher survey also contained the issues questions, but we deleted the presidential preference question because we feared it would be seen as too intrusive to ask such a question of adults who actually might have voted, as compared to asking students to retrospectively speculate about whom they would have supported.

To explain the nature and range of ideological diversity in the classes we studied, it is important to make a distinction between inter-person and intra-person diversity. The first compares students to other students and to the teachers, while the second examines the ideological coherency of one's own views. Information about both of these can give us a sense of the political homogeneity or heterogeneity in the sample as a whole, in the schools, in specific classes, and for individual students. This is important because in order to have the kind of "cross-cutting" political talk that advocates of deliberation support, it is necessary to have at least some level of diversity of viewpoint within a discussion community. Also, it can help explain why some issues spark lively discussions, while others seem to die on the vine. More importantly, it lays the groundwork for exploring whether teachers' views influence their students—which, as we explain in Chapter 6 on teacher disclosure, accounts for much of the controversy about whether schools should engage students in controversial issues discussions.

While our data showed that there are ideological differences among schools and classes, with some much more homogenous than others, there was much more ideological diversity in classes than appeared at first glance. As an example, when we initially analyzed the survey data, we paid a lot of attention to presidential preference, reasoning that this would be a good proxy for a student's overall ideology. And while it was a fairly good indicator, it also masked a good deal of diversity of opinion, a point I return to shortly. Similar to how adults in the states actually voted, a majority of students in Indiana favored President Bush, while the students in Illinois and Wisconsin favored Senator Kerry.

Just as students in the three states "lean" with respect to presidential preference, many of the classes did as well. For example, of the 948 students who answered the presidential preference questions, 47% of them were in classes where more than 70% of the students agreed with their view about who should have won the 2004 presidential election in the first year of the study, and 37% in the second year. In some classes, there was 100% agreement. Moreover, when we compared who the students said they would have voted for in 2004 with how adults in their communities actually did vote, there was a clear similarity, as we shall see with the case studies that follow.

During our classroom observations the first year, we noticed that even in some of the classes that would appear to be ideologically homogenous based on presidential preference, there was quite a bit of difference of opinion with respect to many issues. While this was not surprising, it vividly showed that presidential preference—while a rough proxy for one's overall ideology—still masked quite a bit of difference that existed in the classes.

Consequently, we used the issues questions along with presidential preference to gain a more detailed and nuanced picture of the ideology of individual students and teachers, and their classes, in the second year of the study. The survey in year two included eight questions about important political topics (e.g., death penalty, civil liberties/terrorism, abortion, taxation, civil unions for gay people, etc.) that we used to create a political orientation scale (see Appendix A). The items were structured as statements that imply a particular orientation based on responses that range on a five-point scale from Strongly Disagree (1) to Strongly Agree (5), with Undecided/Don't Know serving as the mid-point (3).

The scale we constructed can be used to assess an individual's or a class's political orientation, described on a spectrum of far-left to far-right in terms of political orientation: 1 = Strong Left; 2 = Left; 3 = Undecided/Don't Know; 4 = Right; 5 = Strong Right. On this spectrum, the mean of the spectrum of the student population in year two was 2.6, suggesting a somewhat left-leaning population of students. For the sample, classroom averages ranged from 1.75 (1 = Political Left) to 3.63 (5 = Political Right). Compared with presidential preference alone, adding the political orientation scale showed that while in some classes students' political views cohere more than in others (that is, some lean left, some right, and some in the middle), there is certainly more diversity of opinion than one would expect if all we knew about this class was presidential preference.

Of course, such summary measures still provide only a cursory view of the political orientations of students, with inadequate information on the extent to which a class consists of a fairly homogeneous group of students (all hold similar opinions, or express similar political orientations), or heterogeneous (a wide range of opinions are represented in the class). For example, it would be theoretically possible to have a class mean of 3.00, which could indicate that the students were undecided, or that there was more diversity, such as a class with half holding strong left views, half with strong right views. Some indication of the range of political orientations expressed within a class can be derived from including the range along with the mean response for a given class. This will become apparent when we turn to the case studies.

However, range only tells us the span of political orientations, not the distribution of students within that span. While range in conjunction with the mean provides some indication of distribution, the standard deviation of the class average political orientation scales provides a better indication of the distribution of political orientations represented in the class.

Ideological Coherence

The descriptive utility of such measures is somewhat limited; however, it does allow us a summary description of a class's political orientation, allowing us to identify, for example, which classes lean furthest in one or another political direction. These measures tell us very little about the issues underlying these measures, or the diversity of opinion represented in one class on any particular issue. For this reason, we turned to intra-student political orientation as another way to flesh out the diversity that exists in each class. Here we examined how consistent (politically speaking) a student's own opinions were across a variety of politically charged issues. That is, do individual students tend to consistently respond across issues with the same political orientation, or do students express more independent thinking, leaning right on some issues and leaning left on others? Finally, can we differentiate between students who hold strong opinions from students who are either undecided or express less conviction on social issues?

While students did tend to lean to the "right" or "left," most were not coherent ideologically, and this often showed up in two ways. First, students were undecided about many issues (a mean of 2.6 per student of the eight issues included in the ideology scale). Second, when students did have views on issues, they were rarely politically coherent in those views. The measures of ideological coherence we used gauge the consistency of political orientation expressed by a student across a variety of controversial social issues. A measure of zero (0) indicates perfect consistency in terms of the political orientation expressed by the student across all controversial issues reported. The mean of the standard deviation for students' ideology scores was 1.22 (compared with their more politically coherent teachers, with a mean of 0.87), and the majority of students in the sample scored between 1 and 1.75 on the ideological coherence scale. Measures above 1.5 indicated that the student responses across the controversial issues spanned two or more categories on the five-point Likert scale for political orientation, e.g. from Strongly Disagree to Undecided/Don't Know; or from Agree to Disagree. This illustrated that many students—even those in classes that appeared to be "red" or "blue"—are politically variegated.

When we performed these same analyses class by class we learned that in many of the classes that appeared to be homogenous, there was actually much more diversity—especially when we factored in the large number of students whose own views were ideologically variant. That is, it was not unusual to see a class where 70% of the students said they would have voted for Bush, but only half supported the death penalty, while the other half did not. Also, they were split on civil unions for gay people and undecided on a number of issues. In sum, our most significant finding with respect to ideological diversity in classrooms is that they are much more heterogeneous than we expected, especially when you factor in how many individual students are undecided on issues, or are all over the board on the issues for which they do have views.

Recognition of Diversity

But, of course, the value of ideological diversity in a classroom is more likely to be pronounced if the teachers and students recognize that it exists. Recall that a central finding of the Hibbing and Theiss-Morse (2002) study was that there is a positive correlation between fear of conflict and the belief that one's views are in the mainstream. In short, ideological diversity could be an untapped resource in classes unless its existence is activated by the opportunity to hear these different views. This accounts for why the second research question about whether students and teachers could accurately describe the diversity in the classes is important. To gauge this, we included the following item on the post-course scaled survey in Year 2: "Most of the students in this class have similar opinions on the issues we are discussing." We also asked students to describe the nature and range of the ideological diversity in their classes during the interviews. We found that teachers were better at describing the diversity in their midst than students, and that teachers and students in classes that we rated as "best practice discussion classes" based on the qualitative data were much better at accurately describing ideological diversity than students in classes with no, or lower quality, discussion. This makes sense: if students are given the opportunity to hear their classmates' views on issues, they are much more likely to recognize the diversity in their midst than if the teacher lectures most of the time, or if the quality of the discussions is low.

Impact on Student Experience and Learning

With respect to the question of how ideological diversity influences students' experiences and learning in these classes, our survey data showed that students in ideologically diverse classrooms were more likely to report that they have a good understanding of political issues, and somewhat more likely to report feeling positive about expressing their opinions in a group. The interviews and observations gave us a much more robust sense of the impact of ideological diversity on the quality of the discussions, the degree to which students reported feeling comfortable with political conflict, and their general interest level in the discussions.

As a general rule, students found hearing viewpoints different from their own extremely interesting, especially if the discussions provided adequate time and the expectation that students explain their views, not just state them. Students routinely mentioned the connection between diversity in discussions and their own thinking. As one student remarked about the impact of hearing disparate views, "it makes me think deeper on every issue, not just government issues." Another, who said her family doesn't "listen to what anyone else has to say," thought that these classroom discussions on controversial issues helped her appreciate the diverse political perspectives of her classmates and others: "if you have an opinion, but then you get to hear what someone else has to say about the other side of it, [it makes you] think about it a little more."

Three Case Studies: A "Blue" Class, "Red" Class, and "Purple" Class

The rest of the chapter focuses on three classes in our study: the most left-leaning (Table 5.1; the teacher is Kushner), the most right-leaning (Table 5.2; the teacher is Walters), and the most ideologically heterogeneous (Table 5.3; the teacher is Voight).

Generating Diversity in a "Blue" Class

I begin with Mr. Kushner and his students in one section of a semester-long elective social issues course at a large comprehensive high school in a medium-sized city. This is the most left-wing class of the 35 classes in the study. All of the students participating in the study in the class indicated they would have voted for John Kerry in the 2004 presidential election. We looked at the election results from the 2004 election to see how adults in this community actually voted and found that John Kerry won more than 75% of the vote in the parts of the community that students who go to this school come from. So, if anything, this particular class is even more left-leaning on the question of presidential preference than the adults in their community. The class average for political orientation is 1.93 (on a scale of 1 = left wing and 5 = right wing), and the teacher is even further to the left (1.63). In terms of ideological coherence—or the degree to which a student is internally consistent in her political views—we see a range from 0.60 to 1.51, and a class average of 1.01. If a student were totally coherent, her score would be zero (0), which would indicate that on all issues she strongly agreed with either a left-wing or right-wing perspective. There are no students in the entire sample who are this coherent, but most are less coherent than the students in Mr. Kushner's class.

Note that the teacher is more coherent than any of his students at 0.52. This indicates that the class is both more left wing and more coherently left wing than is typical (again, the average across the sample for ideological coherence was 1.26).

Looking just at the presidential preference, political orientation, and ideological coherence scores, it would be logical to assume that this class would not be an especially easy one for high-quality discussions of controversial political issues because so many of the students have similar views. As it turns out, this was not an assumption born out in practice. In Mr. Kushner's class we observed some particularly powerful discussions, of such issues as affirmative action,

Table 5.1 Mr. Kushner's Class

	Political Orientation	Ideological Coherence	Presidential Preference	Taxes	Free Market	Abortion	Civil Liberties	Death Penalty	Charity-Welfare	Cons. Adults	Civil Unions
Mr. Kushner	1.63	0.52	N/A	1	2	2	2	2	2	1	1
Student A	2.00	1.00	Kerry	2	4	1	2	2	3	2	1
Student B	1.67	0.71	Kerry	1	3	1	1	1	1	1	1
Student C	1.22	0.67	Kerry	3	3	4	2	3	2	1	1
Student D	2.22	1.09	Kerry	2	3	2	2	2	2	2	1
Student E	1.89	0.60	Kerry	2	4	4	4	1	2	2	1
Student F	2.44	1.51	Kerry	4	2	1	1	1	1	4	1
Student G	1.78	1.30	Kerry	1	4	2	4	1	3	1	1
Student H	2.00	1.32	Kerry	2	3	1	4	3	2	2	1
Student I	1.56	0.73	Kerry	2	4	4	2	2	2	2	1
Student J	2.11	1.05	Kerry	2	3	1	3	4	3	1	1
Student K	2.22	1.09	Kerry	3	4	2	2	3	3	2	1
Student L	2.11	1.17	Kerry	2	2	1	1	3	3	1	1
Student M	2.33	1.00	Kerry	3	4	1	2	2	4	1	1
Student N	1.67	0.87	Kerry	2	2	1	2	1	3	1	1
Student O	2.11	1.27	Kerry	2	3	2	2	2	1	1	1
Student P	1.56	0.73	Kerry	2	3	1	1	2	2	1	1
Class Avg.	1.93	1.01		2.19	3.19	1.88	3.81	2.06	2.31	1.56	1.00

1 = Strong Left; 2 = Left; 3 = Undecided/Don't Know; 4 = Right; 5 = Strong Right.

abortion, and healthcare, and we learned from our interviews with students that they heard disparate views on many issues, even though they said it was common in other classes only to hear what one student called the "left-wing party line."

There were two factors that accounted for the high-quality issues discussions in this class: the actual diversity of opinion that did exist on some (but not all) issues, and the skill of Mr. Kushner. To illustrate, notice on Table 5.1 that there is a great deal of disagreement about the civil liberties and free market questions, quite a few 3s (undecided/don't know) on many of the questions, and some disagreement on most other questions. In other words, in this—the most left-leaning class in the study—there were still some real differences of opinion on important issues that Mr. Kushner mined for discussion. In fact, we noticed that he was very skillful at finding the part of an issue that students disagreed about, even when it appeared that their views were similar. For example, when discussing abortion Mr. Kushner noticed that although most students supported abortion rights, they were divided about spousal or partner consent and so he made sure that their discussion on the issue focused, at least in part, on that disagreement. He told us that "it would be more interesting at the high school to have more of a mix. But now I look at issues that bring out more subtle differences that are significant, but for which students are not as ideologically peg-holed."

But Mr. Kushner recognized that even though the students in his class were generally left-leaning and remarkably similar on some issues, in reality there was both intra- (that is, individual students were left wing on some issues, undecided on others, and right wing on others) and inter- (across the class) diversity. Consequently, he went to great lengths to bring diversity of opinion into the class that did not exist naturally. He did this by ensuring that students were reading high-quality resources on various perspectives of the issues, inviting guest speakers to class to voice views that were radically different from what the vast majority of students believed, and using specific discussion methods that required students to analyze multiple positions—even those they did not initially support. For example, he frequently used Structured Academic Controversy, a form of small group discussion that requires students to prepare for and advocate two sides of policy issues, and moot court simulations in which the students rarely were able to select which "side" they wanted to support. This is not to suggest that students did not get to voice their own views—this frequently occurred. But we also noticed Mr. Kushner playing the role of "devil's advocate" to push his students to consider points that were not being raised.

Over the course of the two school years that Mr. Kushner participated in the study, we observed many classes and conducted enough interviews with students to be confident in our assessment that what was happening in his class was perceived by the students to be markedly different than the "echo chamber" of ideology they encountered in other classes.

When interviewing one male student from this class, he estimated that "at least 90%" of his school's student body would consider themselves Democrats and that he "never really gets opinions on the other side." When asked how he thought how his learning had been different compared with a school that might have been more politically balanced, he leaned in and said, "How did it affect me? I have watched every Michael Moore movie, except *Fahrenheit 9/11*, in the school (holds up two fingers): twice!" He went on: "I have watched *Roger and Me* in Econ class. And then we have watched *Bowling for Columbine* and a few others in film study from that teacher. And we have watched, I mean, so we just watched them all. I think the teachers are also like that [liberal] as well." At the same time, this student praised Mr. Kushner for presenting competing political ideas in their class, and described it as "one of the few classes where you hear both sides."

The success that Mr. Kushner and his students experienced with issues discussions in his class was due not to the diversity of views that existed among the group—but in spite of their ideological sameness. He recognized that just because they agreed on many things did not mean they agreed on all issues, and even when they did, he was able to use facilitation techniques, guest speakers, curricular resources, and specific discussion strategies to create more diversity and analysis than would have happened naturally. That is, Mr. Kushner did not see the ideological agreement that existed in his class as a poison pill—but as a challenge to be confronted.

Issues Discussions in an Evangelical Christian School

Mr. Walters and his students are also in an ideologically homogeneous environment compared with other classes—not surprisingly, given this is a small Christian high school that requires students and their parents to sign a statement testifying that they hold fundamentalist Christian beliefs. Most of the school's teachers also subscribe to these beliefs. Tom Walters is one such teacher. Table 5.2 illustrates that in some ways his class is the mirror opposite of Mr. Kushner's group. Recall, Kushner's class was the most left-wing or "blue" class in the study, and Walter's class is the most right-wing or "red" class in the study. The students are juniors enrolled in a required civics class.

All but one of the students in this class said they would have voted for George Bush in the 2004 presidential election. Because students come from all over the county to attend this school, it was not possible to know precisely who the adults in their neighborhoods voted for in 2004, but the county in which the city was located voted for John Kerry 62% to George Bush's 37%, with Ralph Nader receiving the remainder. In other words, this is a very "blue" county, although not as much as the one in which Mr. Kushner and his students reside. One student told us that because they all come from a similar background, they

Table 5.2 Mr. Walter's Class

	Political Orientation	Ideological Coherence	Presidential Preference	Taxes	Free Market	Abortion	Civil Liberties	Death Penalty	Charity-Welfare	Cons. Adults	Civil Unions
Mr. Walters	3.75	1.49	N/A	2	2	5	5	2	5	4	5
Student A	3.67	1.22	Bush	2	3	5	4	2	4	3	5
Student B	3.00	1.73	Bush	3	3	1	3	1	1	5	5
Student C	3.67	1.50	Bush	3	3	5	5	2	4	1	5
Student D	3.89	1.17	Bush	4	3	3	3	5	5	2	5
Student E	4.00	1.12	Bush	4	4	5	3	2	5	3	5
Student F	3.56	1.59	Bush	1	3	5	4	2	5	2	5
Student G	3.56	1.13	Bush	2	3	4	2	4	4	3	5
Student H	3.33	1.12	Kerry	4	3	3	3	4	4	3	5
Student I	3.22	1.48	Bush	3	3	5	3	1	2	2	5
Student J	3.44	1.33	Bush	3	3	1	3	5	3	3	5
Student K	4.00	1.00	Bush	3	3	5	5	4	3	3	5
Class Avg.	3.58	1.31		2.91	3.09	3.82	3.45	2.91	3.64	2.73	5.00

1 = Strong Left; 2 = Left; 3 = Undecided/Don't Know; 4 = Right; 5 = Strong Right.

tend to have the same political views—especially about whether Bush or Kerry should have won the 2004 presidential election.

The class average for political orientation is 3.58 (on a scale of 1 = left wing to 5 = right wing), but the teacher is slightly less conservative than the students as a group with a political orientation of 3.75. For ideological coherence, the students are slightly less coherent than Kushner's class—at 1.31 (compared with their 1.00). But that is still a much more coherent group than the students in the study writ large, and more than most classes. Not withstanding, it is crucial to point out that even in this, the most conservative class in the study, there is still ideological diversity on some major political issues. Notice too that there are many "3s" in the table, which shows that students do not all have opinions on these issues—and as we were told by many teachers, "undecided" and "don't know" can be a very good place from which to begin controversial issues discussions.

Notably, Mr. Walters has more diverse political views than his students (1.49). He is the *only* teacher in the entire sample, regardless of political orientation (that is, whether they swing left or right) who is less coherent than his students. From our interviews with him we learned that while he shares most of the religious views that dominate in the school community overall, he considers himself a "social justice" Christian, which accounts for why he opposed the death penalty and does not believe the rich are too highly taxed.

Despite the class's relative coherence regarding political orientation, students do report hearing some competing perspectives. One student explains that the all-Christian make-up of the school means students share personal beliefs, but politics can be debated. In terms of gay marriage, he says, "Christians can disagree about the government's rules over the issue, but not over the personal choice of being homosexual." Note, however, that all of the students in the class are opposed to legalizing civil unions between gay and lesbian couples, so it is unlikely that a robust discussion on this issue could occur—at least not without the kind of significant "ideological" intervention that Mr. Kushner attempted when he invited in a guest speaker whose views on the issues were different from those of his students (who, recall, also were in agreement as a class about civil unions—just on the other side from Mr. Walter's students).

The teacher echoes the distinction raised by this student when explaining what he wants them to decide on their own compared to what he hopes they all will believe. He says, "certainly we are trying to train our students to have a Christian worldview. I am going to say this is how I think one would think Christianly about this issue" but "while I would never balk at sharing with a student how I felt about these political and social issues and why I felt it, I wouldn't say this is how you should feel."

Mr. Walters also described the challenges he faced when trying to mediate between a desire to prepare his students for more secular environments (such as secular universities and colleges) where multiple and competing views will more frequently be aired, and doing his job of reinforcing and inculcating the religious beliefs of the school community.

> But sometimes that is a matter of pointing out that everybody in this whole class responded to that question exactly the same. You had all these same points. Now what does that say about the make up of our class? I am trying, and I am very open and honest with them from the beginning. "This is an unusual class. I feel like this last year before you go off to college I want to encourage you to, the class, I think, to think for yourself sort of a thing, but to understand that there are consequences for thinking for yourself. And thinking for yourself doesn't just mean whatever I think is necessarily okay and that there is always some kind of a framework of foundations and consequences that are going to be associated with thinking for yourself, with cutting yourself loose from the party line that has been given to you by your parents, by going to school here, and by the Church that you go to." So I would like to think that I am trying to help them constructively navigate this transition into becoming their own selves when it comes to engaging important issues without just turning them loose and doing the whole *Dead Poet's Society*, think for yourselves, you know. Go wherever you want, there are no boundaries.

While the students' ideological diversity was limited somewhat by the school's policy of allowing only "saved" Christians to attend, Walters took a number of steps to ensure that his students would be exposed to some views that were different than what they heard at home—or in the hallways. He regularly used curriculum materials on international issues containing multiple and competing perspectives, facilitated discussions to bring out as much disagreement as he could on those issues for which he thought it was good to air diverse views, and also looked outside the school and involved his civics students in a multi-school deliberation program to ensure that his students would hear other political views. Although these events allowed the students to be exposed for brief interludes to fellow students holding varied political opinions, the day-to-day homogeneity of their own classroom seemed to limit the impact of such exposure.

Because of the ideological homogeneity in the class, the students were not *regularly* exposed to opinions that sharply departed from their own. As a result, it was hard for them to seriously grapple with differing viewpoints and they sometimes resorted to relying instead on oversimplification and ideological clichés to defend their positions. One student, for example, dismissed all the opposing views that he heard as left-wing ideology, unworthy of respectful consideration and deliberation. He surmised that the interschool deliberation event was predicated on the notion that, "America has made terrible mistakes. We are terrible people, the Right is wrong. Now go from here." However, keep in mind that many of Mr. Kushner's students in the public school described the student population as ideologically homogeneous as well. Just as Mr. Kushner was teaching against the grain of the "big sort" as it applies to schools, so too was Mr. Walters—who, according to his students, was much more open to diverse views than most teachers in the school.

Mining the Diversity in a "Purple" Class

The Deliberative Polling research explained in Chapter 1 (Fishkin & Farrar, 2005) illustrates why naturally occurring diversity can be such a boon to issues discussions. Recall, Fishkin and his colleagues stress the importance of bringing together people who do not agree from the onset in order to ensure that multiple and competing views will be aired. Moreover, they are exposed to high-quality resources and the discussions are carefully facilitated. We saw conditions very similar to this in Mr. Voight's required, non-tracked government class—the most ideologically heterogeneous group in the study. Located in a large town in a rural area that itself is fairly ideologically diverse relative to the two other communities previously discussed (in 2004, 54% of adults in this community voted for John Kerry, and 45% for George Bush), Mr. Voight describes the class as diverse in a number of ways: "We tend to have a wide range socio-economically. We probably have upwards of 40–50% students who are on free or reduced lunch. We have about 20% Ho-Chunk population. We have some other mix of minorities." The class is also academically mixed, "I have everything in there from the very brightest down to the range of what I would say would be a very average student."

The difference in the political orientation and ideological coherence of students in his class compared with the other two classes clearly illustrates the ways in which this group is heterogeneous (Table 5.3).

Note that the class average for political orientation is 2.83 (on a scale of 1 = left wing to 5 = right wing) compared with 1.93 for the "blue" class and 3.58 for the "red" class. A bit more than half of the students said they would have voted for John Kerry, with the rest supporting George Bush. The students in Mr. Voight's class are also less politically coherent than the other two classes, although note that the teacher is exactly as coherent as Mr. Kushner—and much more coherent than his students.

Mr. Voight, who had taught for 27 years when we were in his classroom, described his teaching as much less traditional than it used to be. As a consequence of the school's transition to block scheduling, Mr. Voight has become more student-centered and teaching his students how to participate in issues discussions is a significant focus of his practice now. He told us that while he wants his students to feel free to talk openly, he insists on adequate preparation:

> I'm kind of a stickler, because I want them to have something to talk about. I don't want them to be taking an inch of material and just

Table 5.3 Mr. Voight's Class

Is It Exciting? Fun?	Political Orientation	Ideological Coherence	Presidential Preference	Taxes	Free Market	Abortion	Civil Liberties	Death Penalty	Charity-Welfare	Cons. Adults	Civil Unions
Mr. Voight	1.38	0.52	N/A	1	3	3	1	1	2	1	1
Student A	3.00	1.41	N/A	1	2	3	3	5	2	3	5
Student B	2.88	1.13	Bush	3	3	5	3	2	3	3	1
Student C	2.29	1.25	Kerry	1	3	1	3	4	—	3	1
Student D	1.63	0.92	Kerry	1	3	3	1	1	2	1	1
Student E	3.63	1.30	Bush	3	3	1	4	4	4	5	5
Student F	3.25	1.58	Kerry	1	3	5	3	4	4	1	5
Student G	3.25	1.39	Bush	3	3	1	3	4	2	5	5
Student H	3.88	1.64	Bush	1	3	5	5	5	5	2	5
Student I	2.38	1.06	Kerry	2	3	3	2	4	3	1	1
Student J	3.88	1.13	Bush	4	3	5	2	5	4	3	5
Student K	2.88	1.64	Kerry	2	3	5	2	1	4	1	5
Student L	1.75	0.89	Kerry	2	3	1	1	3	2	1	1
Student M	2.63	1.06	Kerry	2	3	4	3	2	4	2	1
Student N	2.00	0.93	Kerry	3	3	1	2	2	3	1	1
Student O	3.13	1.46	Bush	4	4	1	3	4	3	1	5
Class Avg.	2.83	1.25		2.20	3.00	2.93	2.67	3.33	3.21	2.20	3.13

1 = Strong Left; 2 = Left; 3 = Undecided/Don't Know; 4 = Right; 5 = Strong Right.

expounding on their sort of superficial notion of something. I want them to have some depth on the issue . . . I want them to have to read something that has some meaning to it. My goal in there is to get them to be able to disagree and really disagree and really know how to talk about it and be able to walk away and not go out and poke each other. I think we've lost that in our country.

The students in the class describe robust discussions that are rich in multiple perspectives. One student said, "I think there is a disagreement amongst all of us in the class. There are a lot of us that just disagree with each other so then it becomes a big discussion and then we kind of run out of time." But Mr. Voight's role in producing quality discussion is not lost on the students. They describe him as knowing them well enough that he can facilitate with an eye toward getting differing opinions on the table. One student remarked:

> I feel like Mr. Voight knows the students fairly well, knowing like their political backgrounds just from talking to them and getting to know them. So he will call on a student to voice their opinion and then ask another student to give theirs as well. You know, you get like multiple different opinions. So it is not like one-sided or anything.

It was obvious to the research team that Mr. Voight had an easier time teaching his students how to seriously consider the views that differed from their own than did the other two teachers because there was more natural occurring ideological diversity among his students. That being said, we were also in plenty of classes with high levels of ideological diversity in which the students were unaware that anyone disagreed with their views because the teachers had not allowed for the views to come to the fore. Having ideological diversity in a classroom was an untapped resource. By contrast, Mr. Voight regularly provided his students with opportunities to participate in discussion, insisted that they read and carefully consider a range of perspectives, used role plays and other strategies to encourage them to thoughtfully consider views different from their own, and facilitated discussions with an eye toward amplifying the diversity in the class.

Conclusion

In sum, this analysis of ideological diversity and its effects suggests that classes do look like the communities in which they are embedded to a certain extent, but there is typically more variance in students' own views (intra-diversity) and across students (inter-diversity) than one would imagine—or than could be understood if you only focused on rough proxies, like presidential preference—to make judgments about the nature and range of diversity in a class. We also found that teachers and students were much more aware of the diversity in their midst in classes with high-quality discussions—which shows again that teacher skill and pedagogy matter. Moreover, in classes with wide political differences that are unawakened, there is a high opportunity cost, since most young people are unlikely to engage in such discussions in politically diverse climates elsewhere.

6

To Disclose or Not to Disclose

A Controversial Choice for Teachers

CO-AUTHORED WITH PAULA McAVOY

When I [Hess] started teaching, one of the most controversial political issues facing the body politic was whether the Equal Rights Amendment should be added to the Constitution. I remember searching for good pro/con articles for my students to read and then moderating heated and often exciting discussions about the issue in the social studies course I taught. As a new teacher, I was unsure about how to respond to students' queries about my own views on the issue, but I remember feeling vaguely pleased when I heard two students debating what I thought about the issue as they left the classroom. Their debate was a signal to me that my strongly held personal views were not readily apparent to my students. It was evidence, I thought, that I was not a biased teacher.

At lunch, I shared the students' conversation I had overheard with other teachers, which sparked an intense debate. Some of my colleagues thought I had wasted an opportunity to demonstrate to my students how adults think through political issues. One said I was acting like a "political eunuch," and knowing of my own intense interest in politics, asked, "Why do you want to be a non-political role model?" Other teachers at the lunch table disagreed. "It's our job," said one, "to help our students think through these issues, not to impress our own views upon them." Another added, "The longer I teach the more I understand about how much power teachers have over students. I don't want to abuse that power—and I don't want kids to agree with my views just because I am the teacher."

The controversy surrounding teacher disclosure emanates from the cultural wars that continue to play out in U.S. public schools. In 2005, the Alliance Defense Fund sued Cupertino Union School District on behalf of fifth grade teacher Stephen Williams who was facing district action for over-emphasizing Christian messages in early-American historical documents (Boyer, 2005). In 2006, UCLA graduate Andrew Jones founded the Bruin Alumni Association to expose the "Dirty 30"—a collection of professors Jones deemed to be too radical for the classroom (Jones, n.d.). And in February, 2007, Arizona Senate Majority

Leader Thayer Verschoor presented a bill that would "punish public school teachers and professors for not being impartial in the classroom" (Associated Press, 2007).

As these incidents illustrate, what teachers say and do with respect to voicing their personal views in schools is clearly of interest to the public, policy-makers, interest groups, and the media. The messages from these sources indicate that many believe it is problematic for teachers to disclose their political views. Some even go so far as to suggest that teacher disclosure is synonymous with indoctrination. This apparent consensus against disclosure from outside of schools is markedly different from the views in the educational community, where a robust (and healthy) debate about whether teachers should disclose their political views in class has been going on for quite some time. To clarify from the onset, the disclosure we are interested in for this chapter is when a teacher explicitly shares his/her political views with students. Elsewhere, I [Hess] have described the multiple ways in which teachers' views influence their teaching, ranging from determining what constitutes a legitimate matter of controversy that belongs in the curriculum (see Chapter 7), to the selection of curricular materials (Hess, 2004a). Here we focus more narrowly on the ways in which teachers disclose and their attitudes toward disclosure. In addition, we report findings about what students think about various types of disclosure and what effect, if any, disclosure has on learning and classroom climate.

Until recently, there was a dearth of research that probed how teachers and their students make sense of this critical question. What we do have shows that when teachers tackle controversial issues in the classroom, the question of what role the teacher ought to play in the discussion becomes important and controversial. In a study of 12 middle and high school teachers from rural schools, Miller-Lane, Denton, and May (2006) found that student age and community norms played a role in decisions not to disclose. Of the middle school teachers, all chose the role of neutral facilitator when leading discussion. The high school teachers were slightly more divided, with the three disclosers believing that sharing their views created more authentic discussion, so long as it is clear to students that the teacher's voice is just "one of many in the class" (Miller-Lane et al., 2006, p. 38). McCully (2006) found a similar desire for authenticity among community educators in Northern Ireland who engaged students in discussions about "The Troubles." McCully reported that 19 out of 20 educators did disclose because "as products of a divided society, neutrality was impossible" (2006, p. 62). Thus, if educators chose not to disclose their views, they risked diminishing the trust necessary for group discussions to be meaningful and productive. Other studies have found that teachers who claim to be "neutral" might nevertheless implicitly communicate their views through sarcasm, tone of voice, and line of questioning (Cotton, 2006; Niemi & Niemi, 2007).

These studies, while important, do not constitute a robust literature base from which to understand teacher disclosure. But they do point to the fact that teachers who engage students in discussion of controversial issues make different decisions about the roles they will play during the discussion and that most teachers are intensely aware of the controversies surrounding disclosure. This chapter adds to this literature by further exploring how teachers in multiple states and contexts think about the issue of teacher disclosure. This chapter draws on the ongoing study we are conducting that formed the basis of Chapter 5. It is the first recent study that investigates how high school students feel about disclosure and the impact it may or may not have on engagement and learning (Hess, McAvoy, Smithson, & Hwang, 2008). In the study, we address the following questions:

1. To what extent are students and teachers in favor of or opposed to disclosure, and what are the reasons behind their positions?
2. To what extent do teachers disclose their views, and are students able to accurately identify disclosure? What causes them to assess this accurately or not?
3. Does disclosure cause students to align with the teacher's views? If not, what effect does disclosure have on how students experience and learn from issues discussions?

Attitudes Toward Disclosure

To answer these questions, we gathered data through qualitative and quantitative sources— primarily a survey of students and teachers and interviews. We found that students and teachers reported differing attitudes toward disclosure (see Appendix B).

These responses show that while teachers are clearly divided about the issue of disclosure, the majority of students are in favor, with 80% thinking it was "fine" for teachers to share opinions. We also asked whether students desired more disclosure from their teachers and found they were divided, with 52% wishing they heard from the teacher more often and 46% either comfortable with the amount of disclosure they received, or wishing that they heard less about the teacher's point of view.

We also found that students were quite confused about whether or not they heard disclosure from their teacher. In only five classes did 70–100% of the students consistently identify the teacher's policy.

A Continuum of Teacher Disclosure

When interpreting this confusion between teachers and students, we learned that there are many ways in which teachers disclose. Rather than thinking of teachers as either "disclosers" or "non-disclosers," it is more accurate to think of teacher disclosure along a continuum. On one end, in this study, were several firm non-disclosers who explicitly stated their policy to the students and stuck to it:

> But we, as teachers really have a very strong opinion that to create a safe environment we should not say what our opinions are on any issue . . . we just don't feel it is our place. We will play double dagger every so often with questions. We will restate things just to sort of stir the pot . . . But we will never, no, we never say what we think on any issue . . . we won't. We won't express what we think. I told the kids I will take out a full-page in the *Urban Chronicle*, the school newspaper, the day I retire and let them all know.

This teacher took one of the strongest stands against disclosure, and represented the "pure neutrality" end of the continuum. On the opposite end of the continuum were explicit disclosers who made it clear to the class that they would hear the teacher's opinion:

> The kids know my political point of view. I had made a decision years ago, I lived as a social studies teacher with a fantasy of I . . . would never reveal my personal opinions on things. And I would always stay objective and neutral. I think that is a total fantasy, and I think you can't do that. And so I decided to try differently and it has worked very, very well for me because I handle it very well, and I am very careful about it.

In between these two views were non-disclosers who "try [their] best" to stay neutral, but sometimes "slip," others who answer honestly when asked, and some who stay neutral in discussion, but will share their views afterwards. There were also a few who implicitly disclosed and were aware of it, making comments like "I think they get that I'm liberal . . ." Collectively, these teachers in the middle might be thought of as "occasional disclosers."

It is not surprising that the teachers who took the clearest stands to disclose or not disclose had students who could consistently report their teacher's policy, in part explaining the low consistency in student reporting. In most classes, students reported very different experiences with regards to disclosure. Some nearly split down the middle with half thinking the teacher disclosed, and half thinking the teacher did not. In interviews, teachers in the middle of the continuum admitted that disclosure is something they struggled with, "I mean, it is very hard when I am so heavily invested emotionally, intellectually into these issues, to check that at the door." Without a clear policy and with occasional "slips," it is likely that some students heard and remembered moments of disclosure, and some did not. We also had some preliminary findings that suggested that students often misinterpret what they see in the classroom. For example, some students, particularly those from low socioeconomic status (SES) backgrounds, misunderstood devil's advocacy as teacher disclosure. Others were not clear about how the teacher used humor, or they made incorrect assumptions based on, for example, how long the teacher paused before responding to conservative comments made by students.

This student confusion complicates data interpretation. The mixed methods used in this study proved to be important in attempting to get behind the meaning of what is clearly a muddled understanding of classroom experiences. For analysis, labels became necessary, so we refer to teachers as "disclosers" if they self reported that they regularly shared their views, if they participated in discussions as an equal voice, if they disclosed when asked, or if they were aware of the implicit ways in which they disclose. "Non-disclosers" are teachers who attempted to stay neutral, or see neutrality as the best policy, even though most admitted this is not always easy to do. Under this framework, the qualitative responses aligned with the quantitative findings with 47% of teachers saying they do share their opinions and 52% saying they do not. For students, we considered those who believe their teacher disclosed as students who experienced disclosure, even if there was evidence to suggest that they misunderstood the teacher's practice.

Influence

The common wisdom around disclosure is that when a teacher discloses, they inflict undue influence upon a captive audience. We found that both teachers and students were primarily concerned about two types of influence. The first was "ideological influence," that is, the belief that students are likely to adopt the teacher's views either out of respect for the teacher as "expert" or because the teacher is abusing his or her power. The second is "pedagogical influence." This is a view that the teacher's opinion interfered with the discussions, the classroom climate, or with the student–teacher relationship. Here we report to what extent students and teachers believe that students are influenced by disclosure, whether or not students are being influenced, and the different ways disclosure impacts how students experience the class and the discussion.

Ideological Influence

One clear finding from the data was that what students and teachers worry about most with regard to disclosure is the possibility that teachers will shape student opinion to align with their own. In the quantitative data, 45% of teachers believed that if social studies teachers share their views, students are more likely to adopt those same opinions. Students were nearly in agreement with teachers, 44% thinking students were likely to adopt a teacher's opinions. However, only 23% of students felt that they were likely to change their minds to align with the teacher. In other words, students were twice as likely to think that their classmates would be affected by disclosure but believed their own views would not be affected. Recall also that in the student and teacher "pro-disclosure" we saw that 80% of students say it is "fine" for teachers to share their views, while only 55% of teachers agree with that statement.

The qualitative student data showed that students found it acceptable for teachers to "share" their views so long as they were not "preaching," "pushing," or "forcing" their opinion without giving serious consideration to competing points of view. Fear of this type of influence was the main reason why students in non-discloser classrooms felt that teachers should remain "neutral." Many of these students reported that they worry a personable discloser will sway them, as in "when you like somebody . . . you agree with them because he seems to know a lot." Still others were concerned that teachers would use their power to coerce students. They also imagined that disclosure would come with bad teaching behaviors like "playing favorites" or biased grading. Nearly all of these students were speaking hypothetically, imagining teachers who *could* influence students, and not wanting to find themselves in those classrooms.

Students in the follow-up interviews given after they finished high school were equally leery of disclosure, with 53% saying that their teacher did not disclose, and 96% of those supporting a non-disclosure policy. When asked the reasons why they were against disclosure, the number one answer given was fear of influence. The common argument among the students was that it is not a teacher's "job to influence our opinions, just to teach us to build our own opinions." Similarly, many of the teachers in the study who were against disclosure were concerned that students would adopt their views if they shared them during discussions. As one teacher in a school where all of the twelfth grade government teachers were against disclosure explained, "We don't want the kids to feel pressured to sort of brown-nose and take our opinion."

It is clear that some students and teachers are concerned about indoctrination, and this is, in large part, what causes them to be disclosure-averse. However, in this sample, 47% of teachers said that they do share their opinions about the issues discussed in class, some inserting them during the discussion and others waiting until the end of the activity or unit of study. Students in these classrooms usually report that disclosure is at worst benign and at best desirable. When interviewed, some students who supported teacher disclosure reasoned from a position of fairness: "if the students get to share their opinion, I think teachers should too." Students also wanted to hear their teachers' views out of curiosity and a desire to know their teacher as a person. Disclosure, some believed, "makes him [the teacher] seem more human." Finally, in discussion-rich classrooms, students were interested in hearing "an adult's perspective." The voice of a knowledgeable teacher was a welcome change: "she is obviously educated, and she knows what she is talking about. And I would much rather get her opinion than get a classmate's opinion . . ."

What caused these students to see themselves as inoculated against ideological influence? One factor was that nearly all of the students reported that their teachers were open to disagreement and "wouldn't look down" on students for holding views that differed from the teacher's. Most students described their teachers as "open-minded" and "accepting of the students' opinions." Further, students felt that the material in class was presented in a "balanced" way. This attitude came through in the teacher interviews as well, with comments such as:

> And if they know my opinions, I mean, I can still approach an issue from the opposite side . . . or discuss it or deliberate it very intelligently. And I can back it up with facts. And I can back it up with good information even if I don't believe, or if I don't agree with what it is that is going on.

In the teacher interviews, none reported a desire to influence students' political positions on issues, although many were very explicit about their desire to shape students' conceptions of what it means to be an engaged citizen.

Given that most students felt they were in classrooms where students were allowed to disagree with the teacher, those who experienced disclosure did not feel that they were being pressured to adopt the teacher's views. In the follow-up interviews, students who believed they experienced some form of teacher disclosure remained supportive of this policy. When asked if they remembered whether or not the teacher shared personal views about the issues discussed in class, 35% answered affirmatively. Of those who responded to the question about how they felt about this, 90% were in favor of disclosure, responding that what they experienced was somewhere between "fine" and "the right thing to do." As they did in high school, 42% felt that knowing the teacher's views had no influence on them and an additional 15% thought that disclosure had a positive influence:

> When he presented his own opinions and why he felt that way, it kinda showed us what we should be basing our opinions on, even if we didn't share the same opinion . . . I guess I started to see more sides of issues than I did before, so I thought more about my own opinion.

There were other "positives" that were more questionable. For example, one student remarked, "It is good to be exposed to that so you are not shocked by it in college." Important to note is that 40% of the respondents who reported disclosure said that the teacher did so after the discussion. This, they felt, buffered the class against blindly adopting the teacher's views: "The whole goal was to get us to think get about and discuss political issues rather than just being spoon-fed whatever they want us to hear."

The preliminary data on student opinions of various issues seems to indicate that the majority of students are correct: students do not appear to be swayed by teachers who disclose. In initial analysis of the pre- and post-questionnaires, none of the classes show student views changing to align with their teachers' political ideology. In many cases, students' views on issues (such as the death penalty, abortion, civil unions, and tax policy) changed from the beginning of the course to the end. But to date, the statisticians working on the study have not been able to identify any relationship between teacher disclosure and students' views on issues—with the exception of one teacher in whose class students changed their views on two issues in a direction that aligned with his. This is clearly the exception to the general rule. We have no other evidence that shows that teachers' views on issues influence their students' views.

Pedagogical Influence

Does this mean that disclosure cannot influence students? We do not think so. What we have found is that the teachers in this study who chose to disclose were, for the most part, very careful about disclosure and did their best to present competing views fairly. Further, most were occasional disclosers, who answered questions honestly when appropriate. Consequently, we did not find students moving to align with their teachers' views. But while we found little evidence of ideological influence, disclosure still has a pedagogical effect on the classroom and student learning. The effect can be positive or negative depending on the student hearing it and the way in which the teacher discloses.

Recall that students reported that they did not want teachers to "preach" at them. When some students heard what they perceived to be more aggressive disclosure, or opinions presented in "really, really, strong ways," they were not persuaded to agree, but they did report having negative experiences in the classroom. Of the 200 students interviewed, only seven students, from three different classrooms, felt that the teacher had crossed a line. One who disagreed with the teacher's view described the teacher as "ripping the other side" and "forcing" her point of view on a particular issue "over and over and over again." However, this same student thought "it is nice that Ms. Potter gives her opinions sometimes" as long as she is "civil about it." Other students were ideologically in agreement with the teacher, but felt that the teacher was silencing others:

> [How do you know Ms. Gardner's opinions?] Like just from all her opinions, and then basically, like, by the semester the jig is up. She is not even pretending to be . . . that balanced anymore. Like she is fair, but you can obviously tell she is liberal . . . And like I am too. It is like, I don't like to disagree with her a lot, but I kind of don't think that her approach to it. . . like, I know if she was conservative and so open on conservative issues, I would kind of get mad about that.

In the follow-up interviews from this particular class, 10 of the 12 students said that the teacher did disclose, but all thought it was "good to get a viewpoint as strong as hers" and that she "always provided the disclaimer before she spoke that this is strictly my opinion." Conversely, 15 students in the follow-up interviews who had experienced disclosure felt that teachers should "try to stay neutral." One felt particularly strongly about this, stating that the teacher was "influencing people and if you look up to your teacher and she has completely different views from you, it can feel disrespectful in a way."

While these students appeared to be outliers in the dataset, we feel that they might be "canaries in the coal mine" that have an important perspective. Recall that 23% of students did feel susceptible to ideological influence. Moreover, students who reported this feeling were more likely to be low SES and have low scores on our measures of political knowledge. Conversely, it appears that high SES acts as a "shield" of some sort against the perception that a teacher can influence one's opinions—perhaps because they come in with more political knowledge and are more accustomed to discussions with adults. So, when we consider students who are less accustomed to political talk and might be ideologically different than the teacher, our research suggests that they could feel personally attacked by explicit disclosure, and may not feel secure enough in their skills or knowledge to challenge the teacher—even if the teacher would be open to disagreement.

Additionally, many students reported that it is the likeable, knowledgeable teacher who is most likely to sway student opinion. In one class, a student described that she has "a lot of respect" for her teacher because "he knows a lot." At the same time, she said of his occasional disclosure:

> I think it helps students get more information about the topic, but it can also kind of change how they feel about something. Like it can really influence them too, they believe in one thing and then all of a sudden they will switch over. I don't know. I think it is fine if he told us his opinions after we have been exposed to enough of it. I don't think it is right if it should influence what we think.

It turns out that this perception that the teacher is trying to influence students significantly affected whether or not students move away from being disclosure-tolerant. In our statistical analysis, we dove deeper to investigate whether or not students changed their initial opinions about disclosure and found that slightly more than half of the students (211) changed their views to some extent, with about equal numbers switching to become more or less in favor of disclosure. Using three regression models that held for the student's initial opinion about disclosure, we found that if students perceived disclosure in the classroom, they were more likely to change pre-post to favor disclosure. However, if the students felt that the teacher *was trying to influence* the students to adopt her views, then students were likely to move away from supporting disclosure. To clarify, students were amiable to allowing teachers to share their views, and when teachers did so, they changed students' views on whether disclosure is acceptable, with one important caveat: if they believed that the teacher wanted students to adopt the same political views, then they became less supportive of disclosure.

This worked in the other direction as well—the students who changed from being pro-disclosure to anti-disclosure were more likely to have been in the classrooms of non-disclosure teachers. This was especially the case when the non-disclosure teachers made their policy vividly transparent to their students. For example, in one school with three government teachers—all of whom participated in the study—they agreed as a matter of pedagogical policy not to disclose their views to students and clearly explained this policy and its rationale to students at the beginning of the course. This points to an important finding in that our data shows that teachers do not influence students' views on political issues—but ironically, they do have an impact on what students think with respect to the controversial pedagogical issue of teacher disclosure.

There is another dimension to the teacher disclosure issue, which is what impact it has on the quality of the discussions, and what students think they are learning. Students in non-discloser classrooms generally defended the position of teacher neutrality because of the positive effect they felt it had on student learning. They liked that they felt they were "discovering on our own . . . how we feel about these issues." Many students also reported that they had to work harder and pay attention more when teachers did not disclose. Non-disclosers "[get] you to think more and debate more and actually read what you are learning . . . if she doesn't say [her opinion] you actually have to go through and read all the information and actually decide on your own. You learn more just from not hearing what her opinion is." Students were also concerned about the effect disclosure has on the student–teacher relationship. Many students reported that they would participate less if they knew the teacher disagreed with them. A few also admitted that they felt "conflicted" when they wanted to write about a topic they knew their teacher opposed.

In the follow-up interviews the second most common reason that people gave for supporting non-disclosure (after teacher influence) was that discussion was better and/or people participated more when the teacher facilitated without disclosing; as one student commented, "I think when a teacher expresses . . . his or her own view that sort of makes the students less willing to express their own point of view, at least that's the case with me." Our preliminary analysis of the pre- and post-change shows that there is a positive relationship between non-disclosure and a number of factors that are linked to student participation in discussion. For example, students are more likely to say that they have a responsibility to participate in class discussion in non-discloser classrooms. However, there are some students who see teacher disclosure as a valuable learning opportunity because, when done thoughtfully and well, it can serve as a model of how a knowledgeable adult thinks through an issue. Moreover, some students perceived disclosure as content information coming from the teacher that could be taken with more credibility than that coming from other students. This suggests that disclosure can be used as a pedagogical tool that, when done consciously and reflectively, might further a specific educational purpose.

It is important to point out that the students in this study were in the upper grades in high school (and thus, probably less susceptible to teacher influence). Moreover, while half of the teachers in the sample reported disclosing their political views to students, none of them were even remotely close to fervent indoctrinators. That being said, these findings suggest that the problem that most people who are against disclosure identify—that teachers will influence political views—is not such a problem when teachers are able to respectfully engage competing points of view. Instead, it may make more sense to focus attention on what influence disclosure has on how students experience and learn from discussion, their perceptions of how open the classroom climate is, and what effect these things have on their participation. In short, there may be some important problems that are linked to teacher disclosure, but if so, they are probably not the ones the public and educators have focused on in the past. Another way to think about the effects of disclosure is the distinction between preventing a negative and creating a positive. Many people are against disclosure because they want to prevent the negative of influence. Our data indicate that if there are strong reasons to worry about disclosure, they do not have to do with the ones focused on in the past; instead, we found that teacher disclosure can essentially impede some of the *positive* influences on student learning: students might participate less if they feel their teacher is a discloser, which might impact the quality and breadth of class discussion.

Lessons Learned

The issue of disclosure is obviously complicated and controversial. So, what does this study tell us that could help educators think through this issue? First, we learn three things about what students are looking for in classroom discussions:

1. **Problem solving.** Students clearly want to discuss (it is far and away the activity they report liking the most in discussion-rich classrooms), and they want to feel like they are "figuring it out" for themselves. Further, they prefer it when they are thinking about "adult" problems and engaged in the complexities of the issue—not just "sharing" uninformed opinions. Teachers who teach toward one particular point of view, or take up too much of the discussion, rob students of the opportunity to solve the puzzle themselves.
2. **To be liked.** Students want to know that their teacher respects them and their ideas—even if they disagree. There are certainly students who have great affection for teachers who express ideas with which they disagree with, but there are also students who fear repercussions from a teacher who disagrees with them—especially if the teacher shows disregard for their particular point of view (see point 3).

Students also want to be liked by their peers. A minority of students thrive off "heated" discussions, but most report wanting "civilized" discourse, which allows them to learn about each other as well as how to respectfully disagree.

3. **Fair play.** Students are curious about what their teachers think, and some like to hear the "adult" opinion. But while most want to give teachers the "right" to share their opinions, they do not want the teacher's opinion to dominate the discussion. They also want the tone of the class to be "fair and balanced" insofar as all points of view are given equal consideration. To that end, teachers should be genuinely respectful to the other side. Students can tell through tone of voice, humor, and attitude if the teacher is disparaging a viewpoint while claiming to be "presenting" the other point of view. Teachers should also avoid partisan sarcasm. This type of humor creates an "insider/outsider" climate in the classroom wherein those who agree with the joke are in the "in group" and those who do not are made to feel foolish, or "out." This type of off-handed disclosure is what often leads students holding minority points of view to feel disrespected.

Second, when considering a position about disclosure, teachers should weigh three possible (but not certain) dangers associated with some types of disclosure:

1. Students might talk less. Again, our data show that students feel less responsibility to contribute to discussion when the teacher discloses.

2. Students worry about their own behavior and the behavior of their classmates when the class knows the teacher's view. To be clear, many of the students who reported this fear were in non-discloser classrooms, and were speaking hypothetically. But it is nevertheless important to note that what students feared was a change in the classroom climate that would make them think twice before stating their true views on assignments or in discussion. Again, what we found was that in actual discloser classrooms, students simply spoke less.

3. Some students reported that they work harder to understand the issues when they do not know the teacher's opinion. This is connected to the idea that students want to figure out their own views, but when given the opportunity, they are tempted to write or speak to please the teacher.

In sum, it is clear that when teachers and students share their perspectives about whether a teacher should disclose, the fear that teachers may influence students' opinions looms large. Teachers were especially worried about this—it was the most frequently mentioned reason we heard from the non-disclosure teachers for why they tried to withhold their opinions on political issues from their students. Students worried about this too, although we think it is important to underline the fact that only one in five reported a teacher could influence their views—it is their weaker-willed classmates they worry about. In the main, though, these eleventh and twelfth grade students seem much less worried about this than teachers, which is why so few reported that they perceived the teacher as trying to influence their views. It is important to note that we observed in almost all of the teachers' classrooms and did not find any relationship between our assessment of the overall quality of the teaching and whether the teacher disclosed or not. We saw excellent teaching in discloser classrooms, and excellent teaching in non-discloser classrooms. For that reason, we think it is important to directly challenge the content and tone of some of the rhetoric that exists in the popular media about the disclosure issue. It may be that there are some teachers who unduly influence their students, but we are struck by the fact that virtually all of the students in our study do not feel like *their* teachers are having that effect on their views. Moreover, we have virtually no evidence to suggest that teacher disclosure does influence students' views. It is clear to us that for these students, disclosure and indoctrination do not go hand in hand.

Conclusion

While I have explained our findings about ideological diversity and teacher disclosure separately in Chapter 5 and in this chapter, there are important ways in which they overlap, theoretically and in practice. First and foremost, engaging young people in controversial issues discussions as a form of school-based democratic education is based in large part on the deliberative ideal that depends on a fair-minded and rigorous airing, analysis, and critique of multiple and competing perspectives. While it is possible for teachers to purposely insert these perspectives into a class discussion through the selection of materials, devil's advocacy, and the like, when they arise naturally students come to the deliberation with genuinely different perspectives on issues; thus, the discourse is more authentic, and consequently, more engaging. While these findings about the nature and range of ideological diversity that exist in classrooms demonstrate that some classes are much more ideologically diverse than others, they also show that even classes that initially appear to be incredibly homogeneous are actually much more diverse than many students and teachers realize. Moreover, a central finding from this study is that ideological diversity is much more likely to be recognized by students and teachers alike when the quality of issues discussions is high. Thus, ideological diversity in classes is clearly a deliberative asset—one that can be plumbed by skillful teachers.

The decision that teachers make with respect to disclosing their own views is related to ideological diversity in key respects. Many students indicated that teachers should not disclose because that would influence others' opinions (and even in some cases, their own). This influence would then lessen the educative impact of ideological diversity in a class discussion because one person's views would be so persuasive. Conversely, recall that students who supported teacher disclosure tended to do so because they thought their teacher's views would just add to the mix, which would increase the diversity of views that were available to them for consideration. Thus, one interpretation of the diversity/disclosure connection is that students' views on disclosure (irrespective of what they are) are often linked to the larger goal of ideological diversity in discussions. It appears to me that students have an intrinsic and strongly held view that it is critically important to engage in discussions of important political issues and that such discussions are much more educative if there is genuine disagreement. If disagreement about political views is at the heart of democracy, as many deliberative theorists contend, then there is evidence that the young people in this study are attracted to that ideal.[1]

III
Controversy in the Curriculum

7
Teaching in the Tip
Controversies About What
Is Legitimately Controversial

One of the most controversial aspects of teaching controversial issues revolves around differing opinions of what is controversial in the first place. This plays out in the differing opinions regarding how a question is taught—is there one answer, or are there multiple and competing answers? It is this issue to which I now turn. The reason this is so controversial in schools is because there is often ferocious debate in the world outside of school about whether something is *legitimately* controversial, especially when an issue is tipping. Tipping refers to a number of processes by which topics (which have managed to get into the curriculum in the first place) shift back and forth between their status as open questions (for which we want students to engage in deliberating multiple and competing answers) and closed questions (for which we want students to build and believe a particular answer).

To elaborate, imagine the curriculum as a box. Often the first step for advocates of a topic, or series of topics that represent a particular political perspective, is simply to get inside the box (Zimmerman, 2002). Consequently, many of the controversies surrounding the social studies curriculum emanate from this desire for inclusion (Binder, 2002). Decisions about what will be in the curriculum are significant. For example, when schools include previously forbidden topics in the curriculum, they send a message that legitimizes the topic; this is culturally significant given the ways in which schools are reflective of society writ large. Even more important, what students learn in schools *is* related to the content of the curriculum. I know this point seems self-evident, but I am struck by how often curricular battles are really proxy wars for adults' political disagreements—and what gets lost is the very real impact that different curricula have on what students believe (Thornton, 2003).

Once a topic is put into the curriculum, there is often controversy about whether it should be treated as open or closed. Thus, a "tipping" process often begins. The box can be tipped so that the issue is "open," meaning that the issue is indeed controversial and worthy of discussion, as is, for example, the current issue of capital punishment in the United States. However, the box could also be tipped "closed," as would be the case with an issue such as women's suffrage because it is no longer controversial. While it is relatively easy to identify capital punishment as an open issue and women's suffrage as a closed issue within the context of contemporary United States, teaching becomes more precarious when an issue has not tipped, but rather is in the process of tipping—moving from open to closed or closed to open. Inevitably, there will be those who feel that the issue is closed and therefore not open for discussion in public schools, while there will be others who believe that the issue is very much still open and in need of discussion. This is what makes the teaching of controversial issues so controversial.

Before a teacher can engage her students in controversial issues discussions, she must first identify if the issue is closed, open, or tipping. If it is closed, there is no need for discussion in the form of a controversial political issues discussion (which is not to say that the issue should therefore be left out of the curriculum). For example, in the case of women's suffrage, many teachers include lessons or even units about how women gained the franchise and why it was such an important step in U.S. democracy. Or they may even engage their students in a discussion that places them back in time to deliberate the issue in the historical context.

Conversely, issues that are open in contemporary society are the kinds of controversial political issue that teachers, like those show-cased in Chapter 4, often include in their curriculum. If the issue is tipping, there is also room for discussion, but teachers must be sure to take into account the controversial nature of the controversial issue while designing and implementing the lesson, and recognize that the decision they make about whether to treat an issue as open or closed will undoubtedly be one that sparks some degree of controversy.

To more fully illustrate the concept of tipping, the remainder of this chapter looks first at the construction of controversy, followed by four examples of tipping. I then address how it is decided if an issue is open, closed, or tipping and ask who should be making this decision? Finally, I conclude with a discussion of implications for teaching in the "tip."

The Construction of Controversy

Topics are not controversial by nature. Instead, they are socially constructed in ways that cause them to be more or less controversial. This is why it is common for issues that are considered closed in one nation or region to be controversial in others. For example, the question of whether evolution (or other ideas about the origin of life) should be taught in schools is a matter of bitter controversy in some parts of the United States but does not generate the same level of controversy in much of Europe (Hess, 2006). Similarly, in many parts of the world, healthcare is considered a basic human right that governments should provide their citizens, and thus the basic question of whether people have a right to healthcare is a "closed" matter and is taught as such in schools. In other nations, such as the United States, this question is controversial and is taught that way.

But just as questions are controversial in some places and not in others, over time issues can move from being closed to open and vice versa. For example, as mentioned in the introduction to this chapter, at one time the question of whether or not suffrage should be extended to women was controversial in many democratic nations, while now women's suffrage is widely recognized as a basic right (though not, of course, in all nations). Although it currently would not be controversial in many nations for teachers to present women's suffrage as a closed matter, imagine what it was like for teachers when society was "tipping" from viewing this issue as controversial to one that was settled. This tipping process is a major reason why one scholar deemed the teaching of controversial issues "a multi-risk business" (Cavet, 2007, p. 1). Much of the conflict that arises from the teaching of controversial issues in schools is rooted in disagreements about whether or not a teacher (or school, or curriculum material) communicates the right decision about which side of the "tip" to promote (Camicia, 2007; Hess, 2004a). This is a key point because the decision about whether to construct an issue as open or closed is, by definition, a form of position-taking on the part of the school and teacher, and therefore, controversial.

Examples of Tipping

Teaching Japanese Internment and Evolution in the Classroom: Tips of the Past

To illustrate how tipping works, it may be helpful to analyze a concrete example of a topic that has tipped since I began teaching in 1979: the internment of Japanese Americans during World War II. As a high school history, government, and law teacher in a suburb of Chicago, I was inculcated into a social studies department that believed it was essential to engage students in discussions of highly controversial issues in social studies courses. Consequently, infused throughout all of the required courses and many of the electives were contemporary topics that were quite controversial. There was also a marked distinction between the liberal politics of the majority of social studies teachers and the political values of the larger community, which at the time was one of the most solidly Republican areas in the United States.

In the school's required U.S. History course, we showed a movie about the internment of Japanese Americans that was touted as "balanced" because it gave equal time to what were then widely considered two legitimately opposing views. One view held that the internment was justified because of military necessity (or at least that people at the time had good evidence to believe that to be the case), while the other position was that it was an egregious violation of civil liberties that was driven by racism and the desire to steal land. The textbook we used also presented competing views about the internment, as did the many supplemental curricular materials that were disseminated to teachers.

In our history classes, students were asked to deliberate about which position had the strongest warrant. I recall these discussions as spirited and intense. I had a strong position on the issue, but at that time I did not question whether or not framing the internment as a controversial issues topic was in any way problematic. In fact, we thought we were being hip and edgy in comparison to what some of the veteran teachers in the department told us about how the internment had been treated in the curriculum in the past. In their experience, this topic was either ignored (kept under the historical rug, so to speak) or presented as a military necessity. In other words, it was treated as a closed issue, and the correct understanding of the internment was that is was justified. By approaching it as a controversial issue, we were recognizing that a "tip" had occurred, which seemed like a progressive move.

In 1987, I left high school teaching to work for the Constitutional Rights Foundation of Chicago. While there, I was exposed to a wide array of curriculum materials, and I routinely talked with authors of history textbooks. I began noticing that the curricular treatment of the internment was changing. Another tip was occurring—perhaps in response to a national commission that had issued a blistering 1983 report criticizing the internment as a racist travesty of justice (Commission on Wartime Relocation and Internment of Civilians, 1983). Now it was less likely that students would be asked to deliberate about whether or not the internment was justified, and much more likely that students would study it as a case of the government denying the civil liberties of citizens. The clear intent of this approach was to close the issue so that students would learn that the internment had been wrong. It is important to note that the tip was occurring as the government officially recognized that the internment was a clear violation of civil liberties. The Civil Liberties Act of 1988, a federal law signed by President Ronald Reagan, declared in part: "The Congress recognizes that, as described in the Commission on Wartime Relocation and Internment of Civilians, a grave injustice was done to both citizens and permanent residents of Japanese ancestry by the evacuation, relocation, and internment of civilians during World War II" (The Civil Liberties Act of 1988).

Even a cursory analysis of social studies curriculum materials developed since this law passed shows that students are much more likely to encounter the issue of Japanese internment as closed rather than open and controversial (e.g., Cayton, Perry, Reed, & Winkler, 2005, pp. 858–859). This is not to suggest that there is 100% agreement about how the internment should be taught. Camicia's (2007) study focused on a vocal minority in one community that challenged a curriculum that it perceived as biased because it did not treat the topic as a controversy. However, this is not the norm; even in the community Camicia studied, it was a clear a minority of people objected to the curriculum. The teaching of the internment of Japanese Americans has tipped—twice—from a closed question (the internment was necessary) to an open question (was the internment justified?) to a closed question (the internment was a grave injustice).

While the example of teaching the Japanese internment illustrates how an issue can tip from open to closed, the example of teaching evolution illustrates the possibility of the opposite tip—from closed to open. This phenomena of tipping (from closed to open) can be attributed in part to the rhetoric of openness that is deeply embedded in American classrooms: both sides of an issue should be taught. Advocates for the inclusion of evolution in the school curriculum more than 80 years ago made the argument that evolution should at least have equal time in the curriculum as creationism. The Scopes trial was set up as a way to teach evolution *alongside* creationism—not in its stead (Larson, 1997). This is not to suggest that advocates of evolution did not ultimately want to see it taught as the right answer to a scientific question, but they used the appeal of equal time, which has so much face validity, to at least open the issue.

yeah, this was my first thought

no? how is this not closed?

Current Issues in the Tip—Same Sex Marriage and Global Warming

Attempts to open a previously closed issue create enormous controversy, and this is happening today with the next example of tipping—same sex marriage. Until very recently, the question of whether or not the government should legalize marriage between gay people was absolutely closed in most curricula and classrooms (in the same way that the question of whether inter-racial marriage should be legalized was closed for so long). Between 1979 and 1995, not once did I hear a social studies teacher talk about engaging students on this topic as an open question. That is, students were not asked to deliberate whether marriage laws should be interpreted to include same-sex couples. There was plenty of attention to marriage in the curriculum, especially in personal economics classes where a common simulation involved a faux marriage between two classmates (always a male and female pair), who were sometimes even assigned an egg to care for. While this simulation was ostensibly designed to impress upon teenagers the economic challenges of marrying and having children at a young age, it always communicated powerful messages about which lifestyle was "normal"—and hence preferred.

Increasingly, there are movements to include the topic of gay marriage in the curriculum. When the topic is included in the curriculum in public schools, which is still rare in many parts of the nation, it is most likely as an open issue. While some individual teachers may present same-sex marriage as a closed issue, supporting the position that it should be legalized, curriculum materials on the topic almost always position it as a controversial issue with multiple and competing positions, with the exception of materials from gay rights organizations. While advocating for the inclusion of gay marriage as an open issue in the curriculum often provokes controversy, advocating for the position that supporting gay marriage should be treated as a closed issue is even more controversial.

This next example of teaching in the tip focuses on global warming. I have included it because I believe it masterfully illustrates the controversy that arises as an issue goes through the process of tipping, as it is in the case of global warming, from open to closed. I side with the scientific community and consider global warming to be a closed issue—that is, much discussion could and should revolve around policies concerning global warming, but global warming itself is no longer debatable. However, it became apparent through a teacher's response to a column I wrote for *Social Education* in spring of 2007 (Hess, 2007b) that not all educators agree with me, and our difference of opinion is what complicates the teaching of controversial issues.

My column addressed the use of documentary films in secondary social studies courses. In the *Social Education* column, I wrote:

> While the high rate of documentary film usage by social studies teachers indicates that they are amenable to bringing new films into their classrooms, we also know that some films can provoke uproar in some communities. This is more likely to occur when the film is cutting edge—whether it's ahead of the mainstream consensus on what is considered school knowledge, perceived as taking a position on an issue that is highly controversial, or about a topic that some parents or other community members consider taboo. In these cases, detractors tend to claim that the objectionable film is biased. Underlying this charge is an assumption that materials used in courses—including documentary films—should be unbiased, objective renditions of reality. Just as some people advocate that teachers should keep their political views to themselves, some argue that people who make documentary films should do the same. Failing that, their films should not be used in schools.
>
> Perhaps it's the word "documentary" that causes people to think that such films should be "objective." Documentation implies a neutral process—unearthing evidence rather than making a story out of it. Films that are judged to fail the objectivity test are suspect. When this occurs, accusations erupt that the film lacks "balance," and if shown, must be censored or countered with equally powerful portrayals of competing perspectives.
>
> As a case in point, teachers in Federal Way School District, south of Seattle, were criticized for showing *An Inconvenient Truth* (a 2006 documentary, featuring Al Gore, on the perils of global warming) because, as one parent argued, "Condoms don't belong in school, and neither does Al Gore. He's not a schoolteacher." Charging that the film was biased, one parent, Frosty Hardison, said, "The information that's

being presented is a very cockeyed view of what the truth is . . . The Bible says that in the end times everything will burn up, but that perspective isn't in the DVD" (McClure & Stiffler, 2007). While the School Board did not bow to Mr. Hardison's wishes to ban the film, it decided that if teachers want to show the film they must get the permission of the school principal and make sure that a "credible, legitimate opposing view will be presented." Given that virtually all scientists now believe that global warming is a well-warranted reality (as opposed to one side of a controversial issue), finding evidence on the "other side" that is equally credible as what the film presents may be the rule that swallowed the film. As a staff member of the National Science Teachers Association stated in response to a query about how to teach the opposing view (that global warming is not manmade or that its effects are not damaging), "I wouldn't even know where to find someone, to be honest."

It is not surprising that showing *An Inconvenient Truth* in schools has created controversy. Although there is agreement in the scientific community about the veracity of Gore's central claims, this consensus does not exist among the general public. The latest national survey on the beliefs of adult Americans about global warming shows that while 77% believe it is occurring, fewer than half say it is caused by human activity, and most do not say it is a top priority issue that deserves national attention.[1] In the case of *An Inconvenient Truth*, then, the dispute about whether the film deserves airtime is a classic example of how ideological battles in the world outside of school enter the classroom doors. But even if we accept the veracity of his two central claims, his film is not objective. It is a rallying cry, a call to arms. It is designed to convince viewers that global warming is a tremendous problem and that we need to act on it immediately or our collective future is in peril.[2]

The remainder of the column did not focus on global warming or Al Gore's film; I had simply used this particular film to make a point about the perils of viewing documentary films as "objective" sources. I did not encourage teachers to show the film to their students, nor did I intend to explicitly stake out a position about whether global warming should be treated as a live controversy or as a question for which there is a right answer.

Regardless, a few months after the column was published, I received a message from the journal with the news that a teacher had written a strong letter critiquing the column. I was invited to write a response to the letter, and both would be published in a future issue (Laviano, 2007; Hess, 2007b). The letter was entitled "Dueling documentaries available on man-made global warming debate":

After reading "From *Banished* to *Brother Outsider, Miss Navajo* to *An Inconvenient Truth*: Documentary Films as Perspective-Laden Narratives" from the May/June 2007 issue of *Social Education*, I became disheartened when the author did not mention the extraordinary 2007 British documentary that directly challenges Al Gore's claim that global warming is due to man-made causes.

High school students in my contemporary issues course investigate the international debate over man-made versus naturally occurring climate change. As in any controversial topic I cover, the students begin by gaining a solid foundation of the neutral facts followed by the debatable viewpoints each side of the issue provides.

In the case of the man-made versus naturally occurring climate change debate, I show Al Gore's *An Inconvenient Truth* to present the man-made CO_2 argument. To balance out this debate with a "dueling documentary" I show the opposing British documentary video from Channel 4 called *The Great Global Warming Swindle*. The documentary's website is http://www.channel4.com (click documentaries) and can be downloaded for free from video.google.com. This documentary asserts that our changing climate is ultimately controlled by sun spots as opposed to man-made CO_2 emissions.

What astounded me in this article was that a staff member of the National Science Teachers Association "didn't even know where to find someone . . ." with an opposing view since I was informed about this opposing mainstream video from an economics teacher! For those who like to teach controversial issues, don't dismiss the cause of global warming as a closed case; use both of these engaging documentaries to let your students decide.

Michael Laviano
International Baccalaureate Teacher
Erwin, Tennessee

In response to Mr. Laviano's letter, I wrote:

Teachers, we know, are powerful curricular gatekeepers who often disagree about whether topics should be presented to our students as matters of legitimate controversy or as questions for which there are correct answers. For teachers like Mr. Laviano and myself who engage their students in deliberations about controversial issues, there is perhaps no decision more important than determining whether a topic is a matter of legitimate controversy in the first place. These decisions are often challenging because the nature of what is considered open or closed often "tips" over time, and during this tipping process there is significant disagreement among the public and within our field about which way to go.

Mr. Laviano and I would make different decisions about how to present the topic of global warming in class and whether to use the documentary film *The Great Global Warming Swindle* as evidence supporting one side of the debate. He advocates teaching global warming as an open question and using the film to balance the claims made in *An Inconvenient Truth*. I disagree with him on both points. I don't think that global warming is a legitimate controversial issue that should be presented to students as an open case. Just the opposite: I think the issue has tipped and is now one for which there is a right answer that should be taught to students—especially since the stakes are so high.

While there are some scientists who disagree that global warming is a reality that is caused by human behavior, the *vast* majority of them do not.[3] Keeping in mind that our understanding of what is scientifically credible can change as new evidence emerges, it may be the case that at some point in the future we need to re-open global warming per se as a controversial issue. But just because there is some disagreement about whether something is scientifically accurate does not mean that it deserves open-case status in the curriculum. That said, I do think there are *many* controversial issues related to global warming that belong in the curriculum—but they focus on policy questions about what we should do to address the problem of global warming, not whether it is a problem in the first place.

As an aside, *The Great Global Warming Swindle* does not strike me as a particularly well-warranted source. Given the consensus that has emerged in the scientific community about global warming, I think it would be highly unlikely to find a source that presents a scientifically credible opposing view—which may account for why the staff person from the National Science Teachers Association was not aware of it. While Mr. Laviano characterizes the film as a mainstream source, he may not be aware that after it was shown on Channel 4 in Great Britain, there was a storm of controversy from scientists (including some interviewed for the film who claimed their views had been misrepresented).[4]

What makes global warming so challenging is that there is a striking difference between the consensus that has emerged in the scientific community and the views held among the general public, especially in the United States. Moreover, there is a significant difference in how Republicans and Democrats view global warming, which helps explain why the question of how to teach about global warming in schools is so politically charged.[5]

As an educator who advocates the inclusion of controversial issues in the curriculum, I frequently encounter the view that *all* topics should be presented to students as controversial so they can decide which view to support. I find that view irresponsible. Our job as teachers is to make the best judgments we can about the content of our courses. It is a challenging task that will be done with more integrity if we make *public* our decisions about what questions we present as open or closed and the grounds on which those decisions are based. Even better is to deliberate these questions with our colleagues.

I thank Mr. Laviano for his letter. As the graduate students enrolled in a course I am teaching this semester on controversy in the secondary school curriculum can attest, it provoked a spirited deliberation in class about whether global warming should be presented as open or closed. As readers can imagine, there was lots of disagreement. Students on both sides of this issue made strong and compelling arguments. So while I would make a different decision about how to approach global warming than Mr. Laviano, it is clear to me that reasonable people can (and do) disagree about this—and also that some of the most interesting controversies in our field revolve around what we should teach as controversial.

Issues and Implications

What all of these examples have shown is that it is not easy to come to agreement on the status of an issue as open, closed, or tipping, and it is not clear who should be making this decision. Furthermore, especially if this issue *is* tipping, there are important considerations teachers must make as they include the issue in their curriculum. In the last two sections, I will address each of these issues in turn.

Who Decides?

Michael Hand (2008) provides a definition for teaching something as controversial:

> To teach something as controversial is to present it as a matter on which different views are or could be held, and to expound those different views as impartially as possible. It is to acknowledge and explore various possible answers to a question without endorsing any of them. The intended outcome of such teaching is, at least, that pupils should understand a range of views on a topic and arguments in their support, and at most, that they should hold and be able to defend considered views of their own; it is emphatically *not* that they should come to share the view favoured by the teacher (2008, p. 1).

Thus we are confronted with the central question: Who decides if an issue is indeed controversial? The global warming example above illustrates the many different players involved in this decision—society writ large, political leaders, specialized communities (such as scientists) parents, and inevitably, teachers.

Mr. Laviano believes that the question of whether or not global warming is "manmade" and caused, at least in part, by CO_2 emissions is a matter of contemporary controversy and should be treated as such in the school curriculum. Although I do not know Mr. Laviano, my hunch is that he realizes that there is a lively dispute among the general public, political leaders, and educators about whether or not global warming should be treated as a closed or open issue. As I have already mentioned, I disagree. I see the issue as closed.

If you imagine Mr. Laviano and myself as proxies for a larger dispute, then you can see the consequences that teaching an issue that is tipping might have for teachers and their students. If a teacher approaches the global warming issue as closed—as I recommend—then students would not engage in an analysis of the arguments supporting the opposing view. Instead, the baseline assumption that frames curricular decisions about the topic would be that global warming is a reality that might be taught explicitly, particularly in a science class. This does not mean that if global warming is considered a closed issue then it should be taken out of the social studies curriculum. Instead, one can imagine a social studies class that includes discussions of policies concerning what should be done about global warming. As an example, a class might deliberate about whether the federal tax on gasoline should be increased to discourage driving, thereby reducing CO_2 emissions. Treating global warming as a closed question would most likely be supported by teachers who have become convinced that the evidence supporting global warming is so overwhelming that approaching it as a controversial issue in their classes is irresponsible.

Increasingly, there is a tendency in the United States to avoid making hard intellectual decisions by "teaching the conflicts" as if there were no real difference between what is true and what is false. Under the banners of "balance," fair play, and multiple perspectives," teachers and curriculum designers face extreme pressure to bow to "public" demands (often orchestrated by slick public relations campaigns) instead of making curricular decisions based on disciplinary knowledge. Global warming is but one example of the danger this path poses for people of all political stripes because it means that the content of the school curriculum is really just a matter of who holds the reins of political power at a given moment.

And yet, with respect to most public policy issues, I generally agree with President Bush's exhortation that, "Both sides ought to be properly taught . . . so people can understand what the debate is about" (Baker & Slavin, 2005, p. 1). Moreover, it would be naïve and undemocratic to suggest that the public's views should not have any influence on what is taught in the public's schools. With all of this to consider, it is not easy to decide when "balance" is the democratic approach to a matter of controversy or is simply a cop-out that turns any notion of truth on its head.

So again, we must ask, who decides? Should it—and could it—be the general public? If there were widespread agreement among the general public that global warming is a reality, then treating this topic as a closed issue in schools probably would not cause much controversy, which is the case in many nations.

Or should it be specialized communities, for example, scientists, who decide because society trusts their expertise and it would be inappropriate to teach something that has been determined fact as opinion?

Even though the in-print disagreement reprinted here was civil, it does not take much imagination to envision a heated controversy provoked when the public, parents, students, or other stakeholders in the schools find that Mr. Laviano or Ms. Hess is teaching an issue as closed when they think it should be open or vice versa. And yet, while it is likely that the general public, specialized communities, and parents will in some way shape the understanding of an issue as open or closed, inevitably the decision about an issue's status, and the resulting curriculum that surrounds it, will be decided by the teacher.

Educators are often the "state actors" who make decisions about whether or not a topic will be included in the curriculum, and once in, whether or not it will be treated as open or closed. Even in this era of standards and high-stakes assessments, in most school districts individual teachers still have the power (and the responsibility) to make decisions about the content of the curriculum. Teaching controversial issues during the tipping process is tricky business and accounts for many of the tensions surrounding curricular choices in schools. Complicating this is the fact that it is difficult, if not impossible, to ascertain precisely when an issue has tipped, making it difficult for teachers to stay behind the front wave of the tipping process (Hess & Avery, 2008).

The Challenges of Teaching in the Tip

In the preceding sections, I have explained several different ways issues can tip. The first is when a topic tips from closed (where one perspective is taught as the answer) to open, and then back to closed (with the opposite position taught as a right answer), as illustrated by the case of the internment of Japanese Americans. A second way an issue can tip is from closed to open, as is the case with gay marriage. Finally, a third way an issue can tip is from open to closed, as illustrated with the global warming example. And we must also not forget that even to get an issue in the curriculum box is controversial in and of itself. This discussion is not meant to be an exhaustive inventory of the ways that topics can tip in the curriculum, but simply an illustration of the fact that there is no monolithic tipping process.

Understanding the different ways that issues can tip may help to shed light on some of the challenges not only facing social studies teachers who work in the realm of controversial issues but also teachers of other disciplines who confront serious controversy and controversial issues in their classrooms. I often hear from teachers that treating a topic as controversial is simply too controversial in itself. They are afraid to engage their students in talking about real issues because they fear the emotions such a discussion may ignite among their students. They are also concerned about upsetting the community.

The four studies I have conducted on controversial issues teaching and materials since 1998 (Hess, 2002; Hess & Posselt, 2002; Hess, Stoddard, & Murto, 2008; Hess & Ganzler, 2007) have led me to believe that the tipping process can help us understand why some topics and issues create so much controversy, while others do not. While there is significant disagreement about whether or not a topic should be included in curriculum and whether or not it should be treated as open or closed, there is not all that much controversy about controversial issues teaching in general, unless the teacher is accused of giving unfair advantage to a particular perspective. This is not to suggest that controversial issues teaching is happening in all classrooms, or that it does not engender controversy, but only that treating an issue as an issue has become almost mainstream *as long as the issue is not in the process of tipping*. But teaching during a tip (or teaching in the service of leading or preventing a tip) is much more precarious for teachers because, by definition, there are going to be some people who support the tip and others who do not. All of the "best practices" about controversial issues teaching will not satisfy people who fundamentally disagree with an issue's positioning. That is, having students engage in thoughtful analysis of competing points of view on a topic is exactly what people who advocate closing an open issue do not want (and vice versa).

Implications for Teachers Who Confront Controversial Issues in their Classrooms

Consequently, it is incumbent upon teachers to make decisions about whether or not a topic (such as global warming or gay rights) should be presented as open or closed. My sense is that teachers are much more likely to make wise decisions about this if they are conscious about what criteria they are using when classifying topics as open or closed and if they deliberate these choices with other teachers. It is clearly the case that the political views of teachers influence how and what they teach; rather than a problem to be prevented, this presents a reality to be examined. This examination is more than an intellectual exercise; it allows teachers to recognize both that this reality applies to them and that they should become thoughtful about the ways in which their views inform what happens in their classrooms. My experience has shown that as teachers, it is easy for us to recognize how others' views influence their teaching, but much more difficult for us to recognize the impact of our own views in our classrooms. Toward that end, I conclude this chapter with two stories about how educators think about teaching in the tip, first with an explanation of how I try to address some of these issues in my own teaching of preservice teachers and finally, with an analysis of how practicing teachers are thinking about teaching a controversial issue that is currently in the process of tipping—intelligent design.

Preservice Teachers

For the past several years I have experimented with lessons that help preservice and practicing middle and high school social studies teachers investigate how their political views may influence their teaching. I have used this lesson in the secondary social studies methods courses at the University of Wisconsin-Madison and also as part of short courses I teach on controversial issues discussions at other institutions.

The first class session begins with a brainstorming exercise. I ask students to list all the ways in which they think teachers' political views influence what they teach, how they teach, and what their students learn. This task presupposes that teachers' views inform their teaching. This may seem like a controversial position for me to take, but it is one I arrived at through extensive practice, research, and reflection. It highlights my view that teachers are political beings and that teaching provides multiple opportunities for teachers' political views to influence their work. This is not to suggest that teachers should indoctrinate students into particular political positions, but it reflects the reality that the curricular decisions teachers make will, by definition, be influenced by their own views. The fact that students have no trouble developing long lists during the brainstorming portion of the class has convinced me that this is not an aberrant view but one that is readily apparent to social studies methods students. For example, one student remarked that teachers communicate their political views by how much time they devote to particular issues, while another observed that the posters on classroom walls could reveal teachers' views.

When the students have finished brainstorming, I explain that this lesson will focus on just two ways in which teachers' political views influence their teaching: how they conceptualize what is a controversial issue and teacher disclosure (see Chapter 6 on teacher disclosure). At this point I explain to them that I once thought that teacher disclosure was the primary and most important way teachers' political views showed up in the classroom, but that the first study I conducted on skillful discussion teaching changed my mind. In that study, I asked teachers to explain what criteria they used to determine if they would include a controversial public issue in their curriculum, prompted by a list of issues (on such topics as abortion, gay rights, etc.). I was stunned when it became apparent that the teachers disagreed about whether some of the topics were even issues in the first place (Hess, 2002). For example, one teacher argued that gay rights issues were not controversial. Instead, he characterized them as human rights issues for which there were answers he wanted his students to understand and believe. The results of the study showed that well before the disclosure issue even arises, teachers make an *a priori* decision that is undoubtedly as important as whether or not they share their own views with their students. This decision is to determine whether a question is an issue for which they want their students to examine multiple and competing views, or a question for which there is a right answer that they want students to internalize.

After this discussion, I pass out a short article I wrote for *Social Education* (Hess, 2005), which includes a typology of four ways in which teachers conceptualize what is a matter of "legitimate" controversy and how they approach issues with their students:

1. Denial: It is not a controversial political issue: "Some people may say it is controversial, but I think they are wrong. There is a right answer to this question. So I will teach as if it were not controversial to ensure that students develop that answer."
2. Privilege: Teach toward a particular perspective on the controversial political issue: "It is controversial, but I think there is a clearly right answer and will try to get my students to adopt that position."
3. Avoidance: Avoid the controversial political issue: "The issue is controversial, but my personal views are so strong that I do not think I can teach it fairly, or I do not want to do so."
4. Balance: Teach the matter as genuine controversial political issue: "The issue is controversial and I will aim toward balance and try to ensure that various positions get a best case, fair hearing."

Students read the typology, and I briefly explain each category using examples from the article. Then, I ask them to list issues, phrased as questions (e.g., should the death penalty be outlawed?), that they would put in each of the four categories. Next, each student discusses his/her list with a partner, with an emphasis on *why* he/she placed questions in particular categories. I then write each of the four category labels on the board, and each student writes an abbreviated notation for one item in each of the four categories. When students return to their seats and look at the board, the first thing they notice is that many of same issues are listed under different categories. For example, in the fall of 2007, the Iraq War showed up multiple times and in each of the four categories.

Next, I ask students to talk about what accounts for these differences in order to illuminate the criteria they use to categorize issues. We then talk about the criteria and how these criteria illustrate one way in which teachers' views inform what is in the curriculum, how the topics are treated, and consequently, what students might learn. I conclude this part of the lesson by explaining how important it is for teachers to be aware of, and to reflect critically on, the criteria they use to determine what is a matter of legitimate controversy versus what is a "settled" question. In other words, I do not suggest that it is a problem that teachers' views influence these decisions. Instead, I try to help them understand that people have widely disparate ideas about what constitutes a matter of legitimate controversy as well as what criteria should be used to make that determination. Just as importantly, I try to help my students see how significant it is for teachers to make their decisions transparent and to engage in discussions about them with their colleagues.

Practicing Teachers

This type of discussion is also important for practicing teachers. In early December 2005, I ran a session at the "Colorado Deliberating About Democracy" Conference about an issue that is trying to make it into the curriculum box in science—intelligent design. Much like the "equal time" argument used to get evolution taught alongside creationism, there is an effort to have intelligent design taught as an alternative explanation about the origin and development of human life in sciences classes.

I wanted to know if the 65 teachers who attended my session thought this issue (whether or not to teach intelligent design in science) should be discussed in social studies classrooms. And if so, should be taught as controversial (open), or not (closed)?

I asked the 65 teachers who attended to use three criteria to consider the following four lesson ideas that included intelligent design: (1) an inquiry lesson asking students to determine what accounts for the increased interest in teaching intelligent design in science courses; (2) a constitutional lesson asking students to assess whether or not a school district's policy to include intelligent design violated the Constitution; (3) a comparative lesson, directing students to compare differing philosophies on the origin and development of human life; and finally (4) a lesson that would bring the teaching of intelligent design in science into the social studies classroom as a controversial issue worthy of discussion. The teachers considered this final lesson the most controversial by far. A closer look at some of the teacher's comments illustrates again the controversial nature of teaching an issue whose own status of being controversial (or not) is in flux.

Almost half of the teachers said they would not teach this lesson. For some teachers, it was just not that important; their rationale for its exclusion was simply based on the desire to spend class time on controversial issues they deemed more important. For other teachers, however, the issue was either too controversial or not controversial enough. In some communities, the policy question about whether intelligent design belonged in science courses was simply too hot to handle. One teacher commented, "I wouldn't touch that with a ten-foot pole. There are already serious religious divisions in my school, and I don't want to make them worse." Another teacher said, "This is a classic lose–lose. Parents who have strong feelings about intelligent design in the curriculum—on both sides—will wonder why this is presented as a controversy when they think they have the right answer." One teacher asked her colleagues a series of difficult questions: "What evidence would kids use to make a decision about this policy issue? Wouldn't they decide based on whether they think intelligent design is valid science? And how would they know that anyway? And given that I am not a science teacher, how would I know how to help them know that?" These questions, while challenging, did not go unanswered. A number of teachers who supported engaging students in this policy deliberation pointed out that many public policy questions involve scientific issues and that in a democracy, non-experts weigh in on these issues all the time. Another teacher pointed out that most legislators and school board members are not scientists either, and we should be scaffolding young people into the kinds of policy decisions that are based on contested interpretations of truth.

Some other teachers questioned whether or not they wanted to be seen as taking a stand on the validity of the controversy, when the majority of the science teachers in their school view this as a question for which there is a right answer. "Look," said one teacher, "virtually all scientists agree that intelligent design is not science—why should I fan the flames of ignorance by advancing this as a legitimate public controversy? I would prefer to stand in solidarity with my colleagues who are having a hard enough time just keeping evolution in the curriculum." For some teachers, then, the question of whether or not intelligent design belongs in the curriculum was not a matter of legitimate public controversy that deserved classroom airtime, but a closed issue, a question for which there was already a right answer. Unlike the inquiry lesson that the teachers viewed as having a veil of neutrality, the very act of presenting students with this topic as a controversial issue sent a message that some teachers didn't want to perpetuate.

Conclusion

These examples highlight the critical aspect of teaching controversial issues, particularly issues in the tipping process, which is that teachers should not shy away from teaching such issues as long as they continue to reflect upon the curricular decisions they make about which issues to present, and whether to present those issues as open or closed. In surfacing those decisions, and the underlying criteria used to make them, and in discussing their positions with colleagues, teachers can find ways to continue to bring vitally important issues into the classroom—even during the tipping process.

8
September 11:
"The Ultimate Teachable Moment"
How Supplementary Materials and Textbooks
Deal with Controversy in the Classroom

In the fall of 2002, I went to a Bruce Springsteen concert in Milwaukee, Wisconsin. Shortly after September 11, 2001, Springsteen began writing songs for a new album, *The Rising*. He said that many of the song lyrics emanated from conversations he had had with family members of people who died at the World Trade Center on 9/11. For months after the attacks, the *New York Times* ran short obituaries of the deceased. These "Portraits in Grief" focused on the victims' lives: their families, hobbies, hopes, and dreams. The obituaries were quite different from the norm because the reporters interviewed family members and friends in order to craft detailed, and often quirky, profiles of the people who had died. In some of the obituaries, Springsteen was mentioned. The wife of an executive from Pennsylvania, for example, described her late husband as an ardent fan of The Boss. "Every time you rode in Jim's car, Bruce was on, whether you liked it or not," she told the *New York Times*. Another survivor mentioned that her brother had saved 35 ticket stubs from Springsteen concerts. As he read all the obituaries, Springsteen was startled—and humbled—to see the recurrence of his name. Inspired, he called family members of the deceased and had long conversations with them about the lives of the people they had lost. From those conversations he wrote the songs on *The Rising*. Many of the songs are mournful and serious, illustrating Springsteen's belief that the tragedies of September 11 are of historic importance. Given the origin of these songs, I was interested in whether Springsteen would say anything about the state of the nation at the concert I attended, which took place more than a year after September 11, 2001.

Toward the end of the concert, Springsteen took a break from singing and explained that he had two public service announcements to make. One was to urge concert-goers to donate to Second Harvest, a Wisconsin food bank. In the second, Springsteen explained his views on what it means to be a good citizen in the post-9/11 era. It went something like this: During times of crisis, it is often remarkably easy to allow essential civil liberties to be eroded; we rarely recognize that this process is occurring until it is too late. It is important to be vigilant, he said, to make sure we protect the vital freedoms this nation is based on and to deliberate—to be thoughtful and cautious—when deciding to go to war. That, according to Bruce Springsteen, is what it means to be a citizen. Then he launched into his famous song, "Born in the USA," which had been appropriated by Ronald Reagan in the 1980s as an anthem of patriotic and civic pride. Springsteen was reclaiming his song, and with it, vividly illustrating his conception of what it means to be a citizen.

Springsteen's conception of citizenship is just that: his. All of us have our own ideas of what it means to participate effectively in democracy—and our own definitions of what democracy is or should be. These conceptions and definitions span the ideological spectrum, are informed by our own life experiences, and influence what we think schools should teach young people about democracy, their rights and responsibilities, the nation's history, and America's role in the world. More significantly, these competing conceptions often butt up against one another, and are particularly pitched during times of national crisis.

Controversies About What It Means To Be a Citizen

As a case in point, a controversy about the Pledge of Allegiance that occurred shortly after 9/11 in Madison, Wisconsin, illustrates that even in communities that are unusually ideologically homogeneous, there are widely disparate views about what messages schools should embody and promote with respect to democratic participation.

In July 2001, a newly passed Wisconsin state law required every child in the state's elementary and secondary public and private schools to recite the Pledge of Allegiance or sing the national anthem each day. The law included an opt-out provision so that students who did not want to say the Pledge could remain silent. This opt-out provision is required by the Supreme Court's decision in *West Virginia v. Barnette* (1943), in which the Court held that the First Amendment's Free Speech Clause protects students from being forced to salute the U.S. flag or say the Pledge of Allegiance in school.

The new law went into effect shortly after 9/11, which frames the controversy that ensued. On October 1, 2001, the Madison school board voted to play an instrumental version of the anthem each day, but not to require a recitation of the Pledge. A storm of protest ensued. Conservative talk show hosts such as Rush Limbaugh lambasted the school board, calling the decision un-American. At the school board office, temporary employees were hired to field phone calls on this issue, and so many e-mails arrived (more than 1,000/hour) that the school district's e-mail server crashed.

Two weeks later, on October 15, 2001, I organized a class field trip to the school board meeting held in the auditorium of one of the district's high schools. My class, a graduate seminar in democratic education, joined more than 1,200 people who attended and were hoping to weigh in on whether or not the school board should alter its policy. One of the class members, a new doctoral student who had just arrived from South Korea, was absolutely astonished by the turnout. She turned to me before the meeting began and exclaimed, "Wow, you have some democracy in the United States—do this many people always attend local government meetings?" Unfortunately, I had to tell her that typically just a handful of people attend school board meetings. Some 166 people spoke that night in three-minute bursts that covered the full range of the ideological spectrum. Opinion was divided—although not equally—and at about 2a.m., the school board voted to change its original decision and to allow school principals to choose whether to offer the Pledge or the anthem.[1]

After the meeting, I asked my students to analyze what this controversy was really about. Many said it illustrated the uneasiness that existed in the nation about what people should do in a time of crisis and what message schools should send to young people about what it means to be an effective participant in a democracy. This is one way in which the schools have been influenced by 9/11: the tensions between these competing views on what good citizens should do have become much more public than they were prior to that day. Bringing these tensions into the open is not a bad thing; in fact, one way to interpret the public and very heated debates about the content of schools' approaches to democracy education is that people care about schools. Even people without children can become interested in these debates because they recognize that schools matter. Rhetorically, schools are an important venue, and in many communities, they are one of the few genuine public venues left. Public venues are important because they are the one place in which we communicate who we are and what matters to us. However, this is not just a rhetorical enterprise. The content we teach and the methods we use to teach this content clearly influence what young people learn.

It was not surprising, then, that schools' approaches to teaching about the events of September 11, 2001 and its aftermath would generate controversy. What was surprising to many people—including those well-versed in the curriculum wars of the past—was the extraordinary vitriol that permeated this battle. It was not long after 9/11 that a number of prominent educators and political leaders complained that some of the curricula developed shortly after 9/11 were heavy on multicultural tolerance and light on patriotism (Bennett, 2002). Conservative educator Chester Finn, for example, wrote that the teaching recommendations emanating from some of the most prominent education organizations (such as the nation's largest teachers' union) promoted "rotten advice, relativistic, non-judgmental (except about the United States), pacifist and anything but patriotic" (2002, p. 8). And it was important, Finn argued, to "redress the balance between those who would have the schools forge citizens and those who would have the focus on students' own feelings and on doubts about America" (2002, p. 6). To Finn and many others, the events of 9/11 and their aftermath provided a particularly powerful opportunity for schools to instill in young people essential information about history, while building their understanding of and allegiance to a particular set of civic values. Finn advocated the adoption of curriculum materials that would encourage patriotism, so that young people would know that "It's OK to love your country and love your flag" (2002, p. 11).

Other educational leaders disagreed vehemently with Finn's assessment of what schools should teach about 9/11 and its aftermath. Rethinking Schools, a major progressive educational non-profit organization based in Milwaukee, Wisconsin, prefaces its compendium of essays about the teaching of 9/11 with this goal: "As educators committed to social justice, we believe that students need something different than a daily recitation of the Pledge of Allegiance. We need to direct students' attention to the broad trends that continue to make the world an unequal and dangerous place" (Kohn, 2001, p. 2). Rather than focusing on the development of traditional feelings of patriotism, educator Alfie Kohn advocated assessing whether schools are taking the right approach by analyzing the "extent to which the next generation comes to understand—and fully embrace—this simple truth: The life of someone who lives in Kabul or Baghdad is worth no less than the life of someone in New York or from our neighborhood" (Kohn, 2001, p. 5).

It is important to point out that most of the disputes about what to teach about 9/11 and its aftermath focus primarily on the point of view of the messages embedded in the curricula, as opposed to the question of whether the topic has a legitimate place in the school curriculum. That is, there appears to be widespread agreement among educational leaders that the events of 9/11 and what has transpired because of them are not simply topics that could be taught in schools, but that *should* be taught.[2] Finn argues, "It's right to teach about September 11th because it was one of the defining events of our age, of our nation's history and of these children's lives" (2002, p. 4). Susan Grasack, the executive director of the Choices for the 21st Century Project, agrees that there is no question about whether these events and their aftermath deserve attention in the curriculum. "9/11 was a watershed," she observed. "[B]efore 9/11, the country had two oceans on either side. That was the way we understood ourselves. After 9/11, oceans didn't matter" (2003).[3] Many educators who specialize in developing curricula for schools agree that 9/11 and its aftermath are just too important to ignore. For example, Chuck Tampio, the vice president of Close Up, a national civic education organization, said, "The way to look at 9/11 was sort of what Sputnik was for the sciences, that 9/11 should be for the civic and social sciences" (2003).

Given the perception that 9/11 was important to include in the curriculum, it is not surprising that many educational organizations took up the "teachable moment" and rapidly produced materials—many of them intended for use by students in secondary courses and others as background resources for teachers. Like many other teachers, I began collecting these materials, and even cursory analyses showed that they varied widely in tone, type, and message. For example, consider the focus of two sets of materials developed post-9/11. They are similar because each received considerable media attention; yet they embody and communicate vastly different perspectives.

Justice Anthony Kennedy of the U.S. Supreme Court was behind the development of the first set of materials. While many justices on the Court are quite interested in education, it is not in any way typical for them to become engaged in curriculum projects. After all, they have enormously busy day jobs. So why would Justice Kennedy concern himself with what schools should teach about 9/11 and its aftermath? His interest, he explained, was sparked after reading a *Washington Post* column that quoted Muslim high school students attending U.S. high schools. They displayed—in Kennedy's words—"no empathy, no outrage" over the attacks (Frieden, 2002). In response, he developed a program with the American Bar Association called "Dialogue on Freedom." He wrote a law-school-like hypothetical scenario about the fictional island of Quest, where the government is corrupt, the people are poor, and an anti-American demagogue called The Drummer is on the rise. Students are asked to imagine they are marooned on Quest. They must come up with answers for a people who demand to know what U.S.-style democracy has to offer them. Using the "Dialogues on Freedom," Justice Kennedy (and many other judges and lawyers who participated in the program) aimed to foster among students an appreciation for American values and freedoms.

Another curricular response took a very different perspective on what students should be taught about 9/11 and its aftermath. Rethinking Schools, with funding from the Ford Foundation, developed and disseminated a booklet entitled *War, Terrorism and Our Classrooms: Teaching in the Aftermath of the September 11 Tragedy*. The essays and lesson ideas in this booklet promoted core principles important to Rethinking Schools, such as:

1. Educators need to nurture student empathy.
2. We need to be multi-cultural and anti-racist.
3. We need to ask "Why" questions, such as why the U.S. supported anti-democratic regimes—especially in the Middle East.
4. We need to enlist students in questioning the language and symbols that help frame how we understand global events. They mention, for example, that when Osama bin Laden was fighting Soviet troops in Afghanistan, President Reagan called him a "freedom fighter."
5. Educators need to honor dissent and those who challenge power and privilege as they work for justice (Rethinking Schools, 2001).

Studying Curriculum About 9/11

The American Bar Association and Rethinking Schools were by no means the only organizations that developed curricular materials about 9/11. A wide array of educational organizations that specialize in writing materials on important historical and contemporary events and issues started to develop curriculum immediately after September 11, 2001 that ranged in focus (e.g., constitutional issues about the Patriot Act, choices among different foreign policy options, why voting is an important response to 9/11) and medium (print materials and video). In a highly unusual move, even the U.S. Department of State (2002) developed an instructional video and accompanying lessons about terrorism. I found this intriguing and decided to embark on a more formal study of how 9/11 was presented in curriculum developed for secondary school students.

Supplemental Curricula

The first stage of the study started in 2003 and focused on 9/11 text and video curriculum materials from six major U.S. non-profit curricular organizations, along with materials developed by the State Department.[4] Although previous studies have analyzed the ideological content of textbooks (Loewen, 1995; Ravitch, 2004; Zimmerman, 2002), much less attention has been paid to the content of curricula found in other sources, such as supplemental materials, video, and websites. The paucity of information about these curricula is a problem because the advent of the World Wide Web has made materials produced by educational organizations much easier for teachers to access. Moreover, the web has made it possible for organizations to respond rapidly to teachers' requests for curricula about an event that has just occurred. Given the longer production time for textbooks, it is likely that curricula developed by non-profit educational organizations have become increasingly important as sites of cultural formation. That is, these materials are communicating important messages to teachers and students about the nature of a major event such as 9/11 and what it means for democracy and democratic participation.[5]

In the spring of 2003, I, along with a team of graduate students, searched for curricula about 9/11 and its aftermath intended for secondary-level students via the World Wide Web, traditional library searches, and personal contacts with the staff of organizations that we knew had developed curriculum on contemporary topics in the past. Because our primary interest was to analyze what was communicated to students, our initial screen of materials caused us to set aside the sets of essays and more general resource guides developed for teachers.[6]

We located 15 curricula with materials intended for a secondary student audience, purchased them if necessary (many were disseminated free of charge on the World Wide Web), and performed an initial screening to ensure that the materials contained enough materials related to 9/11 and its aftermath to merit inclusion in the study. An expert panel of educators with extensive professional experience (as curriculum writers, professional development leaders, and researchers) analyzed the 15 examples and rated them using a set of questions we developed. Generally, we wanted to select curricula that illustrated an ideological range, was of sufficiently high quality, and utilized different approaches and pedagogies. We used the experts' ratings, along with our own analyses, to select seven curricula that represented a range of approaches and ideologies. All seven organizations agreed that the authors of the curricula could participate in on-the-record interviews (see Table 8.1).

Textbooks

In the summer of 2005, I worked with Jeremy Stoddard to broaden the study to include top-selling U.S. history, world history, and government textbooks published between 2004 and 2006 that included the events of 9/11 and the war on terrorism.[7] All the textbooks selected were high-school-level texts published by large media companies that market research showed were the most widely selected by schools (Education Market Research, 2005). We selected nine high school textbooks intended for use in different social studies courses—world and U.S. history, civics or government, and law—because we were interested in whether the primary content of the course would influence the 9/11 content (see Table 8.1). For example, from our experience working with high school textbooks in the past, we have found that history textbooks tend to focus on narrating events in a way that does not typically involve competing interpretations, while government and law textbooks tend to focus more on content that explicates the form and structure of government in the United States, explains the meaning of core concepts such as due process and separation of powers, and sometimes presents competing views about what kinds of policy decisions should be made as well as their ramifications. We felt that this general difference also might affect the specific coverage of 9/11 in each of the textbooks.

While impossible to pinpoint precisely, our analysis suggests that these textbooks are used by almost 8 million high school students in the United States. Put more dramatically, it is likely that one of every two students enrolled in a U.S. history, world history, government or law course will be in a class that uses one of the textbooks.[8]

Study Questions

The study had two primary aims. The first was to examine critically what curricula are communicating about 9/11, its aftermath, and terrorism more generally *and* to analyze the messages embedded in supplemental materials as compared to those in textbooks. The second aim related more broadly to

Table 8.1 The Curriculum in the Study

Non-profit Curriculum		Textbooks	
Title	Publisher	Title	Publisher
Terrorism: A War Without Borders (2002)	U.S. Department of State	*American Odyssey* (2004)	Glencoe/McGraw-Hill
First Vote (2002)	Close Up Foundation	*America: Pathways to the Present* (2005)	Pearson/Prentice Hall
Terrorism in America (2002)	Constitutional Rights Foundation	*The Americans* (2005)	Houghton Mifflin/ McDougall Littell
Civil Liberties and Terrorism/Iraq: Should the U.S. Launch a Preemptive Attack? (2002)	Educators for Social Responsibility	*World History: Connections to Today* (2005)	Pearson/Prentice Hall
September 11: Commemorating America's Civic Values (2002)	Bill of Rights Institute	*World History: Patterns of Interaction* (2005)	Houghton Mifflin/ McDougall Littell
Responding to Terrorism: Challenges for Democracy (2002)	Choices for the 21st Century	*World History* (2005) *U.S. Government: Democracy in Action* (2006)	Glencoe/McGraw-Hill Glencoe/McGraw-Hill
Identity, Religion, and Violence: A Critical Look at September 11, 2001 (2002)	Facing History and Ourselves	*Magruder's American Government* (2005) *Street Law: A Course in Practical Law* (2005)	Pearson/Prentice Hall Glencoe/McGraw-Hill

disputes about the kind of democratic participation that schools should promote. In particular, we were interested in what topics or questions related to 9/11 and terrorism were presented to students as genuinely controversial, and which explicitly or implicitly presented a "correct" answer that the curriculum writers expect students to adopt.

Unique Features

While a plethora of fascinating studies examine and critique the ideological messages embedded in school curricula, this study had three distinctive features that are important because they inform not only the content, but the very nature of our key findings. First, the study began shortly after the materials were developed; this means that as researchers, we were doing our work close in time to when the writers did theirs. Curriculum studies are often much more retrospective, with researchers writing in a different political context than the one in which the materials were developed. Our proximity in time to the writers' work enabled us to empathize with the challenges that confront curriculum writers who tackle events that have recently occured, are emotionally vexed, and clearly are not yet fully understood. Developing curriculum is always very hard work—but writing about a "moving target," as one of the writers commented to us, can prove especially daunting. Moreover, it is obvious that the way in which the context of the times influenced the writers would also influence us. However, because we wanted the writers to talk to us about the politics of writing these materials, time could be an enemy: their memories would fade if we allowed a significant amount of time to pass.

The second feature of this study that differentiated it from most research on the content of curricula is that the writers of the supplemental materials agreed to be interviewed, and our conversations were *on the record*.[9] This means that we did not have to infer what they were trying to do solely from the text of the published materials. We had their own answers to a host of important questions, such as why they wrote the materials, what they wanted to convey, what influenced their choices regarding inclusion and exclusion of content, and what issues they perceived were open versus closed.

The third feature that we have not seen before in analyses of curriculum content is the inclusion of both supplemental materials—many which were distributed for free and to a large number of teachers—and textbooks in an analysis that focuses on a particular topic. While it is true that textbooks remain the most commonly used resource in secondary classrooms, technology has dramatically changed, and in my view, improved, the kinds of resources available to teachers. And because it is well known that market forces and factors have an enormous influence on the ideological content of textbooks, it is crucial to determine whether curriculum developed outside the huge, for-profit publishing companies is notably different, or whether the market's "invisible hand" actually has the same kind of influence on non-profit organizations and on the government.

Key Findings

In the remainder of this chapter, I explain four of our key findings from both stages of the study. First, although 9/11 is presented in all the materials as an extremely significant event, it was used in markedly different ways to support the varied missions of the organizations developing the materials and the central disciplinary focus of the textbooks. Second, while there was widespread agreement that 9/11 was an important topic for students to grapple with, many of the materials—especially the textbooks—fail to provide basic details about what happened on 9/11. Third, there is a stark difference between the ideological range represented in the supplemental materials and that of the textbooks. Fourth, attempts within the materials to be perceived as fair and balanced illustrate core tensions about how 9/11 and its aftermath should be dealt with in schools. I conclude by discussing the ways in which curriculum about 9/11 and its aftermath is a case study in ongoing debates about the content and form of democratic education.

Mission Matters

All the authors of the supplementary curriculum whose materials we analyzed agreed that 9/11 was an important and tragic event, defined most significantly as an example of terrorism against the United States. Six of the authors argued that its aftermath (such as the war in Afghanistan, the quick passage of the Patriot Act, enhanced security measures at airports and other public venues in the United States, and acts of hate leveled against Muslim students) was as important for students to learn about as the precipitating event.

Vast differences, however, emerged regarding *which* aspects of 9/11 and its aftermath the organizations interpreted as important enough for young people to focus on and learn about. These widely varying emphases emanated from the different missions promoted by the organizations. For example, the Choices for the 21st Century Program at Brown University focuses primarily on foreign-policy decision-making. This group develops curriculum materials on particular topics (e.g., The Middle East) that present background and engage students in analyzing and deliberating four disparate policy options for the United States. While their materials always look beyond U.S. borders, they are firmly rooted in questions about what the United States should do relative to other parts of the world.

The Choices Program is an example of the deliberation approach to democratic education that focuses students' attention on national decisions about international issues. The Choices Program curriculum, *Responding to*

Terrorism: Challenges for Democracy (Choices for the 21st Century, 2002), mirrors precisely how this organization has framed issues in the past. For example, the capstone activity in the curriculum is a simulation of the U.S. Senate Foreign Relations Committee that requires students to deliberate the following possible U.S. responses to terrorism:

1. Direct an expanded assault on terrorism: This option focuses on military intervention and intelligence, proclaiming, "We have no choice but to take on the job of policeman."
2. Support United Nations leadership to fight terrorism: This option focuses on terrorism as a "universal threat" that will only be solved through an "international effort."
3. Defend our homeland: This option stresses the need to "build up our national defenses" while implementing new policies at home to protect our security.
4. Address the underlying causes of terrorism: This option emphasizes the need to "examine our own policies" and "improve the quality of life of disadvantaged populations."

Susan Graseck, Executive Director of The Choices Program, explained in an interview that their materials were developed several weeks before the United States bombed Afghanistan:

> I remember feeling this curriculum material is landing at the right time. It was the time when the American public as a whole was talking about this issue, thinking about this issue. We were being told at the time that clearly we cannot let this stand, clearly we have to go do something about this, clearly we have to get out the military, and that kind of thing. That's what we were being told the American public thinks. And then you would hear all these interviews on radio. And you would hear the American public talk. And that's not what we were saying at all. We were saying, "Yeah, this is really complex, this is really hard, I am not really sure, I am not really comfortable with this, I don't know what I think about this . . ." Our curriculum was fitting into the middle of that context. It was helping people to talk about this. (2003)

In other words, the materials that Choices developed for students to use in schools mirrored the kinds of actions that Choices believes all citizens should take in response to an event such as 9/11: deliberating with others about the wisdom of various options available to the U.S. government. Even though 9/11 was especially significant and unusual, the Choices Program staff was able to structure the materials to align precisely with the overall mission of the organization.

The flexibility with which 9/11 and its aftermath was interpreted is also evident in the materials developed by the Bill of Rights Institute, a non-profit organization founded in 1999. Claire Griffin, the Institute's vice president in charge of educational programs, said in an interview that the mission of her organization is "to help teachers help their students to better understand the Founding period, the Founders, the Founding documents, and then the significance of those ideas and those ideals in preserving American liberty today" (2003). The Bill of Rights Institute (2002) developed a number of lessons about 9/11 and its aftermath, but the lesson the Institute's staff deemed most significant was titled *September 11: Commemorating American's Civic Values.* This lesson was written specifically for use on the first anniversary of the terrorist attacks. The introduction to the lesson plan describes its purpose:

> In this lesson, students will commemorate the tragic events of September 11, 2001 by focusing on those civic values that enabled the American people to respond—both individually and collectively—to the horrific attacks of that day and to ultimately triumph over adversity. By examining what our nation's Founders and others have said about civic values and then looking for examples of these values in the national reaction to September 11, students will be affirmed in their adherence to these values and inspired to live by them. (Bill of Rights Institute, 2002)

Griffin said in an interview that the lesson was written to marry schools' needs for materials to use on the anniversary of 9/11 to the overall mission of the Bill of Rights Institute: "We knew teachers were going to want to, or be required to, somehow commemorate September 11. We knew that there was going to be a need and so we looked at how we, being true to our mission, could meet that need" (2003).

In a similar fashion, the other organizations whose lessons we studied were remarkably consistent in creating materials that were consistent with their existing missions. The fact that all of these organizations grafted the events of 9/11 and their aftermath onto their existing missions is significant because it demonstrates the pliability of major events and the desire of the organizations' staff to mold 9/11 to suit widely disparate educational objectives. The organizations' missions operated as a form of master narrative that enabled (and directed) the writers to interpret the importance of 9/11 and its aftermath in vastly different ways. The fact that the Choices Program could so easily map 9/11 onto its existing foreign-policy deliberation framework, while the Bill of Rights Institute similarly had no problem connecting 9/11 to its particular brand of character education, shows that the mission matters. That is, the differences in the overall focus of the curricula both represent, and are caused by, the particular niche of democratic education that each organization is designed to meet. Even an event like 9/11 that the writers described as a "watershed" and "unprecedented" could be molded to support each organization's pre-existing ideas about which form of democratic education should be privileged.

In the textbooks, on the other hand, one of the dominant messages was that the attacks of 9/11 are extraordinarily important and severe, especially compared with other terrorist acts in history. The significance of 9/11 was communicated both by the type and quantity of words used. The textbooks utilized such powerful phrases as "horrendous plot" and "unprecedented attack" to describe the events of 9/11. Eight of the nine books characterized the attacks as historically significant for the United States and the world. For people in the United States, 9/11 is a "day imprinted on the minds of many Americans" and an event that people in the United States reacted to "in horror." In other books, the emphasis was on how important 9/11 was for the world. For example, one of the world history texts described 9/11 as a "turning point" in world history and a "crime against humanity" writ large (not just a crime against people in the United States). Clearly, the textbook developers sought not only to describe 9/11, but also to emphasize its importance as the *defining event* of the recent past.

In spite of these commonalities in descriptive language, the manner in which 9/11 was utilized in different types of textbooks varies. Within each textbook, the events of 9/11 and their aftermath are "emplotted"—that is to say, situated within a larger narrative context—in different ways. The emplotment of an event can affect the overall message students receive from its coverage, as Simone Schweber (2004) illustrated in her study of the teaching of the Holocaust in secondary classrooms. In the case of the 9/11 material in the nine textbooks we studied, the U.S. history textbooks tended to discuss 9/11 as a specific event related to the subsequent war on terror. On the other hand, in the world history textbooks, 9/11 is typically emplotted within coverage of global issues, the aftermath of the Cold War, or issues in the Middle East. Finally, the government and law textbooks tended to utilize 9/11 as an example of a larger concept that students should understand, such as the expansion of executive power or the right to writs of habeas corpus and the detention of enemy combatants. Each of these types of textbooks illustrates how the events of 9/11 and their aftermath can be marshaled to serve as an example of various topics, themes, and concepts, depending on the overall goal of the textbook.

Nature of Intellectual Work

In addition to examining what the curricula said about the events of 9/11 and the subsequent war on terrorism, we also analyzed the nature of the intellectual work being asked of students in the materials. Here, too, we found that the range of focus of assessment items aligned closely with the overall mission of the text or organization. These items differed greatly in the amount of intellectual work they asked students to do, from comprehension or identification items to asking students to compare and contrast or even deliberate on issues of controversy related to 9/11 and terrorism. Overall, however, none of the texts or materials we examined challenged students to examine critically the roots of the attacks or to analyze the external policies of the United States, despite conservatives' allegations that curricula developed after 9/11 encouraged excessive or unpatriotic critiques of the United States. In fact, we found just the opposite: the United States was uniformly presented as a victim that deserved and received the world's support in the wake of 9/11.

To analyze the nature of the intellectual work required by these items, we coded them as requiring Higher-Order Thinking (HOT) or Lower-Order Thinking (LOT) as defined by Newmann and Wehlage (1995). HOT items require students "to manipulate information and ideas in ways that transform their meaning and implications, such as when students combine facts and ideas in order to synthesize, generalize, explain, hypothesize, or arrive at some conclusion or interpretation." LOT items require students "to receive or recite factual information or to employ rules and algorithms through repetitive routines" (Newmann & Wehlage, 1993) We looked further to examine the nature of the HOT and LOT items and what they asked students to know and do related to 9/11 and terrorism.

The textbooks contained an average of 10 assessment items related to 9/11 and terrorism, ranging from *American Odyssey* (Nash, 2004) with four items total (1 HOT, 3 LOT) to *Street Law* (Arbetman & O'Brien, 2005) with 21 items (19 HOT, 2 LOT). The textbooks generally utilized LOT items to check comprehension of the text and focus attention on particular content. The goal consistently appeared to be for students to know what happened in an objective way. For example, a LOT item from *Patterns of Interaction* asked students, "What methods do terrorists use?" (Beck, Black, Krieger, Naylor & Shabaka, 2005, p. 1092) and included a list of possible answers in the text (e.g., cyber-terrorism, biological and chemical attacks) for them to identify and write down or recite. HOT items in the textbooks generally engaged students in comparing, contrasting, or synthesizing ideas from the text. For example, an item from *Street Law*, the text that offered the most intellectually challenging and thoughtful items, asked students, "Is the war on terrorism similar to other wars where rights have been restricted? How is it the same? How is it different?" (Arbetman & O'Brien, 2005, p. 206). In order to respond successfully to these questions, students would need to compare and contrast previous examples of the restriction of rights during wartime, such as the detention of Japanese-Americans during World War II, with rights restrictions enacted under the USA Patriot Act. In most of the textbooks, however, students were rarely asked open-ended questions or provided tasks that required them to take a stand on or deliberate a controversial aspect of the events.

As we expected, given their greater length, the materials developed by the non-profits and the Department of State included more assessment items than the textbooks, averaging 42 items and ranging from the Bill of Rights Institute with 10 items (9 HOT, 1 LOT) to Choices with 98 items (56 HOT, 42 LOT). On the whole, the materials created by non-profits included a higher percentage of HOT items than the textbooks and many more items that challenged students to wrestle with some of the controversies that surround the concept of terrorism and the war on terrorism. For example, as part of their lesson on the war on terrorism, Educators for Social Responsibility included a section on the impending war in Iraq that asked students, "What are current major questions about Iraq and weapons of mass destruction? Can you answer any of them with certainty? If yes, which ones? If not, why not?" (Shapiro, 2002).[10] Students were provided with a reading that outlined the major arguments on both sides of the weapons of mass destruction issue and were asked to analyze and interpret what they read.

Attention Without Detail

Although the majority of textbooks and many of the supplemental materials discussed or mentioned 9/11 multiple times throughout the text, the bulk of them, surprisingly, did not go into much *detail* about 9/11. For example, while 9/11 was mentioned 16 times in the textbook *Democracy in Action* (Remy, 2006), there was no connection between the number of words devoted to 9/11 and the level of detail regarding what happened on that day. Only four of the nine textbooks mentioned how many people were killed in the attacks or who was responsible for them, an omission that belies the notion that textbooks always "cover" basic content information. We compared what these same textbooks said about Pearl Harbor and found that most of them went into fairly elaborate detail about the events of December 7, 1941. It was interesting to us that the books took a different tack with respect to 9/11. Perhaps the writers assumed that students would already know what occurred on that day. Bear in mind, however, that a 15-year-old sitting in a high school class in 2009 was only seven years old when 9/11 occurred. We therefore doubt that many students who read these textbooks actually know the details of 9/11. Second, there is evidence that even adults who were old enough to pay careful attention to the details of 9/11 hold many beliefs that are simply not true. To support this claim, consider what a 2005 report issued by the non-profit organization Public Agenda said:

> The Gallup poll found 44 percent believe [Iraqi President Saddam] Hussein was "personally involved" in the Sept. 11 attacks, down from 53 percent in December 2003. When the questions are phrased more broadly, the number who say there is a link also rises. The June 2004 ABC/ *Washington Post* poll found 62 percent of those surveyed believe Iraq provided "direct support" to al Qaeda, and Gallup showed 67 percent who said Hussein had "long-established ties to Osama bin Laden's terrorist organization." (2005)

Given that five of the books we analyzed did not say who committed the attacks of 9/11, and one had the fairly generic "terrorists opposed to U.S. policies in the Mideast" as the explanation, it is likely that students reading these books will not know the answer to this critical (and in some quarters, highly controversial) question. In sum, the materials address 9/11 quite extensively, but many of them fail to provide even rudimentary background information about the event.

Examining the Ideological Range in the Materials

From the first stage of the study, we learned that while the seven curricula had different foci, the ideological range did not extend to the outer reaches of the political spectrum. Even though Finn and others accused schools of promoting a pernicious form of anti-Americanism after 9/11, none of the curricula in our sample advocated civic responses that were even remotely linked to a thorough-going critique of either U.S. history relative to terrorism or the current structures of governance in the United States. But neither did they support the kind of blind patriotism that many conservative commentators called for after 9/11. Even the materials developed by the two organizations in the study with the most conservative missions, the Department of State and the Bill of Rights Institute, failed to advance an extreme rightist form of patriotism.

In *Terrorism: A War Without Borders* (U.S. Department of State, 2002), a video and accompanying lessons developed by the State Department with the assistance of teachers selected by the National Council for the Social Studies, the attacks of 9/11 were described as "the deadliest terrorist attack in history" that "shocked us like nothing before." The narrator continues by saying, "We were the victims and terrorism was a gruesome reality," adding that "people all over the world shared our horror and grief." After a person on the street asks for a definition of terrorism, the narrator responds by noting:

> Terrorism is difficult to define. It is generally accepted that terrorism is the use of violent or intimidating acts against people or property, especially for political purposes. Terrorist acts are deliberately shocking and are intended to cause a psychological reaction to violence in as large an audience as possible. (U.S. Department of State, 2002)

The video then quickly and dramatically shows 12 examples of terrorism: the 1972 Munich Olympics, the Iranian hostages, a Sikh separatist group taking over an Indian shrine, the bombing of Pan Am flight 103, bombings in Peru by Shining Path, the nerve gas attack in a Tokyo subway, the Oklahoma City bombing, an IRA attack on an English shopping center, a bombing in Israel by Hamas, bombings of the U.S. embassies in Tanzania and Kenya, and finally the September 11 attacks on New York and Washington, DC (also described in the opening of the video). The video did not advance or advocate any particular response by the United States government to terrorism generally, or to 9/11 specifically. Instead, it ended with a series of questions:

A young male is shown saying, "Terrorists' intention is to hurt people."

Then a young woman is shown asking, "How do we stop terrorism?"

This is followed by another young woman who asks: "What can I do to stop terrorism?"

The narrator (speaking in an authoritative-sounding male voice) says, "That is the question being asked every day, by every person, in every nation. Sadly, we have yet to find the answer. What do you think?" (U.S. Department of State, 2002)

Susan Holly, an historian in the Bureau of Public Affairs at the State Department, worked with a colleague to develop the script for this video. Holly explained that another branch of the State Department had developed a video for classroom use immediately after 9/11, and that teachers who were charged with reviewing their work and providing feedback had criticized this earlier effort. According to Holly, the content of the first video was problematic:

It was very immediately post-September 11th. It showed a lot of film clips of various government heads saying. "We're going to do something, we are going to do something," and you kind of know what I mean. By the time the teachers saw it, the moment, you know that immediate moment, had passed. They said this is not really appropriate for the classroom, it depicts what happened immediately after September the 11th, and it's— I don't know if I want to say the word "propaganda"—but that is what they said about how it might be received by some people. (2003)

The video script that Holly describes here did not meet muster because it promoted a particular ideological message too bluntly. When asked directly whether the later video was aimed at developing students' support for a particular policy of the U.S. government in response to terrorism, Holly responded, "I suppose you could say yes, in the sense of a broad opposition or a broad understanding of the problem, but I don't think it would be to the point of saying we wanted them to support the Patriot Act or something very specific like that. I don't think that was part of the calculation" (2003). Indeed, the decision to end the video with a series of questions (e.g., "What do you think?") triggered some concern in the Department. Holly explained:

Ending with a question was simply a device we used hoping to spark discussion in the classroom. There were some people in the Department who felt that we should say what should be done. We thought that for students it might be better to let them talk about it and hear their opinion. (2003)

In response to this point, I followed up by saying, "That seems to suggest that even though there were specific ideas you wanted students to have about terrorism, there are things that you think are controversial about terrorism that you want students to discuss." Holly went on to explain her objectives for the video:

> Well, I think we wanted them to think about it in a deeper way or a more sustained way than they might by simply looking at news and hearing the "We're going to get them" kind of way of looking at problems, [versus] saying, "Well, you've heard some of the background, and how do we attack this problem?" Yeah, I think there is definitely room for discussion there. (2003)

Perhaps the fact that the State Department's video project was in the hands of historians—who are civil service employees, not political appointees—accounts for why the content of the video was not designed to lead students to support a particular government response to terrorism. Clearly, there is nothing in the video that would cause students to question the honor or veracity of the government, or its ability to deal effectively with terrorism. And certainly there is nothing in the video that would even remotely support the charges of Noam Chomsky (2002) and others that the U.S. government has historically supported terrorism. Yet it is important to note that even the government did not develop curricula about 9/11 that boldly asked for students' allegiance, either to the nation or to a particular response to terrorism.

In a similar fashion, the organizations with a more leftist or progressive tradition (Educators for Social Responsibility and Facing History and Ourselves) developed materials that failed to promote what some may see as the mirror opposite of blind patriotism: some form of radical transformation or reconstruction. While their materials included critiques of historic and contemporary government policies related to 9/11 and its aftermath, the overall structure of the system and its ideals—in democracy, liberalism, deliberation, and so on—was presented as sound.

While the curricula were not ideologically similar, it is notable that the range of their fundamental dissimilarities did not extend to the far reaches of either side of the political spectrum—especially since these positions were, at least to some extent, given play in the media. Recall that even many journalists (and virtually all politicians) fell into a patriotic trance after 9/11. Dan Rather, who in 2001 was one of the most powerful television journalists in the United States, appeared on an evening newscast shortly after 9/11 and said, "George Bush is the President, he makes the decisions, and, you know, as just one American, he wants me to line up, just tell me where."[11]

Creating an Iconic Image

The images that the materials developers selected to illustrate 9/11 also invoked this "patriotic trance" and were remarkably similar across the various curriculum. All nine textbooks and two of the other resources contained images that show rubble after the destructive attacks of 9/11. Two of the books depicted rubble from the Pentagon, while the other seven showed rubble at the World Trade Center site in New York City. The pictures of New York City were especially striking because all of them included New York City firefighters. Of the seven, six included the U.S. flag raised at Ground Zero. Three of the textbooks had the exact same picture of three firefighters raising the U.S. flag (Figure 8.1), while two others had a different image of the same event, probably taken soon after the flag was raised; one other included both firefighters and a U.S. flag.

By selecting firefighters raising the U.S. flag as the main image to represent 9/11, the text developers chose to emphasize patriotism, nationalism, and heroism. This image reinforces the view that when the U.S. faces significant challenges, its people rise to the occasion, rally around the flag (literally and symbolically), and put their personal needs aside to engage in individual acts that further national interests. Conversely, if the texts emphasized pictures of the destruction caused by 9/11 (such as planes hitting buildings) or people grieving those who were killed that day, the message would be quite different, with the U.S. depicted as harmed and weakened.

What is Terrorism?

One especially notable difference among the materials is how they approached the concept of terrorism. We were particularly interested in whether the materials provided one definition of terrorism or presented multiple and competing definitions, what examples of terrorism were presented, and whether there was alignment between the definition of terrorism and the examples. All but two of the textbooks provided explicit, authoritative definitions of terrorism, while two contained no definition. *The Americans* states that "Terrorism is the use of violence against people or property to try to force changes in societies or governments" (Danzer, de Alva, Krieger, Wilson, & Woloch, 2003), while one of the government texts includes this definition: "Terrorism: the use of violence by nongovernmental groups against civilians to achieve a political goal." Note that there is a significant difference between these definitions, with the first allowing for the possibility of state-sponsored terrorism and the second explicitly limiting terrorism to activities propagated by groups that are *not* part of a government.

While there are differences among the definitions of terrorism given in the textbooks, none of them allowed for the possibility that its definition could be contested or wrong. That is, they presented terrorism as an established concept that means the same thing everywhere. By contrast, terrorism is presented as a contested concept in the written materials that accompany the U.S. Department of State (2002) video (although not in the video itself), and in those developed

Figure 8.1 "Firefighers Raise a U.S. Flag at the Site of the World Trade Center." (Collection: Getty Images News Photographer: Thomas E. Franklin/ The Bergen Record)

by the Constitutional Rights Foundation (2002) and the Choices for the 21st Century (2002) Project (the only three sets of materials that explicitly dealt with the conceptual meaning of terrorism). The Constitutional Rights Foundation introduces the materials with quite a different approach to thinking about what terrorism means:

> Because terrorism implies killing and maiming innocent people, no country wants to be accused of supporting terrorism or harboring terrorist groups. At the same time, no country wants what it considers to be a legitimate use of force to be labeled terrorism. An old saying goes, "One person's terrorist is another person's freedom fighter." Today, there is no universally accepted definition of terrorism. Countries define the term according to their own beliefs and to support their own national interests. (2002, p. 21)

As this passage demonstrates, a major distinction among the texts and materials is whether students are brought into the debate about what terrorism means and what events and people should be considered examples of terrorism or terrorists. For example, in the Constitutional Rights Foundation's curriculum and in the written materials that accompany the State Department video, students are given multiple and competing definitions of terrorism and are asked to determine whether actual and hypothetical events are examples of the concept (see Table 8.2). In the Choices for the 21st Century (2002) materials, students engaged in a similar activity where they analyzed whether Nelson Mandela and others should be considered terrorists or something else (freedom fighters, for example).

Conversely, while the textbooks gave numerous examples of terrorism, they provided no opportunity for students to analyze whether a particular incident was actually an act of terrorism. Even more striking is that many examples of terrorism given in the texts did not match how the book defined the concept. We found that only one of the texts, *Patterns of Interaction* (Beck et al., 2005), included domestic terrorism in its definition, but all three U.S. History textbooks included the Oklahoma City Federal Building bombing as an example of terrorism. While four of the texts claimed that terrorism is conducted against civilians, they included examples that were directed at military targets, not civilians. For example, *American Odyssey* (Nash, 2004), *Democracy in Action* (Remy, 2006), and Glencoe *World History* (Spielvogel, 2005) all refer to attacks on the U.S.S. *Cole*, a U.S. Naval destroyer; *American Odyssey* (Nash, 2004), Glencoe *World History* (Spielvogel, 2005), and *Connections to Today* (Ellis & Esler, 2005) include the insurgencies in Afghanistan and Iraq as terrorist acts, even though they are directed primarily at U.S., Afghani, and Iraqi military and police forces. Finally, two texts, *American Odyssey* (Nash, 2004) and *Democracy in Action* (Remy, 2006), state that terrorism is conducted by "non-governmental groups," which would eliminate state-sponsored terrorism. However, at least two

Table 8.2 *Terrorism in America*, 2nd ed. (Constitutional Rights Foundation). Decision is Left to Student about Whether Each is an Example of Terrorism

Hypothetical Situations

1. "A radical environmental group burns down a vacant hotel that was recently legally built in a wilderness area."
2. "Country X, during a time of war, accidentally kills civilians while conducting bombing raids in Country Z."
3. "Country X hires an organized crime group in Country Z to assassinate civilian leaders of a group opposing the international policies of Country X."
4. "A national separatist group in Country X blows up a railroad station in Country Z to discourage that government from supporting policies of the government in Country X." (p. 23)

Actual Events

1. Columbine High School, 1999
2. Bombing of Los Angeles Times, 1910
3. Murder of former Idaho Governor Frank Steunenberg, 1905
4. Murder of two employees of Slater and Morrill Shoe Company, 1920
5. Bombing of 16th St. Baptist Church, 1963
6. Unabomber, 1985–1995
7. Ku Klux Klan:
   a. During Reconstruction
   b. In the 1920s
   c. During the Civil Rights Movement
8. Tylenol murders in Chicago, 1982
9. Assassination of William McKinley, 1901
10. John Brown's raid, 1859
11. Attack on Lawrence, Kansas, led by William Quantrill, 1863
12. Boston Tea Party, 1773
13. Bombing of abortion clinics, 1980 to present

examples in *American Odyssey* (Nash, 2004), the bombing of a Beirut night club in 1986 and the bombing of Pan Am flight 103 over Lockerbie, Scotland, have been attributed to intelligence agents from Libya and led to U.S. military retaliation against Libya and U.N. sanctions, respectively.

It is misleading to state that terrorism has a clear definition and then give examples that do not meet that definition. Research on concept understanding makes it clear that there needs to be a connection between how a concept is defined (its critical attributes) and the examples used to illustrate it (Taba, 1967; Parker, 1988). While we recognize how difficult that is to do with a concept such as terrorism, it is reasonable to expect textbooks to cite examples that support their authoritatively stated definition of terrorism—or to adopt the tack taken in the other materials and explicitly engage students in the controversy about what the concept itself means.

Finally, it is important to point out that the vast majority of terrorist acts in the textbooks and materials involve the United States or its allies. The resulting message is that terrorism is a more significant problem for the United States than it is for other nations, despite the fact that North America as a region had the lowest number of terrorist attacks—17 between 1997 and 2003. While the terrorist attacks that have occurred against U.S. targets are significant, the U.S. Department of State identifies 274 attacks in Western Europe during that same period and a staggering 820 attacks in Latin America, including South America (U.S. Army Training and Doctrine Command, 2005).

Fair and Balanced?

Given the accusations by Finn and others about the "biased" and "anti-American" teaching about 9/11, it is not surprising that the curriculum writers were keenly interested in creating materials that portrayed a "balanced" view of controversial issues. John Milewski was the executive producer of the "First Vote" video that the Close Up Foundation developed about 9/11, the history of the struggle for voting rights in the United States, and reasons for why young people should vote. Milewsky explained how the organization defines "balance":

> To some degree for us, balance is like pornography. You know it when you see it, and we've being doing this for a long time. Sometimes we know it's balanced when we know it's balanced. In other words, we keep tweaking it and maybe it's taking a line out here, a line out there, and if it sort of feels right to us, that we've paid homage to a variety of different perspectives and points of view. But every piece has its own peculiarities in that regard, and in this one it is a much more subtle balance than something like the death penalty, where there are obviously major camps of thought there that need to be represented to achieve anything that anyone would consider balanced. (2003)

When determining how to achieve ideological balance within their materials, the authors were especially comfortable raising domestic policy issues that came to the forefront because of 9/11. For example, civil liberties issues related to the Patriot Act are topics for debate and deliberation in several of the curricula. Alan Shapiro, the author of three lessons on "civil liberties and terrorism" for Educators for Social Responsibility, explained how important it was for students to treat policy responses to 9/11 as controversial issues:

> [A]s a response to 9–11, most Americans are very concerned about their security and rightfully so, and therefore Congress passes legislation that's designed to help provide greater security in the country. That comes in turn in conflict, or at least it would appear to come in conflict, with passages in the Constitution and the Bill of Rights and also with past American history that raise significant questions. So I would want students to come away with some idea of competing points of view about that Patriot Act. (2003)

While it may seem obvious that curriculum materials about 9/11 and its after-math would include the Patriot Act as a controversial topic, it is important to remember that it was hardly controversial at the time it was signed into law on October 26, 2001—just 72 hours after it was first introduced and barely six weeks after 9/11, when many of the curricula were being written. By including the Patriot Act as a controversial issue instead of a necessarily correct response by the government to the horrors of 9/11, the writers were, in fact, taking a position that a measure the government wanted citizens to view as a matter of necessity might actually be wrongheaded policy.

Shapiro was well aware that the inclusion of particular issues in the curriculum developed by Educators for Social Responsibility was a political act. He said in an interview conducted for our study, "I try to avoid pushing any particular political point of view, except insofar as focusing on the issue in itself, which I think is a political statement. I have long held that as a personal principle, that by focusing on an issue, which means you're not going to focus on something else, you're going to make a political statement of sorts" (Shapiro 2003). And yet Shapiro shared with all the other authors the view that the lessons *per se* were not ideological. During the interview, I asked the question, "If you were to place these lessons on the ideological spectrum, where would you put them?" He responded, "I don't exactly put them on an ideological spectrum. I try, maybe not always successfully, to be as evenhanded as I can be on these various issues" (Shapiro, 2003). What he seems to mean is that there is a distinction between making a political statement about which part of the ideological spectrum should be privileged via issue selection (which is inevitable and acceptable), versus presenting just one position on an issue—which would be a violation of the goals of democratic education.

Similarly, Marshall Croddy, the director of publications for the Constitutional Rights Foundation, explained that the very mission of the organization made it necessary to include multiple and competing perspectives on controversial issues in the curricula they develop. Croddy reported:

> Our bylaws are non-partisan/non-profit, so we have a publications board that monitors and supervises our process. One of the things that we're supposed to provide is a balanced perspective on the issues, make sure multiple sides are expressed, [and] not be conclusive in terms of the issues we raise—that is, leave it to the learner to make those decisions. So we emphasize critical thinking and analytical skill development, rather than for us to advocate any one particular viewpoint or conclusion that we would want the student to draw. We try to do that and obviously we have our own biases, but we test the materials to try to make sure that as little of that bias is represented. (2003)

While the responses to our questions about the ideology embedded in the curricula were thoughtful and often extremely sophisticated, they seemed to suggest that the authors held an ideology of neutrality with respect to the issues. For example, while Shapiro was willing to acknowledge that the selection of issues was itself a political statement, he steadfastly denied that the curricula he wrote illustrated or represented any particular ideology. This was the case for all the authors: not a single one reported that their organization's curricula staked out a particular position that could be labeled "ideological." Instead, the authors said they were advancing a fair-minded (i.e., non-biased) approach to democratic education by providing students with policy choices (as in the foreign-policy curricula developed by the Choices Program), or with pro and con arguments for existing policies (such as the Patriot Act).

Yet, as previously mentioned with the Patriot Act example, the curricula *did* promote particular ideological positions. By putting the Patriot Act in front of students as a matter of controversy, the authors were sending a clear message that the actions of government—even in a time of crisis—could be wrong or misguided.

Conversely, many of the curricula lend support to positions that the U.S. government has taken on terrorism. For example, in the Choices for the 21st Century (2002) curricula, a lesson plan titled "Revolutionaries or Terrorists?" presented five case studies and asked students to use the "standards of the international community" to determine whether the case represented terrorism or some other form of political violence. The cases were the IRA in Northern Ireland, the separatists in Chechnya, the Zapatistas in Chiapas, the ANC in South Africa, and the Weatherman in the United States. Elsewhere in the curriculum, Osama bin Laden was clearly labeled a terrorist.

One of the writers, Sarah Fox, explained the Choices for the 21st Century's decision-making process about which cases to include by focusing on the ANC and Nelson Mandela: "To have kids required to think about whether Mandela is or was a terrorist is so completely different from the way they've been taught about him in the past. I think it is an interesting question for kids to think about and important for them to think about that way" (2003). I then asked, "What about Osama, who is presented here as a terrorist, as opposed to a question for which kids should decide how to classify him in the same way that they classify Mandela? What is the distinction?" The Choices Program writers believed that while a legitimate debate could take place about whether ANC activities (and the acts of Mandela specifically) were examples of terrorism, the same sort of debate was not possible with respect to Osama bin Laden. Implicitly, the materials suggest that it would be wrong and perhaps even dangerous to encourage students to question the conclusion that Osama bin Laden is a terrorist.

Lucy Mueller, one of the Choices Program staff members, remarked that it was without dispute that bin Laden should be labeled a terrorist: "I think this may be an excuse, but the logical explanation on this is because we are Americans. In the aftermath of 9/11, how could we think otherwise? We had the whole world agreeing with us on that issue, I think. At least, countries of the world did, not every individual" (2003). Her statement sparked an interesting exchange among other staff participating in the interview:

> Sarah Fox: It is a very interesting question, because some of that may be what Lucy was saying—it's the timeframe in which the lesson was being written.
>
> Andy Blackadar: I think also, let's be honest. We have to make decisions, too, about . . . I personally think that I am comfortable with labeling him a terrorist. I think that's fine. What purpose will it serve to have that debate? I think it would have actually distracted us from what we have tried to accomplish with the rest of the unit.
>
> Hess: In what way?
>
> Blackadar: Well, a unit would have become controversial about a topic that we don't believe was controversial, rightly or wrongly. Is that fair to say?
>
> Mueller: That's exactly what I was thinking, that there would be people who wouldn't touch this material if we had somehow tried to present bin Laden in another way. Ah, but I would admit, I don't think I really thought about that until you raised the issue now. I guess in my mind it was a given.

Just as the curricula supported official government views on who is a terrorist and what constitutes terrorism, they also represented the position that the U.S. government has never supported terrorism. While there were many examples of terrorism laced throughout the materials, there was never even a hint that the government of the United States has either explicitly engaged in or implicitly encouraged terrorism. Moreover, the allies of the United States did not engage in terrorist activities, according to the curricula we examined. Instead, they protected themselves from other nations and organizations that promote terror. The United States and its friends were presented as blameless victims of terror.

While the authors were concerned about presenting balanced materials on controversial issues, the curricula did take strong positions on a number of topics that could rightfully be considered highly controversial. Domestic issues (such as the Patriot Act) were open for deliberation, and many of the curricula made reference to mistakes that the U.S. government has made in the past *within* the United States. For example, The Constitutional Rights Foundation curriculum included strong language that explained why the internment of Japanese-Americans during World War II was a mistake. But there was very little criticism of how the United States has treated other nations—either historically or more recently.

Conclusion

The public rhetoric about the nature of the ideological messages embedded in school curricula—especially textbooks and other materials used in social studies courses—often centers on accusations that schools are propaganda machines that work to indoctrinate an impressionable youth. Conservatives argue that the schools are full of teachers who have been duped by left-wing professors working in Schools of Education, as a report from the Thomas B. Fordham Foundation recently charged:

> Schools of education often appear more interested in producing social studies teachers with politically correct ideologies than producing competent instructors . . . These theorists have created and promoted a philosophy of social studies education that has proven to be both educationally ineffective and contrary to the values of most Americans. The perspectives of these social studies theorists rest upon three premises: 1. American society is morally bankrupt; 2. an elite band of university professors, infused with a passion for social justice, knows best how to reform our flawed society; and, 3. classrooms in our nation's public schools are an essential battleground for this societal transformation. The theorists' passion for radical social change and their propensity to use the public schools as a tool to do so, is undoubtedly one reason why social studies is in crisis. (Leming, Ellington, & Porter-Magee, 2003, p. i)

From the left, social studies teachers are critiqued because the content of what they present to students is right-wing, overtly patriotic, and dangerously sexist and racist. For example, Gloria Ladson-Billings writes that social studies is flawed because we "continue to tell our students lies about our history, our world views, and our culture" (2003, p. 1). Research suggests that Ladson-Billings is more accurate in her assessment of what students are learning in social studies courses than the Fordham Foundation. Peter Levine and Mark Lopez (2004) report that when a random sample of young U.S. citizens (ages 15–25) was asked to pick the one theme that had been most emphasized in their social studies or U.S. history classes, their top choice was "the Constitution or the U.S. system of government and how it works." The second most common choice was "great American heroes and the virtues of the American system of government." In contrast, just 11% selected "problems facing the country today," while 9% chose "racism and other forms of injustice in the American system" (Levine & Lopez, 2004, p. 1).

The curricula we studied communicated a much more complex and nuanced picture of the ideological terrain in social studies education. Instead of teaching young people a "truth" about 9/11 and its aftermath, the ideological range evidenced in the lessons we studied was wide. Clearly, however, it was not as wide as either Finn or Ladson-Billings charge. That is, neither the far-right nor the far-left wings of political thought in the United States would see their positions clearly and consistently represented in these curricula. Instead, there is tremendous variance among the curricula with respect to which aspects of 9/11 and its aftermath are given attention and which issues are presented as controversial.

Several of the curricula took pains to showcase mistakes that the U.S. government has made in the past with respect to domestic policies—perhaps as a way to attract students' attention to the danger of making unwise decisions hastily in the midst of a crisis. In attempting to understand why the authors might have been unwilling to apply the same critical lens to U.S. policies toward other peoples and nations (and especially to the international mistakes made by the United States), a family analogy might prove useful: sharing criticism within a family is considered acceptable (and sometimes even laudable), but sharing beyond the family is considered a breach of trust. Regardless of the reason, the refusal to engage students in meaningful critique of the actions of the U.S. government outside national borders is extremely problematic because so much of what the government has done in response to 9/11 has been in, and has had a profound effect *on*, other nations.

One impetus for conducting this study was to examine whether curricula developed by educational organizations (as opposed to large corporate publishers) presented young people with a broader or more interesting range of information about an important event than is typically found in textbooks. If so, we reasoned, then these organizations were making a contribution by diversifying the views that young people are asked to consider and analyze. Moreover, the lessons in many of the materials developed by the non-profit organizations were highly engaging—and without exception, they were much less expensive than traditional texts (several were distributed free of charge). While there is much to critique in many of the lessons, it is important to point out these organizations were operating to expand the range of possibilities available to teachers who wanted to infuse their curriculum with information and activities about 9/11 and its aftermath.

There is an "American Tale" of 9/11 presented in everything we examined—both in what is given attention and what is left out. But convergence does not equal sameness: some of the materials asked students to think deeply about difference (how terrorism should be defined, for example, or what policies the United States should adopt), while others did not. Given that much of what people in the United States seemed to agree about immediately after 9/11 has become quite contested, the materials that embody and breathe life into those differences are clearly more authentic to the actual political community we inhabit. Interestingly, many of the materials developed in the year after 9/11 anticipated these disputes, while the textbooks written five years after 9/11 omitted them. To us, that is a difference that matters when creating materials designed to help young people engage in the process of analyzing and reflecting on what it means to be a citizen in our democracy. This is the same process that Bruce Springsteen was inspired to engage in following 9/11, and it is far more than a theoretical exercise. It is, instead, a deliberative process predicated on reaching concrete conclusions about citizens' rights and responsibilities—and about the actions that are inseparable from this conception of citizenship.

9
Creating More Controversy in Classrooms

I was born into a family where political discourse mattered. My parents, grand-parents, and siblings all relished spirited discussions of the issues of the day, and newspapers, news magazines, and books about both contemporary issues and history littered the living room. My parents watched the news each night during "martini hour" and afterwards happily lured our friends into the living room to get their opinions about what was happening in the world. My father was a college debate coach in the early years of his university career, and my mother taught high school government and journalism in addition to being the sponsor of the high school newspaper, *The Spartan*. Not surprisingly, this was a family where to care about politics—deeply—and to engage in discussions about what was and what *should* be going on and *why*, held real cachet.

It is not surprising, then, that I resonated with the discourse-rich curriculum present in the high school where I started my teaching career in 1979. Developed by Donald Oliver and James Shaver in the early 1960s as part of the "new social studies," the Public Issues Model of classroom discussion formed the core of the required history course (at that time called "American Studies") in the school. As an aside, this was the same model of discussion that I later encountered as a researcher when studying the teaching of Bob, one of the teachers whose practice I describe in Chapter 4. In the school where I began my career, new teachers were expected to learn how to facilitate high-quality classroom discussions—especially those that focused on highly controversial historical and contemporary issues. Teaching that was primarily targeted toward generating content-rich classroom talk was the norm in this school. Because this was my first teaching position, I thought my norm was *the* norm in schools. However, as I continued my career beyond this one high school, I learned how uncommon it was to have a social studies department largely united around teaching students to do the intellectual labor of classroom life— with discussion as both the workers' tool and the intended outcome. Clearly, learning how to teach from colleagues who not only valued this kind of demo-cratic education, but also knew how to put it in practice had a formative and lasting impact on my views about what schools should and could help young people learn.

I have argued throughout this book that a particular kind of democratic education is needed in U.S. schools—education that includes discussion of controversial political issues. In this chapter, I will briefly review the argument with which I began. Then, I will turn to concrete suggestions about what should be done to make it more likely that all students will be taught how to engage in discussions of controversial political issues in schools. And to conclude, I will broaden my focus by exploring recent evidence that suggests that democratic education is important now more than ever before—in large part because we are experiencing a severe and growing "democracy divide."

Democratic Education, Controversial Issues Discussion, and Our Schools: A Review

Why Democratic Education Demands Controversial Issues Discussions

Democratic education without controversial issues discussions would be like a forest without trees, or an ocean without fish, or a symphony without sound. Why? Because controversies about the nature of the public good and how to achieve it, along with how to mediate among competing democratic values, are intrinsic parts of democracy. If there is no controversy, there is no democracy. It is as simple as that. If we want democratic education to be both democratic and educational, then we have to teach young people about controversial political issues. Again, I define controversial political issues as authentic questions about the kinds of public policies that should be adopted to address public problems. The precise content of such issues is different in different times and contexts, but contemporary examples in the United States include some of the following questions: Should the federal government grant amnesty to people living in the United States without legal documents? What should be done in our country to lower the high school drop out rate?

We should want young people to learn a plethora of things about controversial political issues. Specifically, we need to teach them that such issues are the nature of the democratic beast and therefore not to be shunned, feared, or ignored; that they can be talked about in civil and productive ways and that there are strategies for engaging in such discussions; that these issues are important and linked to their lives, and deserve both their own and the public's attention. Most significantly, we need to teach young people that what they think about such issues deserves airtime—both in and out of school. Their views matter, not because there is something special about young people, but precisely because there is not. Their views matter because *all* views should matter in a democracy.

Schools as Prime Locations for Controversial Issues Discussions

When asked why I focus so much of my work on school-based democratic education instead of democratic education in other venues, I tell the bank robber tale. When asked why he robs banks, the robber says, "because that is where the money is." Similarly, schools are especially good sites for issues discussions because that is where we are most likely to find young people, and young people are central to the continuation of democracy.

However, I commonly encounter people who are profoundly interested in democratic education but have decided that schools are not very good venues in which to do this kind of work. While I think it a very good idea to investigate the potential that other venues (such as video games, after-school programs, and various forms of "new" media) have for fostering political and civic engagement in our youth, I think it would be harmful to pay attention only to these venues and ignore schools. There are currently almost 50 *million* young people in K-12 schools in the United States. Moreover, there is solid evidence that high-quality democratic education in schools works. Therefore, there is no good reason to give it up.

In addition to being good places to access young people, schools also possess a number of deliberative assets to be mined: courses that lend themselves to controversial issues discussions; access to an increasingly rich array of instructional resources that will ensure that those discussions are high-quality; teachers who are already adept at or who are open to learning how to moderate discussions; and, finally, a wide range of ideological diversity. Thus, it seems that schools are in many ways better venues for democratic education than settings occupied by adults, or spaces inhabited by young people when not in school.

Making Schools Even Better Venues for Controversial Issues Discussion

Even though schools are exceptionally good places to teach young people how to discuss controversial political issues, it is clear that in many schools it is quite difficult for teachers to engage in this kind of teaching. There are many barriers to the inclusion of controversial political issues discussions in schools, ranging from the way schools are structured to the lack of sufficient preparation some teachers have for this kind of teaching. Recent educational trends that privilege the acquisition of low-level knowledge, and the desires of some community members and parents who want schools to reflect their own views on controversial political issues, or to shun them all together, can also stand in the way.

What can be done to ensure that more students are taught how to engage in high-quality discussions of controversial political issues? One of my suggestions is to build on the assets articulated above that make schools potentially rich environments to engage in the task of teaching young people how to discuss controversial political issues.

In addition, there are concrete actions schools can take to improve the likelihood that controversial issues discussions are being taught and being taught well. In this section, I discuss two of them: eliminating tracking and providing teachers with high-quality professional development in this section. Doing these two things will strengthen schools' abilities to engage students in the important work of democracy: controversial issues discussions.

Eliminate Tracking

Tracking, as it is practiced in many schools today, is itself an inherently undemocratic action. If democracy is about equality, then the unequal access students have (due to their position in lower- or upper-level tracked classes) to content, pedagogy, and even good teachers, is deeply problematic. In this section, I focus on how tracking affects controversial issues discussions in two major ways: it prevents many students from gaining access to discussions, and it curtails the ideological diversity among students in classrooms, which we know is a key ingredient in promoting successful discussions.

I am arguing essentially that schools should be structured in ways that readily provide opportunities for *all students* to take courses that include controversial issues discussions. Although this is not happening often, when it does, the result is clearly positive. Take Bob's school, for example. Bob's school has created an unusual and in my view, unusually successful, required *untracked* course. When I interviewed his students, a number of them told me how unusual it was to be in a class with such a range of students because typically they are in classes that are tracked, either officially or by default, by ability level.

In the study I described in Chapters 5 and 6, I encountered another school whose social studies teachers had successfully fought back attempts to track their classes. As one teacher noted of her Social Studies department's decision to refrain from tracking Social Studies courses, "one of the big beliefs of our former department chairman and the department chairman before him was that . . . we are all in the country together and we are all in this government together and so we probably should learn about all of it together." As a result of this strongly held belief within the department, every senior student in the high school takes a similar Government class. Although "Sheltered" classes exist for English Language Learners, even for this group of students, the school maintains its commitment to the equal distribution of high-quality democratic education and to exposing students to a wide range of political viewpoints through their use of school-wide simulations. Students in every senior Government class, including the Sheltered classes, participate equally in senior class-wide legislative simulations with their peers. The teacher of the Sheltered Government class notes a personal belief that English Language Learners should "experience the things the mainstream kids do . . . for these kids to be part of the simulation, take on leadership roles, have their own legislation, get up [to] speed, is really powerful." This teacher highlights one of the important reasons to involve all students in high-quality democratic education, which is the impact on students who are often not given access to this type of education.

This school has maintained a focus on equity by refusing to track the required government course in an era when so many schools are tracking courses—especially required courses—and adding many Advanced Placement courses. In regard to the teaching of controversial issues discussions, this tracking trend is potentially problematic for at least two reasons. First, when social studies classes are tracked, there is a tendency to lower the intellectual demands that are placed on students in the lower tracks. Given the difficulty of controversial issues discussions, they may be reserved only for students who are viewed as already capable of participating effectively in them (presumably students in upper-level classes). Moreover, the most skillful teachers are often placed with students in the upper track classes. Given the amount of teacher skill required to orchestrate controversial issues discussions, it seems likely that controversial issues discussions would happen most often under the direction of the skilled teachers in upper-level classes.

We also need to ask some hard questions about Advanced Placement (AP) Government classes. Enrollment in these classes is increasing at a fast pace—a development that many applaud—and there are many exceptionally talented teachers who have created fabulous AP Government courses. One administrator recently told me that he had to make sure those who taught AP "really knew their stuff" because test scores depended on it, and powerful parents demanded it. Unfortunately, this kind of teacher tracking, which often rations the most experienced and capable teachers to those students who are routinely privileged, is happening in many schools.

Conversely, the trend toward creating Advanced Placement American Government courses in high schools may not only preclude the teaching of controversial issues discussions in lower-tracked classes, it might also work to deprive the upper-tracked students of exposure to controversial issues because teachers fear taking time out of the demanding content-drive curriculum that must be followed to align with the tests.

If education is to be truly democratic, tracking impedes this aim. All students deserve access to controversial issues discussions, and they should be engaging in these discussions *together*, which leads to the second problem associated with tracking.

When students are tracked in the name of ability, what often occurs is the funneling of students into homogeneous groups in regard to race and socioeconomic status. Often, White, wealthier students enroll in honors and AP classes, while minority, poorer students are placed in basic and lower-level classes. The homogenous nature of these classes, consequently, can prevent the ideological diversity that we know greatly benefits controversial issues discussions. For example, AP Government classes rarely mirror the larger student body from which they are drawn (Kahne & Middaugh, 2008). Problems and policies and differentially impact diverse groups in the United States, and in democracy education, we should expose students to the differing views and experiences that exist in their schools. This is especially important in courses where the interchange between students demands different social positioning in order to be authentic and helpful. If AP Government classes do not contain diversity of race and class, we may be thwarting the democratic process in the very place it could do the most good: social studies classrooms.

High-Quality Professional Development

It would be virtually impossible to overestimate the importance of skillful teaching to the enterprise of controversial political issues discussions. As I demonstrated in Chapter 4, teachers who are successfully teaching their students how to engage in thoughtful and productive discussions are masterful teachers.

As a quick review, skillful issues discussion teachers create classroom environments and courses that encourage the airing of multiple and competing views and the participation of all students. Such teachers recognize that peer relations within a class are undoubtedly going to influence students' willingness to participate, as well as the nature and tone of the interaction. While there are many aspects of peer interactions teachers cannot control, they can ensure that expectations about appropriate behavior are clear, and that within-class grouping does not reify existing power hierarchies among students. Teachers can help students understand the value of learning and the power of using one another's names; they can help students learn to discuss without resorting to the taunts and put-downs that unfortunately characterize some of the political talk we see in the world outside of school.

Skillful discussion teachers also recognize that many of their students do not come into their classes already possessing the background knowledge, communicative skills, and/or deliberative dispositions necessary to participate effectively in thoughtful civic discussions of highly controversial issues. Consequently, simply providing students with the opportunity to engage in such discussions is not sufficient, especially if the goal is to reach *all* students, as opposed to simply providing a forum for students who are already proficient discussants. Instead, teachers who are unusually good at this form of teaching work hard to align their theories to their practice and intentionally develop instruction that leads to effective controversial issues discussions. This work involves choosing a model of discussion that will help achieve the goals of discussion, developing lessons that teach *with* and *for* discussion, spending a significant amount of time preparing students for discussion (both through the explicit instruction of discussion techniques and by engaging students in content related to the issue to be discussed), thoughtfully implementing assessment, and creating forums in which students can take ownership.

Although teachers may vary greatly in the nuances of their approaches, the basic components of effective controversial issues discussions teaching cut across their varied techniques, offering a good starting point for teachers who wish to engage students in controversial issues discussions to examine their own practice. Enter—high-quality professional development.

Just as successful discussion teachers know that "far from coming naturally, discussion has to be learned," it is also the case that few teachers are "naturals" with respect to teaching their students how to engage in issues discussions.

Since 1987, I have spent a considerable amount of time experimenting with various forms of professional development for teachers on controversial political issues and have carefully followed what others are doing in this regard. For example, there are a number of democratic education organizations that develop materials and professional development programs for teachers on controversial political issues, such as the National Issues Forum, the Choices for the 21st Century Project at Brown University, and the Deliberating in Democracy Project of the Constitutional Rights Foundation Chicago and Street Law, Inc.[1]

While these organizations and others each have their own approach to professional development, I have noticed some key features that many of them share. First, they explicitly teach what discussion/deliberation is, especially as it compares to other forms of classroom discourse. The professional development programs often begin with a particular model of discussion that has attributes that distinguish it from other approaches and provide teachers with immersion experiences with the model. Second, they are all supported with high-quality materials that are created by professional writers with expertise in content and curriculum design. Third, there is some type of ongoing support given to teachers as they hone their skills in facilitating issues discussions.

While I think the features these professional development programs share are powerful, I doubt that the principles I advocate will be realized in practice unless a school or school district takes seriously the charge to ensure that all students learn how to discuss political issues. A major concern is that typically only one teacher from a school comes to a workshop, institute, or course on issues discussions, and then that teacher returns to school as a "solo practitioner." In the best-case scenario, the teacher will do well with issues discussions—but only his/her students benefit. In the worst-case scenario, the teacher needs more support and follow-up via ongoing professional development to become proficient with issues discussions. After a few failures and no easily-accessibly support network from similarly-trained colleagues, the teacher gives up, and issues discussions become just one more educational reform that did not work.

As an alternative, I would recommend tapping into the programs run by organizations with expertise in issues discussions, and then adding school-based professional development that provides ongoing follow-up and support to teachers. There are many models for how to do this, but one I have seen work particularly well is teacher study groups that convene regularly throughout the school year. These study groups enable teachers to reflect on what is working and what is not in respect to issues discussions.

There are additional school-wide structures that would support teachers that are well worth considering. A written policy that explains the purpose of controversial political issues discussions and states explicitly that this form of democratic education is endorsed in the school can be extremely helpful. Not only does such a policy make clear that these types of discussions are encouraged (instead of merely tolerated), but it can also establish specific guidelines to serve as guideposts of practice. For example, one school district's policy calls for teachers to work to develop a classroom atmosphere in which pupils feel free to express opinions and to challenge ideas, to teach respect for the opinions of others and develop skills of critical thinking, and to choose suitable instructional materials presenting data on varying points of view on issues being discussed (Board of Education, Madison Metropolitan School District, 2002).[2]

But formal written documents will probably have little impact on what happens in classrooms unless they are a piece of a much broader policy that is more specifically geared toward practice. For that reason, I highly recommend sustained, high-quality professional development for teachers, beginning with the teachers who teach courses where the "fit" with controversial issues is immediately apparent (such as a middle school civics class or a high school government course).

High-quality professional development can also bring controversial issues discussions to many grade levels. Although I generally support secondary-level courses specifically dedicated to controversial issues discussions (such as required, issues-based government courses in high school), research shows that young children can deal successfully with ideas that are developmentally appropriate and highly scaffolded (Paley, 1992; Beck, 2003). Consequently, I think it is a mistake for schools to wait until students are older to introduce these discussions. Ideally, by the time students get to high school, they will have had multiple opportunities throughout their elementary and middle school years to begin developing the skills and dispositions needed to participate effectively in issues discussions.

My critique of tracking and call for more high-quality professional development are not intended to negate the fact that schools are *already* excellent sites for controversial issues discussion. Instead, my intention is to provide concrete suggestions about how to make our schools even *better*.

The Democracy Divide

After teaching for many years, I began working at the Constitutional Rights Foundation Chicago (CRFC), where my principal task was to design and teach professional development programs for teachers in the United States. For the first few years I focused my work in Mississippi and Arkansas, but by the time I left to study with Walter Parker and his colleagues at the University of Washington seven years later, I had traveled to most states. I worked in schools that were so poor their teachers had to work at convenience stores at night to pay their bills. Such teachers had only ancient textbooks that talked about Batista's Cuba as if he still ruled that nation, and they dealt with class sizes so large that even the most attentive teachers struggled to learn all of their students' names.

During my tenure at CRFC I also experienced the material riches of schools in some suburban districts and urban private schools. These were schools where individual teachers had travel budgets to attend conferences, tuition reimbursement for graduate coursework, class size limits enforced through the bargained contract, and curriculum materials galore. A quick example to illustrate the stark contrast: in 2008 I investigated teacher salaries in two radically different districts with which I had worked—a very poor one in Mississippi, and a very wealthy one in Illinois. In Mississippi, starting salaries began at $33,100 and inched to $60,630 for the most experienced teacher; in Illinois, starting teachers earned $48,788, with salaries rocketing to $116,218 for the most experienced teachers.

We have become so used to hearing about educational inequality in the United States that it almost seems besides the point to lay out these stark differences once again. But in a book that is about a particular kind of democratic education in the United States, it is imperative to make clear the importance of the context of equality—or lack thereof—that, not surprisingly, has such a powerful impact on what gets taught, by whom, to whom, and in what ways.

Defining the Democracy Divide

It is crucial to examine the connection between education and political participation. And when we do so it becomes clear that there is a serious, persistent, and growing "democracy divide" in the United States, where some citizens have access to democracy and others do not. Evidence suggests that young people with low educational attainment are not "aging into" political participation in the way many did in the past. On virtually every measure of political and civic activity (e.g., voting, attending meetings, buy/boycotting, paying attention to the news, deliberating with others about public issues), young people who graduated from high school participate at a much higher level than those who did not, and the participation rate for those who attended college is higher still. During the 2008 presidential primary season, for example, one in four eligible young people with college experience voted on Super Tuesday, while only *one in 14* of the non-college youth did so.[3] Although the relationship between education and political participation is not a new story, never before has educational attainment been so predictive of whether young people will participate politically.

We can also see the divide playing out within our schools. Recent and powerful evidence supports the claim that democratic education opportunities are meted out in a manner that privileges wealthier students, students who are also more likely to be White. Most notably, a series of recent studies by Kahne and Middaugh (2008) have demonstrated clearly that the elements of high-quality democratic education recommended in the Civic Mission of the Schools Report are much less likely to be experienced by students who are poor, African American, or Latino. As just one example, students in classes with higher average SES levels are 1.42 times more likely to report participating in debates or panels discussions in their social studies courses than students in lower SES classes.[4] In my most recent study, we are also finding a relationship between students' SES and the likelihood that they are in classes that are rich with issues discussions. This is not to suggest that there are not powerful exceptions—recall that Mr. Dunn, whom we met in the beginning of the book, teaches in a school where all of the students are African American or Latino, and most are from families with little wealth. But as a general rule, we see the same kind of inequalities with respect to democratic education that we see in schooling writ large.

Is the democracy divide the only divide? Is it that students are not otherwise "gapped" and there is an especially pernicious effect of inequality with respect to democratic outcomes that we do not see in assessments of other goals that schools are supposed to be meeting, such as literacy or math? I think not. While the important research that Kahne and Middaugh (2008), Levinson (2008) and others are doing to document the democracy divide do not compare civic outcomes to those same students' scores on academic tests, we know from the national and international studies that there is clearly an inverse relationship between wealth and opportunities to high-quality democratic education in schools. And this same effect is seen in standard assessments of academic achievement in other areas. So I think that it is safe to say that students who are on the wrong side of the democracy divide are on the wrong side of the achievement gap generally.

The Democracy Divide—One Part of a Larger Inequality

We cannot be shy about owning up to just how entrenched and difficult it is to solve this problem, which I was reminded of by my good friend Barbara Perry at the United States Supreme Court Institute for high school teachers in 2003. That was the blockbuster year when the Court handed down two decisions about affirmative action (*Grutter v. Bollinger*, 2003). In one, writing for the barest possible majority, Justice O'Connor said that the affirmative action program at the University of Michigan law school was constitutional—for now.

After extolling the virtues of a diverse student body, she wrote: "the Court expects that 25 years from now, the use of racial preferences will no longer be necessary to further the interest approved today." Quite frankly, I was so relieved by the decision that I did not even catch the implications—and the assumptions from which they sprang—in the "25 year limit." But I remember Barbara Perry (whose opinions on affirmative action I do not know and am not referring to here) being astonished and saying something to the effect of, "imagine what it would take in the United States for these inequalities that are deeply steeped in hundreds of years of history to be erased in a mere 25 years."

This raises real questions about what can be done about the democracy divide in a system that has so many entrenched inequities. It is one thing to say students, especially poor students who are more likely to be students of color than White, need more and better democratic education. But the reality is that these students need more and better of all manner of education. In short, it is hard to imagine closing the democracy gap without paying serious and sustained attention to closing the achievement gap that exists in regard to race and wealth, both of which are still such powerful influences in our schools. And yet it is hard to expect that under-funded and under-supported schools and the students within them who are being attacked by the *hard bigotry* of inequality should do any better with respect to democratic education outcomes than they do with any other outcomes. And while there are complex and multiple causes of the inequities that exist, we know that some of them are deeply rooted in the unequal distribution of resources that high-quality education demands. As Jonathan Kozol (1991) and others who preach the social gospel of school equality have remonstrated to the nation on so many occasions, the way in which we dole out resources—financial and otherwise—is a symbol of who is perceived as "counting" and by whom.

Efforts to End the Democracy Divide

Clearly, the democracy divide is a manifestation of a larger problem. For those of us in democratic education this creates a challenge. On the one hand, it makes sense to work on the turf that we know. As people with expertise in this field we should try to make an impact in the area where we can matter the most. For me, that means the focus will, and I would argue should, stay directed toward ensuring that all young people get more and better democratic education. And it may be that adding the "democracy divide" to all the other divides and gaps that the public has been told about (and so many experience so profoundly) could be a catalyst—a lever of sorts—to focus attention on the intrinsic connection between democracy and equality. But it is critical to realize that the forging of this connection—not just rhetorically, but practically—will not happen in a vacuum. As King wrote so powerfully in 1963, "We are caught in an inescapable network of mutuality, tied in a single garment of destiny." In a nation where the most recent electoral results show that unemployment is almost three times higher than the rate of voting of non-college attending young people, it should come as no surprise that the connections between what is happening in the economy generally, the quality of educational opportunities afforded to young people, and the ways in which the young participate in democracy are intrinsically connected.

A number of changes are needed to address the democracy divide that so powerfully correlates with education. First, educators should be deeply concerned about the recent increase in the high school drop out/push out rate, an increase that is especially dramatic in urban schools. There are way too many young people on the wrong side of the schoolhouse gates. Serious and sustained attention must be directed toward reducing this rate, given the powerful connection that exists between educational attainment and civic and political participation. We must recognize that effective dropout prevention programs *are* a form of democratic education, even if they focus more on academic achievement than democratic literacy.

Second, it is important to stop spending such a disproportionate share of the resources in the field on the youth who are already are on the privileged side of the democracy divide (and who are most likely to attain high levels of education). We need a Marshall Plan for education in this country, but in the meantime we must triage the resources we have (Forum for Education and Democracy, 2008). Our standard needs to be quality *and* equality. High-quality programs that do not serve a broad cross-section of youth fail to meet that standard.

By looking carefully and critically at what is taught and to whom, we can better assess how to distribute effective forms of democratic education in equitable ways. Such an assessment serves as a democracy divide audit. We can use it to gauge whether we are standing on the right side of history as this nation approaches one of the most serious challenges it has ever faced: the disparate education that our youth are receiving. We can own up to, investigate, and work to remediate this democratic divide or face its lasting, harmful effects. The effects are real, as illustrated by a look at which sectors of United States society have influence on the political system, and access to healthcare and higher education. These effects undermine our democracy. They also challenge all of us in democratic education to concentrate our efforts on ensuring that all students have access to what we know enhances political and civic participation. High-quality education that does not serve the goals of equality is really not high-quality at all.

Making the Case to the Public

I imagine that most people who have read this book are involved in some direct way in democratic education: teachers and future teachers, school administrators, staff of democratic education organizations, education researchers, academics, and perhaps even school board members. But people in these categories—and I obviously include myself here—are in other roles, too: as members of the public, and perhaps as parents or guardians, aunts and uncles, and grandparents. Consequently, I conclude the book by speaking directly to you in your other roles, to make the case for why the *public* should support high-quality democratic education of all types, but specifically teaching young people how to discuss controversial political issues in schools.

We should want the children in our own and each others' families to learn how to engage in thoughtful and productive cross-cutting political talk and to value such engagement. This, as we know, would be a marked change because relatively few adults in the United States currently participate in such discussions. Specifically, then, I am suggesting that we should want young people to encounter, to speak, to hear, to critically evaluate, and to learn from viewpoints that may be starkly *different* from what they hear elsewhere—in such places as their homes and perhaps their faith communities.

This may be an uphill battle because we know that many people want schools to reflect and inculcate their own political ideologies and views on particular issues. It may just be human nature to want our institutions, such as our schools, to mirror our ideas back to us. And given that so many of us are living in ideologically homogenous communities, it is increasingly easy to imagine that the views we and our neighbors hold are right—so right, in fact, that to consider others' just makes no sense (why learn something that is wrong?) or deeply troubling because they so fundamentally challenge our beliefs. Recall, as one of Zimmerman's (2002) students remarked, "You'll never see a parents' group called 'Americans in Favor of Debating the Other Side.'"

People in the United States should be in favor of hearing the other side because the consequences of not doing so are so dangerous—to our own thinking, to the decisions we make about how to solve the public's problems, and to democracy itself. Therefore, we must resist our impulse to demand that what young people in schools experience reflect our views—because we need schools to do their job, which is to make democracy work.

Of course, I am not suggesting that we want to give free reign to teachers who are purposely and powerfully trying to indoctrinate students into a particular point of view on controversial political issue that is different from our own. But the larger point is we should also not want teachers to indoctrinate young people into the views that comport with our own either—that would be equally dangerous to democracy. While there may be some teachers who are attempting to do this, in my experience they are few and far between. I do not think the problem with respect to controversial political issues in schools is indoctrination into particular views. I think the problem is that there is not enough controversy in the school curriculum. It often gets shunned or stripped out of the curriculum because administrators and teachers either fear intense criticism from the public or they have not formed an understanding of why this kind of teaching is so important.

I am not arguing that we should merely tolerate young people engaging seriously with views other than our own in schools. What we need to do is much bolder, much stronger than tolerate. We need to promote the importance of issues discussions in schools, support them by keeping the conversation going at home, and demand them if our local schools are not currently teaching young people how to engage in such discussions with civility and skill. If your child is not in classes where she is being taught how to engage in public political talk, ask, why not? Be the kind of parent who actually does demand to hear the other side in school, and be the kind of teacher who can put that into practice. In short, it is time to make *all* schools work for democracy.

Appendix A

Methodological Overview
of Study Used in Chapters 5 and 6

The case study of Mr. Dunn and his students, and all the data relied on for Chapters 5 and 6, come from the Discussion of Controversial Issues Study that is housed at the Wisconsin Center for Education Research, and for which I am the principal investigator. The major purpose of the study is to identify the ways in which issues deliberation in social studies classes influence what young people learn and how they act politically. Two research questions guide the work:

1. How do high school students experience and learn from participating in social studies courses that emphasize the deliberation of controversial international and/or domestic issues?
2. Do such deliberations influence students' political participation after they leave high school? If so, what are the pathways to participation?

The study began in the spring semester of 2005 when we selected schools in Illinois and Indiana where at least one teacher in each school participated in a deliberation project coordinated by a democracy education non-profit organization. The deliberation programs selected for the purposes of the study were the Choices for the 21st Century Program and the Constitutional Rights Foundation Chicago (CRFC) Youth Summit Program. Both of these programs provide professional development for teachers, written curricula on international (Choices for the 21st Century) or domestic (CRFC) issues that utilize deliberation as a primary pedagogical strategy and outcome, and opportunities for students to deliberate with their peers from other schools at large-scale deliberative events (Choices sponsors the Capital Forum and CRFC sponsors the Illinois Youth Summit).

In Wave Two (2005–2006 school year), we retained some of the teachers from the first wave, but also broadened our sample to a third state (Wisconsin) and recruited teachers who reported engaging their students in issues discussions using other curricula or materials they developed.

In Wave Three (2007), we conducted phone interviews with 400 students who had participated in the first two waves, 95% of whom had completed high school, some in the spring of 2006, and others in the spring of 2005. The percentage of students we interviewed was roughly proportional to the numbers of students in the two previous waves. It is important to note that we were able to obtain parent and student consent from slightly over 600 students from Wave One and Wave Two for participation in the Wave Three interviews. Consequently, while our overall response rate of 400 Wave Three interviews (after high school) is roughly 40% of our total sample, it is more than 70% the portion of the sample that we could draw from given the consent situation. In Wave Four we added 100 students and one additional school to the sample. Pending funding, we will do a final phone interview with the 400 students who were interviewed in Wave Three, and an additional 75 students who came into the study in Wave Four and have consented to participate in the follow-up phone call. In sum, there are 1,100 students and 35 teachers from 21 schools in three states participating in the study.

There are at least two important limitations in our study that relate to the nature of our sample. The first is that the number of students in each class who participated in the study ranged dramatically across classes. In some classes, more than 80% of the students took the questionnaires, while in other classes fewer than 50% participated. We think this is due primarily to the detailed nature of the parent consent and student assent form. We made every effort to assess whether the students who did elect to participate in each class were roughly representative of the gender and race/ethnicity in the class as a whole and are satisfied that the sample looks very similar to the classes from which it was drawn, with a slight overrepresentation of females and of European Whites. However, we lost a slightly higher percentage of students of color from pre- to post-survey, and from post-survey to the follow-up than was the case with European Whites.

Ideological Diversity

In Wave One, students only completed one questionnaire, which was given toward the beginning of the course. For Wave Two, we made significant changes to the pre- and post-questionnaires in order to obtain more information about forces and factors present in the first wave that our interviews and observation data suggested were important. We also developed a teacher questionnaire that was virtually identical to the student instrument and made some small adjustments to our interview protocols. It is important to note that we did not remove any items that we used in Wave One in order to make comparisons across Waves One and Two. However, our pre-post findings that assess what influence the class had on students are only drawn from the data we collected in Wave Two.

To address our questions about ideology, we included items on the student and teacher surveys about important political issues, such as taxation, civil unions for gay people, and the death penalty. On the survey the students took while in high school, we also asked for whom they would have voted in the 2004 presidential election had they been legally eligible, and on the follow-survey we asked about political party affiliation. The teacher survey also contained the issues questions, but we deleted the presidential preference question because we feared it would be seen as too intrusive to ask such a question to adults who actually might have voted, as compared to asking students to retrospectively speculate about whom they would have supported.

During both waves, the researchers observed classes and interviewed the teachers and one-fifth of the students while they were in high school ($n = 230$). To select the students to interview, we used the pre-course survey to ensure that the students represented the range of the sample in the class with respect to political orientation, gender, race, and affinity for classroom discussion (as assessed by students' answers to survey questions about their participation in and enjoyment of discussion in class).

When we interviewed students and teachers, we asked them to describe the range of political difference that existed in their class, how much disagreement among students was voiced during issues discussions, whether they thought students were encouraged and/or felt comfortable voicing their true opinions in the class, and the like. During our observations we also carefully noted the range of opinions that were voiced by the students and teacher during issues discussions and the general tone and tenor of the discussions with respect to the airing of conflicting views.

Appendix B

Views about Issues Discussions

Please choose the answer that best reflects your opinions about the sharing of views about issues during class discussions in the social studies class you teach/have just completed.

Table B.1 Teacher and Student Views on Disclosure

	Teachers		Students	
	Disagree	Agree	Disagree	Agree
1. I wish my social studies teacher would share his or her opinions on issues more often.	N/A	N/A	49.61	50.39
2. I think it is fine for social studies teachers to share his or her opinions about the issues in class.	45.45	54.55	20.74	79.26
3. I would prefer that social studies teachers not share their opinions about the issues discussed in class.	47.83	52.17	78.21	21.60
4. I feel like I need to have the same opinion on issues as my students do/as the rest of the class.	91.30	8.70	88.78	11.22
5. Most of the students in this class have similar opinions on the issues we are discussing.	82.61	17.39	45.81	54.19
6. I feel that when a social studies teacher shares his or her opinions on the issues we are discussing in class students are more likely to adopt those same opinions.	54.55	45.45	58.80	41.20
7. I feel that when my social studies teacher shares his or her opinions on key issues we are discussing in class that I am more likely to adopt those same opinions.	N/A	N/A	76.94	23.06
8. I feel like my students want me to have the same opinion on issues as they do/I feel like my teacher wants students to have the same opinion on issues as she/he has.	65.22	34.78	90.35	9.65
9. Students do not know/I do not know my teachers opinions on the issues we are discussing in class.	47.83	52.17	56.56	43.44

Table B.1 Continued

	Teachers		Students	
	Disagree	Agree	Disagree	Agree
10. I do not share my/My social studies teacher does not share his or her opinions about issues we are discussing in class.	47.83	52.17	53.82	46.18
11. I only share my/My social studies teacher only shares his or her opinions about issues when asked directly by a student in class.	52.17	47.83	62.50	37.50
12. I do not think it is a good idea for social studies teachers to tell students his or her opinions about the issues they are discussing in class.	50.00	50.00	72.76	27.24

Data from Discussing Controversial Issues Study, Principal Investigator, Diana Hess, 2008.

High School Social Studies Teachers (*n* = 22)/High School Social Studies Students (*n* = 518) (most in 11–12th grade).

Notes

Introduction

1. In 2004 Jeremy Stoddard was commissioned by Street Law, Inc. to analyze state social studies standards documents to determine which specifically listed United States Supreme Court cases and which cases were listed. Not surprisingly, he found an inverse relationship between the likelihood that a case was included in the many standards and the extent to which the case continued to generate controversy.

Chapter 1

1. More generally, the study focuses on what impact controversial issues discussions in high school classes have on the political and civic engagement of young people after they leave high school.

Chapter 3

1. For information about how teachers define issues, and which issues students think are important, I rely primarily on the studies explained in Hess (2002), and Hess and Posselt (2002).
2. As explained in the previous chapter, talking about political issues, especially in a diverse "public," can have salutary effects that can extend well beyond influencing the decision on a particular issue.
3. For an explanation of this method for teaching concepts, see Chapter 9 in Parker (2009).
4. For examples of curriculum materials that clearly show the distinction between narrowly and more broadly worded questions, see the National Issues Forum (NIF) (2008) materials in comparison to those of the Deliberating in a Democracy (2008) Project of the Constitutional Rights Foundation Chicago (DID). The NIF materials are framed broadly; the immigration issue on the list (#10) is from the NIF. Conversely, most of the DID materials use a more narrow framing, as represented by the public protest issue on the list (#2), which is from the DID Project.

Chapter 4

1. The teachers' names used in this publication are pseudonyms.
2. During the semester of the study, another teacher also taught this course.

Chapter 5

1. Thanks to the many UW-Madison students who have worked on this study: Louis Ganzler, who served as the primary research assistant on this study from 2004–2006, Ana Collares, who completed much of the original statistical analysis on the Wave Two data, and Julie Posselt, who did the preliminary analysis on the Wave One data. Also Wayne Au and Jeremy Stoddard collected much of the data in Wave Two, and during the last year, Sam Roecker, Melani Winter, Alison Turner, Ru Dawley Carr, Mike Kopish, Hyunseo Hwangh and Sarbani Chakraborty have assisted with data analysis and collection in Wave Four. We would also like to thank the staff at the UW Survey Center who collected the data in Wave Three (the follow-up phone calls). We received important advice from our advisory committee: Joe Kahne,

Walter Parker, and Wendy Richardson. And, of course, thanks to the teachers and students who participated in the study—without them, there would be no study.

Chapter 6

1. Parts of this chapter have appeared in a paper presented at the March 2008 meeting of the American Educational Research Association (Hess, McAvoy, Smithson, & Hwang, 2008) and are used here with permission.

Chapter 7

1. Pew Research Center (2007).
2. To read the complete column, see Hess (2007a).
3. United Nations Intergovernmental Panel on Climate Change Working Group III (2007).
4. To read the letter from an MIT scientist claiming that the producer of the film "swindled" him by misrepresenting his views in the documentary, see Wunsch (2007).
5. Pew Research Center (2007).

Chapter 8

1. For more information about the Pledge of Allegiance controversy in Madison, WI, see Singer (2001).
2. I do not mean to suggest that the question of whether 9/11-related topics should be included in the curriculum was without controversy. Some school administrators were sufficiently concerned about the volatility of these topics that they forbid or sharply curtailed teachers' inclusion of them in the curriculum.
3. Throughout this chapter I use direct quotes with (2003) and no page numbers. All of these quotes are from interviews with the authors who participated in this study.
4. I worked with a team of graduate students on the first stage of the study analyzing the non-profit and U.S. State Department curricula; team members included Kristen Buras, Ross Collin, Hilary Conklin, Eric Freedman, Jeremy Stoddard, and Keita Takayama. Jeremy Stoddard was co-investigator for the study's second stage, which focused on textbooks. Shannon Murto worked on this as well. The first stage of the study was funded by the Graduate School of the University of Wisconsin-Madison. The data presented, the statements made, and the views expressed are solely the responsibility of the author.
5. Research about the creation of textbooks clearly shows that content that could be perceived as controversial rarely makes it through the review processes. Because materials developed by educational organizations are typically considered "supplemental," they are not subject to the same degree of official scrutiny. Consequently, another reason to study curricula not in textbooks is to investigate what effect this freedom has on curriculum writers.
6. Ironically, this criterion ruled out the teacher resource guides developed by two organizations whose ideological differences were among the starkest: The Fordham Foundation (run by Chester Finn) and Rethinking Schools.
7. For additional information about the key findings from both phases of the study, see Hess and Stoddard (2007). The textbook study is described in detail in Hess, Stoddard and Murto (2008).
8. Our estimated figures are based on enrollment statistics for grades 9–12 from the National Center for Education Statistics (U.S. Department of Education, National Center for Education Statistics, 2008) and the combined 63.8% share that these texts hold in the Social Studies textbook market for grades 9–12. As textbooks are often purchased once every five to six years, it will be several years before schools will have these most recent editions.
9. We did not interview the authors of the textbooks because we knew that some of the books have authors in name only, and are actually written by teams of anonymous writers (Schemo, 2006). In retrospect, this is a major flaw of the study because we are not able make any judgments about whether the ideological messages embedded in the textbooks were intended

by the writers, or even by those who vetted their work. During the interviews with the supplemental curricula writers, we found that the conversations about what ideologies we were identifying in the materials compared to what they were purposely or consciously trying to communicate were among the most enlightening and interesting.

10. Educators for Social Responsibility in the Metropolitan Area are now known as the Morningside Center for Teaching Social Responsibility.

11. Rather made these comments as the anchor of the CBS News broadcast on September 18, 2001.

Chapter 9

1. For information about the National Issues Forum, go to: http://www.nifi.org/; Choices for the 21st Century Program, go to: http://www.choices.edu/; Deliberating in Democracy, go to: http://www.deliberating.org

2. These are excerpts from the controversial issues policy of the Madison Metropolitan School District in Madison, WI. Available at: http://www.madison.k12.wi.us/policies/3177.htm

3. For information about youth voting in the 2008 presidential primaries, see: http://www. civicyouth.org/PopUps/FactSheets/FS_08_NH_FL.pdf

4. Joseph Kahne & Ellen Middaugh (2008). Democracy for some. *CIRCLE Working Paper, 59*, 16.

Bibliography

Arbetman, L., & O'Brien, E. (2005). *Street law: A course in practical law.* Columbus, OH: Glencoe/McGraw-Hill.

Associated Press. (2007, February 28). "Arizona bill would bar teachers from sharing political views in class."

Avery, P. G., Bird, K., Johnstone, S., Sullivan, J. L., & Thalhammer, K. (1992). Exploring political tolerance with adolescents. *Theory and Research in Social Education, 20,* 386–420.

Avery, P. G., Simmons, A. M., & Freeman, C. (2007). *The Deliberating in a Democracy (DID) project evaluation report: Year 3.* http://www.deliberating.org/

Baker, P., & Slavin, P. (2005, August 3). Bush remarks on "intelligent design theory" fuel debate. *The Washington Post,* 1.

Barton, K. C., & Burroughs, R. (n. d.). "I see the same fuckin' movies you do, man": Film genre and the depiction of teaching and learning. Unpublished manuscript.

Beck, R. B., Black, L., Krieger, L. S., Naylor, P. C., & Shabaka, D. I. (2005). *World history: Patterns of interaction.* Evanston, IL: Houghton Mifflin/McDougal Littell.

Beck, T. (2003). If he murdered someone, he shouldn't get a lawyer: Engaging young children in civics deliberation. *Theory and Research in Social Education, 3,* 326–346.

Bennett, W. J. (2002, September 10). Teaching September 11: American schools should teach patriotism. *The Wall Street Journal.* http://www.freedomworks.org/informed/issues_template.php?issue_id=1843

Bickmore, K. (1993). Learning inclusion/inclusion in learning: Citizenship education for a pluralistic society. *Theory and Research in Social Education, 21,* 341–384.

Bill of Rights Institute. (2002). *September 11: Commemorating America's Civic Values.* Arlington, VA: Bill of Rights Institute.

Binder, A. J. (2002). *Contentious curricula: Afrocentrism and creationism in public schools.* Princeton, NJ: Princeton University Press.

Bishop, B. (2008). *The big sort: Why the clustering of like-minded American is tearing us apart.* New York: Houghton Mifflin.

Bolgatz, J. (2005). Revolutionary talk: Elementary teacher and students discuss race in a social studies class. *Social Studies, 96,* 259–264.

Boyer, P. J. (2005, March 21). Jesus in the classroom. *The New Yorker, 81,* 62.

Bridges, D. (1979). *Education, democracy and discussion.* Windsor: NFER.

Brookfield, S., & Preskill, S. (1999). *Discussion as a way of teaching: Tools and techniques for democratic classrooms.* San Francisco: Jossey-Bass Publishers.

Camicia, S. P. (2007). Teaching the Japanese American internment: A case study of social studies curriculum contention. (Doctoral dissertation, University of Washington, 2007; Obtained from the author).

Campbell, D.E. (2005). Voice in the classroom: How an open classroom environment facilitates adolescents' civic development. *CIRCLE Working Paper 28.*

Carnegie Corporation of New York & the Center for Information and Research on Civic Learning and Engagement (CIRCLE). (2003). *The Civic Mission of the Schools.* New York: Carnegie Corporation of New York.

Cavet, A. (2007). Teaching "controversial issues": A living, vital link between school and society? *Service de Veille scientifique et technologique.* http://www.inrp.fr/vst

Cayton, A. R. L., Perry, E. I., Reed, L., & Winkler, A. M. (2005). *America: Pathways to the present.* Upper River, NJ: Pearson/Prentice Hall Inc.

Choices for the 21st Century. (2002). *Responding to Terrorism: Challenges for Democracy.* Providence, RI: Watson Institute for International Studies, Brown University.

Chomsky, N. (2002, September 7). What Americans have learnt – and not learnt – since 9/11. *The Age.* http://www.chomsky.info/articles/20020907.htm

Christoph, J. N., & Nystrand, M. (2001). Taking risks, negotiating relationships: One teacher's transition toward a dialogic classroom. *Research in the Teaching of English, 36,* 249–285.

Commission on Wartime Relocation and Internment of Civilians. (1983). *Personal justice denied.* Washington, DC: Commission on Wartime Relocation and Internment of Civilians. http://www.nps.gov/history/history/online_books/personal_justice_denied/intro.htm

Conover, P. J., & Searing, D. D. (2000). A political socialization perspective. In L. M. McDonnell, P. M. Timpane, & R. Benjamin (Eds.), *Rediscovering the democratic purposes of education* (pp. 91–124). Lawrence: University of Kansas Press.

Conover, P. J., Searing, D. D., & Crewe, I. M. (2002). The deliberation potential of political discussion. *British Journal of Political Science, 32,* 21–62.

Constitutional Rights Foundation. (2002). *Terrorism in America.* Los Angeles: Constitutional Rights Foundation.

Cotton, D. (2006). Teaching controversial environmental issues: Neutrality and balance in the reality of the classroom. *Educational Research, 48,* 223–241.

Dahl, R. A. (1998). *On democracy.* New Haven, CT: Yale University Press.

Danzer, G. A. de Alva, J. J. K., Krieger, L. S., Wilson, L. E., & Woloch, N. (2005). *The Americans.* Evanston, IL: Houghton Mifflin/McDougal Littell.

Deliberating in a Democracy. (2008). *Deliberating in a Democracy – Home.* http://www.deliberating.org/

Dewey, J. (1927). *The public and its problems.* Chicago: Swallow.

Dillon, J. T. (1994). *Using discussion in classrooms.* Philadelphia: Open University Press.

Education Market Research. (2005). *The complete K-12 report: Market facts & segment analyses.* Rockaway Park, NY: Education Market Research & Open Book Publishing.

Ellis, E. G., & Esler, A. (2005). *World history: Connections to today.* Upper Saddle River, NJ: Pearson/Prentice Hall.

Engle, S., & Ochoa, A. (1988). *Education for democratic citizenship: Decision making in the social studies.* New York: Teachers College Press

Facing History and Ourselves. (2002). *Identity, religion & violence: A critical look at September 11, 2001.* Retrieved June 2, 2003 from http://www.facing.org

Fineman, H. (2008). *The thirteen American arguments: Enduring debates that define and inspire our country.* New York: Random House.

Finn, C. (2002). *September 11: What our children need to know.* http://www.edexcellence.net/detail/news.cfm?news_id=65&id=

Fishkin, J. (1991). *Democracy and deliberation: New directions for democratic reform.* New Haven, CT: Yale University Press.

Fishkin, J., & Farrar, C. (2005). Deliberative polling. In J. Gastile, & P. Levine (Eds.), *The deliberative democracy handbook* (pp. 68–79). San Francisco: Jossey-Bass,

Forum for Education and Democracy. (2008). *Democracy at risk: The need for a new federal policy in education.*

Frieden, T. (2002, January 27). Supreme Court justice to launch morals program. *CNN.* http://archives.cnn.com/2002/US/01/27/scotus.morals/index.html.

Gastile, J., & Levine, P. (2005). *The deliberative democracy handbook: Strategies for effective civic engagement in the 21st century.* San Francisco: Jossey-Bass.

Gimpel, J., Lay, C., & Schuknecht, J. (2003). *Cultivating democracy: Civic environments and political socialization in America.* Washington, DC: Brookings Institution Press.

Gray, D. (1989). Putting minds to work: how to use the seminar approach in the classroom. *American Educator, 13,* 16–23.

Gross, R. E. (1948). Teaching controversial issues can be fun. *Social Education, 12,* 259–260.

Grutter *v.* Bollinger (2003) 539 U.S. 306.

Gutmann, A. (1999). *Democratic education* (2nd ed.). Princeton, NJ: Princeton University Press.

Gutstein, E. (2003). Teaching and learning mathematics for social justice in an urban, Latino school. *Journal for Research in Mathematics Education, 34,* 37–73.

Gutstein, E. (2006). "The real world as we have seen it": Latino/a parents' voices on teaching mathematics for social justice. *Mathematical Thinking and Learning: An International Journal, 8,* 331–358.

Hahn, C. L. (1996). Research on issues-centered social studies. In R. W. Evans, & D. W. Saxe (Eds.), *Handbook on teaching social issues* (pp. 26–39). Washington, DC: National Council for the Social Studies.

Hahn, C. L. (1998). *Becoming political: Comparative perspectives on citizenship education*. Albany, NY: State University of New York Press.

Hahn, C. L., & Tocci, C. M. (1990). Classroom climate and controversial issues discussions: A five nation study. *Theory and Research in Social Education, 18*, 344–362.

Hand, M. (2008). What should we teach as controversial? A defense of the epistemic criterion. *Educational Theory, 58*, 213–228.

Harris, D. (1996). Assessing discussion of public issues: A scoring guide. In R. W. Evans, & D. W. Saxe (Eds.), *Handbook on teaching social issues* (pp. 289–97). Washington, DC: National Council for the Social Studies.

Hemmings, A. (2000) 'High school democratic dialogues: Possibilities for praxis', *American Educational Research Journal, 3*: 67–91.

Hess, D. (1998). *Discussing controversial public issues in secondary social studies classrooms: Learning from skilled teachers*. (Doctoral Dissertation, University of Washington, 1998).

Hess, D. (2002). Discussing controversial public issues in secondary social studies classrooms: Learning from skilled teachers. *Theory and Research in Social Education, 30*, 10–41.

Hess, D. (2004a). Controversies about controversial issues in democratic education. *PS: Political Science and Politics, 37*, 253–255.

Hess, D. (2004b). Is discussion worth the trouble? *Social Education, 68*, 151–155.

Hess, D. (2005). How do teachers' political views influence teaching about controversial issues? *Social Education, 69*, 47.

Hess, D. (2006). Should intelligent design be taught in social studies courses? *Social Education, 70*, 8–13.

Hess, D. (2007a). From *Banished to Brother Outsider, Miss Navajo to an Inconvenient Truth*: Documentary films as perspective-laden narratives. *Social Education, 71*, 194–199 [followed by my response to a letter to the editor].

Hess, D. (2007b). Teaching about global warming (Letter). *Social Education, 71*(7).

Hess, D. (2008a). Democratic education to reduce the divide. *Social Education, 72*, 373–376.

Hess, D. (2008b). Teaching and learning about controversial issues in social studies. In L. Levstik, & C. Tyson (Eds.), *Handbook of research in social studies* (pp. 123–136). New Jersey: Erlbaum.

Hess, D. (2008c). Controversial issues and democratic discourse. In Levstik, L., & Tyson, C. (Eds.), *Handbook of research in social studies education* (pp.124–136). New York: Routledge.

Hess, D. (2009). Creating comprehensive controversial issues policies to improve democratic education. In J. Youniss, & P. Levine (Eds.), *Engaging young people in civic life*. Nashville: Vanderbilt University Press.

Hess, D. (in press). Teaching student teachers to examine how their political views inform their teaching. In E. Heilman (Ed.), *Social studies and diversity teacher education: What we do and why we do it*. New York: Routledge.

Hess, D., & Avery, P. (2008). Discussion of controversial issues as a form and goal of democratic education. In J. Arthur, I. Davies, & C. Hahn (Eds.), *The SAGE handbook of education for citizenship and democracy*. (pp.506–518). London: SAGE.

Hess, D., & Ganzler, L. (2007). Patriotism and ideological diversity in the classroom. In J. Westheimer (Ed.), *Pledging Allegiance: The politics of patriotism in America's schools* (pp. 131–138). New York: Teachers College Press.

Hess, D., McAvoy, P., Smithson, J., & Hwang, H. (2008 March). *The nature, range, and impact of ideological diversity and teacher disclosure in high school democratic education courses*. Paper presented at the meeting of the American Educational Research Association, New York, NY.

Hess, D., & Murto, S. (in press). Teaching against the threats to democracy in democratic education. In S. Mitakidou, E. Tressou, B.B. Swadener, & C.A. Grant, (Eds.), *Beyond pedagogies of exclusion in diverse childhood contexts: Transnational challenges*. New York/London: Palgrave/Macmillan.

Hess, D., & Posselt, J. (2002). How students experience and learn from the discussion of controversial public issues in secondary social studies. *Journal of Curriculum and Supervision, 17*, 283–314.

Hess, D., & Stoddard, J. (2007). 9/11 and terrorism: "The ultimate teachable moment" in textbooks and supplemental curricula. *Social Education, 71*, 231–236.

Hess, D., Stoddard, J., & Murto, S. (2008). Examining the treatment of 9/11 and terrorism in high school textbooks. In J. Bixby & J. Pace (Eds.), *Educating democratic citizens in troubled times: Qualitative studies of current efforts* (pp. 192–225). Albany, NY: State University of New York Press.

Hibbing, J., & Theiss-Morse, E. (2002). *Stealth democracy: America's beliefs about how government should work.* New York: Cambridge University Press.

Horwitt, S. (Director). (2002). *First vote* [instructional video and pamphlet]. Alexandria, VA: Close Up Foundation.

Hunt, M. P., & Metcalf, L. E. (1955). *Teaching high school social studies: Problems in reflective thinking and social understanding.* New York: Harper and Row.

Johnson, D. W., & Johnson, R. (1995). *Creative controversy: Intellectual conflict in the classroom* (3rd ed.) Edina, MN: Interaction.

Johnston, J., Anderman, L., Milne, L., Klenck, L., & Harris, D. (1994). *Improving civic discourse in the classroom: Taking the measure of Channel One, Research Report 4.* Ann Arbor, MI: Institute for Social Research, University of Michigan.

Jones, A. (n.d.). UCLA Bruin Alumni Association: Who we are. *UCLA Bruin Alumni Association.* http://www.bruinalumni.com/aboutus.html

Kahne, J., & Middaugh, E. (2008). Democracy for some: The civic opportunity gap in high school. *CIRCLE Working Paper* 59. http://www.civicyouth.org/?p=278

Kahne, J., Chi, B., & Middaugh, E. (2006). Building social capital for civic and political engagement: The potential of high school civics courses. *Canadian Journal of Education, 29,* 387–409.

Kahne, J., Rodriguez, M., Smith, B., & Thiede, K. (2000). Developing citizens for democracy? Assessing opportunities to learn in Chicago's social studies classrooms. *Theory and Research in Social Education, 28,* 311–338.

Kerr, D., Lopes, J., Nelson, J., White, K., Cleaver, E., & Benton, T. (2007). *Vision versus pragmatism: Citizenship in the secondary school curriculum in England's Citizenship Education Longitudinal Study: Fifth Annual Report.* Research report 845: National Foundation for Educational Research.

King, M. L. Jr. (1963). Letter from Birmingham Jail. In *Why we can't wait* (pp.76–95). New York: Mentor.

Kohlberg, L. (1981). *The philosophy of moral development: Moral stages and the ideas of justice.* San Francisco: Harper and Row.

Kohlberg, L., & Mayer, R. (1972). Development as the aim of education. *Harvard Educational Review, 42,* 449–496.

Kohn, A. (2001). Teaching about Sept. 11. In *War, terrorism, and our classrooms: Teaching in the aftermath of the September 11 tragedy.* http://www.rethinkingschools.org/special_reports/sept11/pdf/911insrt.pdf

Kozol, J. (1991). *Savage inequalities: Children in America's schools.* New York: HarperCollins.

Ladson-Billings, G. (2003). Lies my teacher still tells. In G. Ladson-Billings (Ed.), *Critical race theory perspectives on the social studies: The profession, policies, and curriculum* (pp. 1–11). Charlotte, NC: Information Age Publishing.

Larson, B. E. (1997). Social studies teachers' conceptions of discussion. A grounded theory study. *Theory and Research in Social Education, 25,* 113–136.

Larson, B. E. (2003). Comparing face-to-face discussion and electronic discussion: A case study for high school social studies. *Theory and Research in Social Education, 31,* 347–397.

Larson, E. J. (1997). *Summer for the gods: The Scopes trial and America's continuing debate over science and religion.* New York: Basic Books.

Laviano, M. (2007). Teaching about global warming (Letter). *Social Education, 71*(7).

Leming, J., Ellington, L., & Porter-Magee, K. (2003). *Where did social studies go wrong?* Washington, DC: Thomas B. Fordham Foundation.

Levine, P. (2005, December 15). Why schools and colleges often overlook civic development. http://www.peterlevine.ws/mt/archives/000751.html

Levine, P., & Lopez, M. H. (2004). *Themes emphasized in social studies and civics classes: New evidence* [CIRCLE Fact Sheet]. College Park, MD: The Center for Information & Research on Civic Learning & Engagement, University of Maryland.

Levinson, M. (2008). The civic achievement gap. *CIRCLE Working Paper* 51. www.civicyouth.org

Levy, T. (1998, November/December). Only a teacher: Break out of the stereotype. *The Social Studies Professional, 148,* 3.

Lockwood, A. L., & Harris, D. E. (1985). *Reasoning with democratic values: Ethical problems in United States history.* Vol. 1. New York: Teachers College Press.

Lockwood, A. L., & Harris, D. E. (1985). *Reasoning with democratic values: Ethical problems in United States history, 1877 to Present.* Vol. 2. New York: Teachers College Press.

Loewen, J. W. (1995). *Lies my teacher told me: Everything your American history textbook got wrong.* New York: New Press.

Mansbridge, J. (1991). Democracy, deliberation, and the experience of women. In B. Murchland (Ed.), *Higher education and the practice of democratic politics: A political education reader* (pp. 122–135). Dayton, OH: Kettering Foundation.

Martin-Kniep, G. (1998). *Why am I doing this? Purposeful teaching through portfolio assessment.* New Hampshire: Heinemann.

McClenghan, W.A. (2005). *Macgruder's American Government.* Upper Saddle River, NJ: Pearson/Prentice Hall (in association with Close Up Foundation).

McClure, R., & Stiffler, L. (2007, January 11). Federal Way schools reject Gore film: 'Inconvenient truth' called too controversial. *Seattle Post-Intelligencer.* http://seattlepi.nwsource.com/local/299253_inconvenient11.html

McCully, A. (2006). Practitioner perceptions of their role in facilitating the handling of controversial issues in contested societies: A northern Irish experience. *Educational Review, 58*, 51–65.

McDevitt, M., & Kiousis, S. (2006). *Experiments in political socialization: Kids voting USA as a model for civic education reform.* CIRCLE working paper 49. http://civicyouth.org/PopUps/Working Papers/WP49McDevitt.pdf

Miller, B., & Singleton, L. (1997). *Preparing citizens: Linking authentic assessment and instruction in civic/law-related education.* Boulder, CO: Social Science Education Consortium.

Miller-Lane, J., Denton, E., & May, A. (2006). Social studies teachers' views on committed impartiality and discussion. *Social Studies Research and Practice, 1*, 30–44.

Morse *v.* Frederick, 127 s. ct. 2618 (2007).

Mutz, D. C. (2006). *Hearing the other side: Deliberative versus participatory democracy.* New York: Cambridge University Press.

Nash, G. B. (2004). *American odyssey: The twentieth century and beyond.* Columbus, OH: Glencoe/McGraw Hill.

National Conference on Citizenship, CIRCLE & Saguaro Seminar. (2007). *America's civic health index: Renewed engagement: Building on America's civic core.*

National Conference on Citizenship. (2008). *America's civic health index: Beyond the vote.*

National Issues Forum. (2008). *National Issues Forum—Home.* http://www.nifi.org/

Newmann, F. M., & Wehlage, G. G. (1995). *Successful school restructuring: A report to the public and educators.* Madison: University of Wisconsin, Center on Effective Secondary Schools.

Niemi, N. S., & Niemi, R. G. (2007). Partisanship, participation, and political trust as taught (or not) in high school history and government classes. *Theory and Research in Social Education, 35*, 32–61.

Northwest Association for Biomedical Research. (2008). *The science and ethics of stem cell research.* Northwest Association for Biomedical Research website: http://nwabr.org/education/stemcellrequest.html

Nystrand, M., Wu, L., Gamoran, A., Zeiser, S., & Long, D. (2003). Questions in time: Investigating the structure and dynamics of unfolding classroom discourse. *Discourse Processes, 35*, 135–198.

Oliver, D. W., & Newmann, F. M. (1967). *Taking a stand: A guide to clear discussion of public issues.* Middletown, CT: Xerox Corporation /American Education Publications.

Oliver, D. W., & Shaver, J. P. (1974). *Teaching public issues in the high school.* Logan, UT: Utah State University Press. (Originally published by Houghton Mifflin, Boston, 1966).

Paley, V. G. (1992). *You can't say you can't play.* Cambridge, MA: Harvard University Press.

Parker, W. C. (1988). Thinking to learn concepts. *The Social Studies, 79*, 70–73.

Parker, W. C. (2003). *Teaching democracy: Unity and diversity in public life.* New York: Teacher's College Press.

Parker, W. C. (2006). Public discourses in schools: Purposes, problems, possibilities. *Educational Researcher, 35*, 8–18.

Parker, W. C. (2009). *Social studies in elementary education* (13th ed.). Boston: Allyn & Bacon.

Parker, W. C., & Hess, D. (2001). Teaching with and for discussion. *Teacher and Teacher Education, 17*, 273–289.

Pew Research Center. (2007, January 24). *Global warming: A divide on causes and solutions: Public views unchanged by unusual weather.* http://pewresearch.org/pubs/282/global-warming-a-divide-on-causes-and-solutions.

Public Agenda. (2005). *Special report on terrorism.* http://www.publicagenda.org/specials/terrorism/terror_pubopinion10.htm

Ravitch, D. (2004). *A consumer's guide to high-school history textbooks.* http://www.edexcellence.net/institute/publication/publication.cfm?id=329&pubsubid=1018

Remy, R. C. (2006). *United States government: Democracy in action.* Columbus, OH: Glencoe/McGraw-Hill.

Rethinking Schools. (2001). *War, terrorism, and our classrooms: Teaching in the aftermath of the September 11 tragedy.* http://www.rethinkingschools.org/special_reports/sept11/pdf/911insrt.pdf

Richardson, W. K. (2006). Combining cognitive interviews and social science surveys: Strengthening interpretation and design. In K. Barton (Ed.), *Research methods in social studies education: Contemporary issues and perspectives* (pp. 159–182). Greenwich: Information Age Publishing, Inc.

Rossi, J. A. (1995). In-depth study in an issues-orientated social studies classroom. *Theory and Research in Social Education, 23,* 88–120.

Schemo, D. J. (2006, July 13). Schoolbooks are given F's in originality. *New York Times.* http://www.nytimes.com/2006/07/13/books/13textbook.html?_r=1&scp=5&sq=textbooks%209/11&st=cse&oref=slogin

Schkade, D., Sunstein, C. R., & Hastie, R. (June 2006) What happened on Deliberation Day? U Chicago Law & Economics, Olin Working Paper No. 298. AEI-Brookings Joint Center Working Paper No. 06–19. http://ssrn.com/abstract=911646

Schweber, S. A. (2004). *Making sense of the Holocaust: Lessons from classroom practice.* New York: Teachers College Press.

Shapiro, A. (2002). *Civil liberties and terrorism: Three lessons for high school students.* Educators for Social Responsibility Metropolitan Area. Retrieved August 8, 2002 from http://www.esrmetro.org/civilliberties.html

Shapiro, A. (2002). *Iraq: Should the U.S. launch a preemptive attack?* New York: Educators for Social Responsibility in the Metropolitan Area.

Shulman, L. W. (1983). Autonomy and obligation: The remote control of teaching. In L. S. Schulman & G. Sykes (Eds.), *Handbook of teaching and policy* (pp. 484–504). New York: Longman.

Singer, M. (2001, November 26). I pledge allegiance: A liberal town's school system meets the new patriotism. *The New Yorker.* http://www.newyorker.com/archive/2001/11/26/011126fa_FACT1

Spielvogel, J. J. (2005). *World history.* Columbus, OH: Glencoe/McGraw-Hill.

Stiggins, R. J. (1997). *Student-centered classroom assessment* (2nd ed.). Englewood Cliffs, NJ: Prentice-Hall, Inc.

Taba, H. (1967). *Teacher's handbook for elementary social studies. Introductory edition.* Reading, MA: Addison-Wesley Publishing Co., Inc.

The Civil Liberties Act of 1988. (Pub.L. 100–383, title I, August 10, 1988, 102 Stat. 904, 50a U.S.C. § 1989b *et seq.*). http://www.civics-online.org/library/formatted/texts/civilact1988.html

Thornton, S. J. (2003). Silence on gays and lesbians in the social studies curriculum. *Social Education, 67,* 226–230.

Torney-Purta, J., Lehmann, R., Oswald, H., & Schultz, W. (2001). *Citizenship and education in twenty-eight countries: Civic knowledge and engagement at age fourteen.* Amsterdam, The Netherlands: International Association for the Evaluation of Educational Achievement.

U.S. Army Training and Doctrine Command. (2005). *A military guide to terrorism in the twenty-first century.* http://www.terrorism.com/modules.php?op=modload&name=Documents&file=get&download=276.

U.S. Department of Education, National Center for Education Statistics. (2008). *Digest of education statistics, 2007.* http://nces.ed.gov/fastfacts/display.asp?id=65

U.S. Department of State. (2002). *Terrorism: A war without borders.* [video recording and supplementary materials]. Washington, DC: U.S. Department of State.

United Nations Intergovernmental Panel on Climate Change Working Group III. (2007). *Working group III fourth assessment report.* http://www.mnp.nl/ipcc/pages_media/ar4.html

West Virginia State Board of Education *v.* Barnette, 319 U.S. 624 (1943).

Westheimer, J. & Kahne, J. (2004). Educating the "good" citizen: The politics of teaching democracy. *PS: Political Science and Politics, 37.* http://www.mills.edu/academics/faculty/educ/jkahne/ps_educating_the_good_citizen.pdf

Wunsch, C. (2007, March 11). *Partial response to London Channel 4 film "The Great Global Swindle."* http://ocean.mit.edu/~cwunsch/papersonline/channel4response

Yamashita, H. (2006). Global citizenship education and war: The needs of teachers and learners. *Educational Review, 58,* 27–39.

Zeidler, D. L., Sadler, T. D., Simmons, M. L., & Howes, E. V. (2005). Beyond STS: A research-based framework for socioscientific issues education. *Science Education, 89,* 357–377.

Zelman *v.* Simmons-Harris, 536 U.S. 639 (2002). *Official arguments transcript.* http://www.supreme courtus.gov/oral_arguments/argument_transcripts/00–1751.pdf

Zimmerman, J. (2002). *Whose America: Culture wars in the public schools.* Boston: Harvard University Press.

Zukin, C., Keeter, S., Andolina, M., Jenkins, K., & Delli Carpini, M. X. (2006). *A new engagement?: Political participation, civic life, and the changing American citizen.* Oxford, UK: Oxford University Press.

Index